# The Dynamics of American Ethnic, Religious, and Racial Group Life

# The Dynamics of American Ethnic, Religious, and Racial Group Life

## An Interdisciplinary Overview

PHILIP PERLMUTTER

PRAEGER

Westport, Connecticut
London

Library of Congress Cataloging-in-Publication Data

Perlmutter, Philip.
  The dynamics of American ethnic, religious, and racial group life :
  an interdisciplinary overview / Philip Perlmutter.
      p.   cm.
  Includes bibliographical references and index.
  ISBN 0-275-95533-8 (alk. paper)
      1. United States—Ethnic relations.   2. United States—Race
  relations.   3. Ethnicity—United States.   4. Group identity—United
  States.   5. Pluralism (Social sciences)—United States.   I. Title.
  E184.A1P394   1996
  305.8′00973—dc20        95–50470

British Library Cataloguing in Publication Data is available.

Library of Congress Catalog Card Number: 95–50470
ISBN: 0-275-95533-8

First published in 1996

Praeger Publishers, 88 Post Road West, Westport, CT 06881
An imprint of Greenwood Publishing Group, Inc.

Printed in the United States of America

The paper used in this book complies with the
Permanent Paper Standard issued by the National
Information Standards Organization (Z39.48-1984).

10  9  8  7  6  5  4  3  2  1

Copyright Acknowledgments

   Grateful acknowledgment is made to the following publications and periodicals
from which adaptations of parts of this book were published: "Inter-Minority
Group Differences, Ethnocentrism and Freedom of Association," *Ecumenical
Trends,* June 1994; "Segregation: Coming Back in Style," *Journal of Intergroup
Relations,* Summer 1994; "Time to Smarten Up Rather than Dumb Down," *The
Freeman,* October 1994; "Speak Out Against Hatemongers!" *Journal of In-
tergroup Relations,* Winter 1994–95; "The Ideal of Equality," *Boston Globe,*
March 10, 1995; "Justice and Cultural Diversity," *The Freeman,* August 1995;
"Affirmative Action Myths," *Christian Science Monitor,* September 9, 1995;
"Group Rights and Individual Wrongs," *Lincoln Review,* Summer-Fall, 1995.

My deepest appreciation to Susan Sunderman for her superb copyediting and suggestions.

*To my darling wife Rosanne,*
*children Jeff and Cathy,*
*son-in-law Alan, and grandson Eli*
*for in their own way helping*
*make a better world.*

# Contents

# Figures

# Introduction

[T]he Bosom of America is open to receive not only the opulent and respectable stranger but the oppressed and persecuted of all Nations and Religions.

—George Washington,
Message to Irish immigrants in
New York City, 1783

Never before have there been so many people of different religious, racial, and ethnic groups in America, whose numbers and diversity continue to be viewed as an inspiring example of evolving American democracy or as an ominous sign of its beginning decline.

However one feels about such developments, they provoke a number of simultaneous questions:

Why have and do so many people from all over the world come to and remain in America?

Why are so many people asserting interest and pride in their group being and demanding that their societal rights be based on group origins?

Why, after four decades of dramatic civil rights reforms, do interracial problems, tensions, and conflicts still seem to exist—and multiply?

Why is it that some solutions to intergroup problems seem to generate new ones, and why do some problems resist solutions, at least ones that are acceptable to succeeding generations?

Why is it that people still argue over what America's basic ideals are, as well as how to best preserve national unity?

Would that there were some simple answer to each of these questions. However, simple answers don't exist because in group life, as in individual life, there are multiple complexities, ambiguities, and contradictions. Political, socioeconomic, and generational differences abound over how to resolve various group problems such as maintenance of religious rituals, retention of ancestral languages, funding separate schools, marrying nongroup members, or, most recently, supporting group proportional representation on all levels of society.

In grappling with such problems, it is essential to remember that America is indeed a land of immigrants. Not only is every American descended from someone who came from somewhere else, but for most of American history people came in a group, as part of a group, or to rejoin a group, either voluntarily or involuntarily. From their very beginnings in America some 12,000 to 29,000 years ago, newcomers were held together by a variety of factors not altogether different from those of today: family, tribe, language, religion, geographic origin, economic class, political beliefs, adventurism, and the lure of food, land, wealth, or booty.

Variety also characterized the reasons why the first Puritans came to New England. Though "the advancement of the Gospel" motivated most of them, wrote John White in 1630, for others it was "private interest. . . . One brother may draw over another, a son the father, and perhaps some man his inward acquaintance. . . . Necessity may press some, novelty draw on others, hopes of gain in time to come may prevail with a third sort. . . ." Subtler and rather unholy motivations were noted by Governor William Bradford: "Many were sent by their friends, some under hope that they would be made better; others that they might be eased of such burdens, and they kept from shame at home that would necessarily follow their dissolute courses."[1] Alas, the New World also attracted family deserters, prostitutes, convicts, thieves, military deserters or avoiders, and even people running away from retaliation for some wrong they had committed.

Among the groups that came voluntarily, some were primarily interested in producing profits for their financiers, discovering natural resources, serving as an outpost for surplus population, escaping religious or political persecution, missionizing the natives and unchurched, and somehow living a life better, easier, safer, richer, or more religiously fulfilling than the one they left back home. All of the early groups needed armed protection against Indians and other colonial powers, as well as financial assistance to survive, which was provided by government, private investors, or group members themselves.

A few groups came involuntarily—or were already here and became involuntary dependents, wards, or citizens of America. The largest group of involuntary arrivals of course were Africans, who were kidnapped, captured, purchased, branded, and transported across the Atlantic, often with the cooperation of other Africans. Both in their native countries and in America, families were torn apart, with children and spouses sold to different white purchasers. Of all transplanted groups, only African slaves were denied a right to maintain their language, culture, and religion (whether animistic or Muslim), to send remittances to families left behind, or to visit or return home.

Much fewer in number were the seventeenth- and early eighteenth-century whites shipped here against their will—English prisoners of war, assorted European convicts, debtors, prostitutes, and kidnapped youngsters. A third group of involunteers consisted of the inhabitants of territories seized, conquered, or purchased without their consent, such as Indians in the path of national expansion, French and Spanish settlers in the South and Southwest, and the aboriginal residents of Alaska and Hawaii.

Whether voluntary or involuntary, group cooperation was essential in crossing the ocean; in clearing the forests; in building homes and farms; in defending against or attacking rival European powers or Indians; in revolting against the British; in developing communities, organizations, and churches; in keeping Africans from rebelling or running away; and, of course, in creating a government increasingly of, by, and for the people. While some came as individuals, they did not long survive by themselves, whether they were lost seamen or mountain men of yore, or today's social isolates. To be a human was to be group dependent.

Group being, however, was not all benign, particularly in its ethnic, religious, and racial dimensions. Group pride, power, and prejudice always created more victims than individuals did. Long before the white men arrived, Indian tribes warred with each other over land, possessions, women, or assorted grievances—real or imagined. The coming of white Europeans, technology, liquor, and diseases exacerbated those differences, as various Indian tribes allied themselves with one or another European power.

Meanwhile, each of the invading European powers wanted to replicate itself, and so a New France, New England, New Netherland, New Sweden, and New Spain were created in what each believed to be a New World, into which only people of their own kind would settle. Moreover, as in the Old World, the invaders differed over imperial claims and religious beliefs, whether between Catholics and Protestants, Catholics and Catholics, Protestants and Protestants, or all Christians, non-Christians, and nonbelievers.

Least welcomed in any of the imperial colonies were Quakers, Jews, Muslims, and dissenters of any kind. Protestant colonists didn't want Catholics and vice versa. Whatever the foreign power, it looked down on the Indians and blacks, whom it had little hesitancy in enslaving and oppressing, and whom it believed were racially inferior and biblically doomed to serve white Christians.

And so from our earliest days as a nation, there was a constellation of problems that minority groups faced: how to survive and preserve their group identity in a New World; how to define and pass on that identity to the next generation; how to relate to members of other groups; how to respond to bigotry and intergroup conflict; how to resolve conflicts between their group's goals and those of the surrounding society; and how to maintain the group's traditional values and beliefs in an increasingly permissive and pluralistic America.

The nation as a whole also faced innumerable problems: how to preserve national unity and domestic tranquillity among former British subjects and colonies, as well as with blacks and Indians; how to absorb and relate to a steadily increasing and diverse racial, religious, and ethnic population; how to prevent tyranny by the few or the many; and how to ensure a maximum of individual freedoms with a minimum of local or federal government intrusion. What most Americans agreed on was that the United States was or should become a new kind of nation where the wrongs of European governance would not be repeated and where the particular geographic, biological, or cultural identities of its citizens would be made secondary to that of national unity and survival.

Then, as today, no sure solutions were found, though many were offered and adopted. Ambiguities, tensions, and conflicts still exist over what the rights and limitations of the executive, legislative, and judicial branches of government are, as well as between them and the rights of individual citizens, all of which are made more complex—and controversial—by the recent growth of claims that the rights of some racial, ethnic, and sexual groups are as important or more important than the rights of other groups or other citizens.

In trying to depict the complexity of such problems, I felt it important to explore the many social, psychological, and historical factors involved. Each of the following chapters focuses on a different and, at times, overlapping, aspect of group life in America: how and why America is becoming more pluralistic; how and why groups form, identify themselves, and change; what the political, social, and generational differences are within and between groups; how and why groups continue to be stereotyped and discriminated against—and how they react to bigotry; what goals groups and the nation have for themselves and each other; and what the benefits and disadvantages of group identity are.

Against that backdrop, I conclude with a discussion about the changing relations between government and groups, the growing dependence of groups on government for their power and continuity, the increasing legitimation of group rights over individual ones, the escalating tensions and conflicts between many groups, and the possibilities of America replaying the separatist, secessionist, and nationalistic strife that characterizes many European, African, and Asian countries. Throughout the book, my focus is on ethnic, religious, and racial groups whose differences among and between themselves elsewhere in the world have caused some of history's greatest calamities. Other groups, such as those based on gender and sexual preference, will be discussed briefly, mainly as they intersect with the above issues.

Wherever I could, I tried to present examples from different time periods in American history, because all too often today's problems are discussed as if they occurred only in the past, or as if they were new to American history, or as if no other people had grappled with similar ones. While each generation tends to slight the advice of its elders, it is no less true that each generation eventually discovers that many of its problems existed before they were born and that their forebears also confronted them.

At the same time, I have deliberately sought to provide a variety of group examples of specific behavior so that readers will realize (if they don't already) that "those people" or "that group" is *just* like or unlike, *much* like or unlike, or *somewhat* like or unlike their own group—whether for the better or worse.

All too often books and studies on racial, ethnic, and religious groups are written for scholars and serious students, aside from those obviously produced by and for the filiopietistic within a particular group. In writing this book, however, I had a broader audience in mind, believing that group life in America is simply too fascinating and exciting to be read about by the few.

In particular, this book will hopefully be helpful to issue-concerned citizens, teachers, social workers, community relations professionals, social policy analysts, journalists, personnel officers, and business leaders, who are: trying to understand what is happening in the world of intergroup relations; seeking to improve intercultural understanding and cooperation; working with minority group members; assessing the impact of group life on America and vice versa; and hoping to maintain a united, democratic, pluralistic country.

To such an audience there is no one way of looking at the subject, nor one all-encompassing solution. Wisdom, nevertheless, is universally recognized, but only if one is patient with complexities and is willing to view problems from a variety of perspectives. Helpful in forming such an outlook is a story I heard years ago from a professor whose name I have regretfully forgotten. He told of how people seated in a cathedral can look through different window panes and see different scenes outside. And yet, he said, if each person looked through the separate windows deep enough, they would all see the same thing.

## NOTE

1. David Cressy, *Coming Over: Migration and Communication between England and New England in the Seventeenth Century* (Cambridge: Cambridge University Press, 1989), 84–85.

# 1

# The Pluralization of American Population

And if a stranger sojourn with thee in your land, you shall not vex him. But the stranger that dwelleth with you shall be unto you as one born among you, and thou shalt love him as thyself; for ye were strangers in the land of Egypt.

—Leviticus 19:33–34

Ever since the first Europeans started forming communities some 500 years ago, America has been in a continuous process of change, with increasing numbers of people of different religions, races, and ethnicities. And yet, though more people come or want to each year than to all other countries of the world combined, America retains a uniquely recognizable identity, which extremely few of its citizens are willing to abandon, and which many foreigners die to obtain.

From a population of almost 3 million at the time of the American Revolution (excluding Indians), the nation grew to almost 250 million people in 1990, representing some 200 different ancestral groups, in which people claimed partial to full roots. According to the census of 1990, there were:[1]

| German | 58 million |
|--------|-----------|
| Irish | 39 million |
| English | 33 million |
| Afro-American | 24 million |
| Italian | 15 million |
| Mexican | 12 million |

| French | 10 million |
| Polish | 9 million |
| American Indian | 9 million |
| Dutch | 6 million |
| Scotch-Irish | 6 million |

Other ethnic ancestral groups with populations of 5 million to at least 1 million were: Scottish, Swedish, Norwegian, Russian, French Canadian, Welsh, Spanish, Puerto Rican, Slovak, Danish, Hungarian, Chinese, Filipino, Czech, Portuguese, British, Hispanic, Greek, Swiss, and Japanese. Some immigrant groups had only a few thousand, such as Ugandan, Nepali, and Singaporean. In all, as of 1990, nearly 20 million residents were foreign-born, representing about 7.9 percent of the total national population. Almost 32 million spoke a language other than English at home, and of some 170 non-American Indian languages reported, the ten most used were: Spanish, French, German, Italian, Chinese, Tagalog, Polish, Korean, Vietnamese, and Portuguese.[2]

In recent years, about 800,000 legal immigrants have arrived annually. Most in the fiscal year 1992 were from Mexico (91,332), Vietnam (77,728), the Philippines (59,179), the former Soviet Union (43,590), and the Dominican Republic (40,840). Also, hundreds of thousands of illegal immigrants try and often succeed in entering each year, aside from tens of thousands of people who come in search of political asylum, claiming they are persecuted or have a well-founded fear of such if they return home. By 1993, for example, some 370,000 refugees were waiting for government approval of their request for asylum, almost half of whom had entered that year from more than 100 countries. Since then, eligibility for asylum was broadened to include those fleeing persecution because of sexual orientation, as in the case of a Mexican gay, as well as women subject to rape, domestic abuse, and such violence as infanticide, genital mutilation, and forced marriage.[3]

The countries of origin of political refugees are slightly different from those of legal and illegal immigrants, but are no less global, and vary in size according to political and/or economic conditions back home, as well as the relations of those lands with America. For example, the top ten countries in 1993 were: Guatemala (34,681), El Salvador (15,362), China (14,354), Haiti (11,377), Mexico (6,192), India (5,902), Pakistan (4,653), Nicaragua (4,286), Philippines (4,107), and Bangladesh (3,759). However, for the longer period of 1982 to 1994, the top ten countries were: Vietnam (424,000), the former Soviet Union (313,000), Laos (119,000), Cambodia (91,000), Iran (38,000), Romania (37,000), Poland (36,000), Ethiopia (30,000), Afghanistan (27,000), and Cuba (19,000).[4]

Though the diversity of people coming to America is unparalleled, it is not new. In pre-Columbian times, estimates of the native population in North and South America range from 8 million to more than 75 million; and north of the Rio Grande, from 1 million to 18 million. Dozens of different languages and hundreds of different dialects were spoken by members of some 500 tribes, who had more variations in height, facial features, and color than the white European invaders. Like the latter, they had their intergroup rivalries and wars.[5]

One foreign power after another established settlements, military bases, missionary outposts, or trading stations in different, overlapping, or similar areas—the Vikings in and off coastal New England; the English, Dutch, Swedes, and Scotch mainly along the East Coast; the French in the north and south central areas; the Spanish in the Southwest, Southeast and Far West; and the Russians in the Pacific Northwest. To varying degrees, they looted and warred with each other, competed for Indian allies, expropriated or destroyed Indian lands and lives, utilized white European indentured laborers, transplanted criminals, and brought or bought enslaved Africans to do the work that they and the Indians could not or would not do.

When the first census of the United States was taken after the American Revolution, in 1790, almost all of the white residents of European descent lived within fifty miles of the Atlantic Ocean: 60.9 percent English; 14.3 percent Scotch and Scotch-Irish; 8.7 percent German; 5.4 percent Dutch, French, and Swedish; 3.7 percent South Irish; and 7 percent unidentifiable. At that time, African Americans represented a higher percentage of the population than today—some 19 percent or 500,000 people.[6]

Like today, clear residential patterns for colonists and native Indians were evident, though their bases were more ethnic, nationalistic, or tribal than socioeconomic. Virginia and Massachusetts had the majority of people of English descent, while Pennsylvania had the largest number of Germans. The Dutch mainly lived in "the zone of tolerance"—New York, New Jersey, and Pennsylvania. New Jersey, which had the fewest English, had the largest number of Irish. Among the native Americans on the East Coast, the major concentrations included the Natchez in the lower Mississippi region; Creeks and Cherokees in the lower Appalachians; Apalachee, Calusa, and Timucua in Florida; Cofitachiqui and Powhatan on the coastal plain; and the Delaware, Iroquois, Huron, Narragansett, Massachusetts, and Wampanoag in the northern woodlands.[7]

In the following decades, dramatic and unanticipated population changes took place as Americans moved westward and compelled the Indians in their path to do likewise, but to ever more restricted land areas. First the states and then the federal government welcomed, or, at least, tolerated immigration from abroad, except in the latter nineteenth century when Chinese and assorted European criminals were specifically banned by law. Between 1820 and 1860, 95 percent of legal entrants were from northern and western Europe, but as a result of the massive immigration beginning in the 1880s, their percentage in 1907 dropped to 19 and that of south, central, and eastern Europeans soared to 81 percent, including the first large number of Jews. In the same year, Japan and America agreed to restrictions on Japanese worker-immigrants. The outbreak of World War I all but stopped immigration, after which it was heavily restricted and subject to quotas in the 1920s along nationality lines—and then thwarted by the Great Depression. Not until after World War II did restrictions ease somewhat, though allowances had been made earlier for American farmers to bring in temporary Mexican laborers, some 5 million of which entered between 1942 and 1960. However, the nationality quotas of prior decades were largely reaffirmed in the 1952 McCarran-Walter Immigration Act, though race was eliminated as a bar to immigration.[8]

In the 1960s overall immigration from Europe began rapidly declining, while that from Latin America, Asia, and North America progressively increased, facilitated ironically by a number of immigration reforms designed to end invidious quotas and to discourage illegal immigrants. The 1965 Immigration Reform Act, which President Johnson signed in front of the Statue of Liberty, ended historically restrictive quotas favoring Europeans, particularly northern and western ones. To its supporters, the act was not meant to increase total immigration, change the ethnic or racial mix of the population, or, as Senator Edward Kennedy said, to "inundate America with immigrants from any one country or area, or the most populated and economically deprived nations of Africa and Asia."[9]

The Refugee Act of 1980 broadened the definition of refugees to include those from non-Communist countries, as well as providing federal financial assistance to those resettling here, so that more than a million refugees entered the United States between 1981 and 1990, mostly from Asia. Six years later, the Immigration Reform and Control Act granted legal status to some 3 million illegal aliens who had been residing here, while imposing penalties on employers who knowingly hired new ones. After the Vietnam War, the Amerasian Homecoming Act allowed the immigration of children of American soldiers and Vietnamese mothers as well as their immediate family members. The 1990 Immigration Act was enacted to favor more highly educated and trained immigrants, as well as Europeans disadvantaged by previous legislation, such as the Irish; in addition, illegal Salvadoran immigrants were given temporary protected status, and some 100,000 Filipinos who had served with our armed forces were offered immediate citizenship.

In spite of the intentions of such legislation, no diminution of legal or illegal immigration occurred, nor did any return to earlier nationality patterns of immigration. By the late 1970s, 42 percent of immigrants were coming from Latin America and 39 percent from Asia, while those from southern, central, or eastern Europe had declined to 8 percent and those from northern and western Europe to a mere 5 percent. For the next decade, 1981 to 1990, only 10 percent of immigrants came from all of Europe.[10]

Just as today's multicultural composition would be unimaginable to America's Founding Fathers, so it is to most immigration reformers of the twentieth century. By 1990, minorities represented at least one-fourth of the population, twice that of the 1970s, wherein 75 percent of the total population had European origin, 12 percent were black, 9 percent Hispanic, 3 percent Asian, and 1 percent American Indian. Also unforeseen were dramatic changes in the numbers and percentages of foreign-born residents, 20 million of whom in 1990 represented almost 8 percent of the total population, the highest number since 1940, but lower than the 1910 peak of 15 percent. More specifically, while from 1960 to 1990 the number of Asians among the foreign-born zoomed from 5 percent to 25 percent and for Latin Americans from 9 percent to 43 percent, the number of Europeans dropped from 67 percent to 20 percent. Then, four years later, the Census Bureau reported that the foreign-born had risen to 8.7 percent of the population: Mexicans 6.2 million, Filipinos 1 million, Cubans 805,000, Salvadorans 718,000, Canadians 679,000, Germans 625,000, Chinese 565,000, Dominicans 556,000, South Koreans 533,000, and Vietnamese 496,000.[11]

Still greater changes are currently in the making, generated largely by increasing legal and illegal immigration from non-European countries, as well as by a declining fertility rate of American-born whites, which is below replacement level—generally considered 2.1 children per woman. Census predictions are that out of an estimated total American population of 383 million in the year 2050, the number of Asians and Pacific Islanders will have grown from 9 million in 1992 (3 percent of the total population) to 41 million (11 percent of the population; Hispanics from 24 million in 1992 (9 percent) to 81 million (21 percent of the population), making them the nation's largest minority group; blacks from 32 million (12 percent) to 62 million (16 percent); and the number of American Indians, Eskimos, and Aleuts will double to 4.6 million (1.2 percent). In contrast, while the non-Hispanic white population will grow from 191 million to 202 million, its percentage of the total population is expected to decline from 75 percent to 53 percent (see Figures 1.1 through 1.5).[12]

No one knows exactly how many illegal immigrants there are in America or from where they came. Guesstimates vary from a few million to over 10 million, as each year some 200,000 to 300,000 illegals successfully elude government authorities. More accurate are the arrest figures, which in recent years averaged 1 to almost 2 million annually, representing 170 nationalities in 1993, mostly from Mexico, followed by El Salvador,

Figure 1.1
U.S. Population in 1993 and 2050 by Race/Ethnicity, with and without
Immigration after 1993

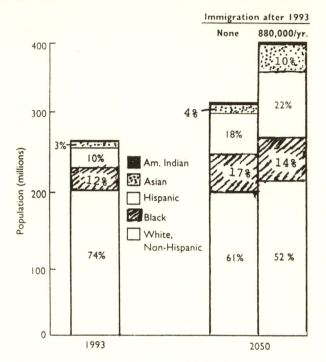

*Source:* U.S. Bureau of the Census.

Note: American Indians make up 1 percent of the population in each bar.

the Dominican Republic, Guatemala, Canada, Honduras, Colombia, Jamaica, China, and Nicaragua. While slightly more than a million voluntarily agreed to leave, some 42,000 were expelled (see Figure 1.6).[13]

Illegals enter—or try to enter—by a variety of ways: plane, ship, speed-
boat, raft, or foot, with many losing their lives by sailing on unsafe vessels
or hiring unscrupulous smugglers who charge a few thousand to $30,000
and then abandon or kill them en route, or will threaten to do so if they
or their families fail to pay the amount owed. As with the drug trade,
international criminal syndicates formed to smuggle immigrants from Sri
Lanka, Bangladesh, Afghanistan, Africa, and the Middle East to western
Europe and America, using former Communist countries in eastern Europe
as transfer points. In addition, large numbers arrived as legal tourists, students, or business people, and then, in violation of their visas, remained
permanently—totalling some 2 million in 1994, mostly Mexicans, fol-

lowed by Poles, Filipinos, Haitians, Bahamians, Canadians, Italians, Guatemalans, Salvadorans, and Nicaraguans. Some illegals paid as much as $5,000 for a bogus marriage with an American citizen, thereby enabling them to legally remain. And some women who were smuggled into the country were forced to work as prostitutes and earn $40,000 to $50,000 to purchase their freedom, as in the case of Thais who were originally told that good restaurant jobs awaited them.[14]

There are also ethnic criminal gangs, as well as corrupt U.S. government officials, who sell would-be immigrants fraudulent visas, social security cards, certificates of naturalization, and instructions on what to say if they are caught: They are political refugees who if returned home would be persecuted or killed. Some immigrants themselves have engaged in highly questionable or fraudulent practices. Some of the 20,000 young people and 60,000 family members who entered the country under the 1987 Amerasian Homecoming Act allegedly took bribes from nonfamily Vietnamese to say they were close family members, thereby making them eligible for immigration to the United States.[15]

In a desire to help illegal immigrants, particularly those claiming to be political refugees from El Salvador and Guatemala, a number of cities and religious groups in the mid-1980s declared their area or buildings "sanctuaries," in which local police, city officials, and clergymen refused to help federal officials identify, arrest, or deport illegals.[16]

So prized is American citizenship that many pregnant Mexican women

**Figure 1.2**
**Immigrants Admitted: Fiscal Years 1900 to 1993**

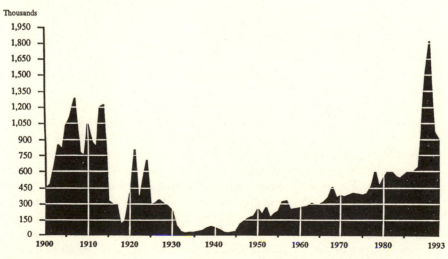

*Source: 1993 Statistical Yearbook of the Immigration and Naturalization Service.*

Figure 1.3
Immigrants Admitted by Region of Birth: Selected Fiscal Years 1955 to 1993

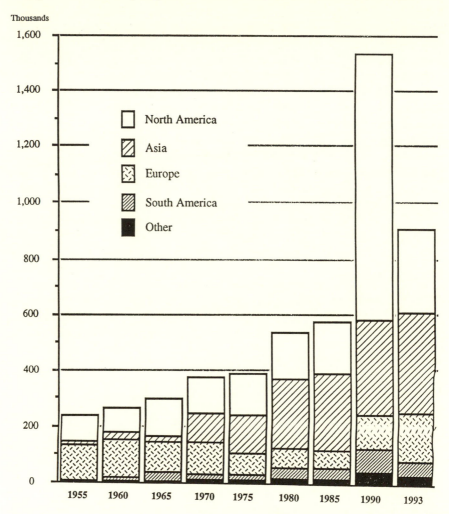

*Source: 1993 Statistical Yearbook of the Immigration and Naturalization Service.*

crossed the border illegally or legally in order to give birth in an American hospital, thereby making their children American citizens under the rule of *jus soli* (the law of soil) rather than *jus sanguinis* (law of the blood)— while they themselves become eligible as guardians of an American to receive Aid to Families with Dependent Children (AFDC). According to one former government immigration official in 1994, approximately two out of three babies born in Los Angeles county hospitals were of illegal alien mothers.[17]

Legal immigrants, and particularly refugees, have readily availed them-selves of America's welfare system. According to the census of 1990, while 8.4 percent of all households were foreign-born, they received 13.1 percent of public assistance funding, especially those who came as legal refugees. Other research found that in the latter households, some 16.1 percent were on welfare, compared to 7.8 percent for nonrefugee immigrant households and 7.4 percent of native-born households. For refugees who came in the latter half of the 1980s, the percentage was even higher—31. As of 1990, the ten largest refugee household groups on welfare were from:[18]

| | | | |
|---|---|---|---|
| Cambodia | 48.8 percent | Cuba | 16 percent |
| Laos | 46.3 | Mexico | 11.3 |
| Dominican Rep. | 27.9 | China | 10.4 |
| Vietnam | 25.8 | Haiti | 9.1 |
| Soviet Union | 16.3 | Korea | 8.1 |

While those who came as legal immigrants were not eligible for three to five years for many government assistance programs, during which time their sponsoring families or friends were supposed to help them, those who were "aged, blind or disabled" could obtain Supplementary Security

**Figure 1.4**
**Percent Foreign-Born: 1900 to 1994**

| Year | Percent |
|---|---|
| 1900 | 13.6% |
| 1910 | 14.7% |
| 1920 | 13.2% |
| 1930 | 11.6% |
| 1940 | 8.8% |
| 1950 | 6.9% |
| 1960 | 5.4% |
| 1970 | 4.8% |
| 1980 | 6.2% |
| 1990 | 7.9% |
| 1994 | 8.7% |

*Source:* U.S. Bureau of the Census.

Figure 1.5
Immigrants Admitted to the United States from the Top Five Countries of Last
Residence: 1821 to 1993

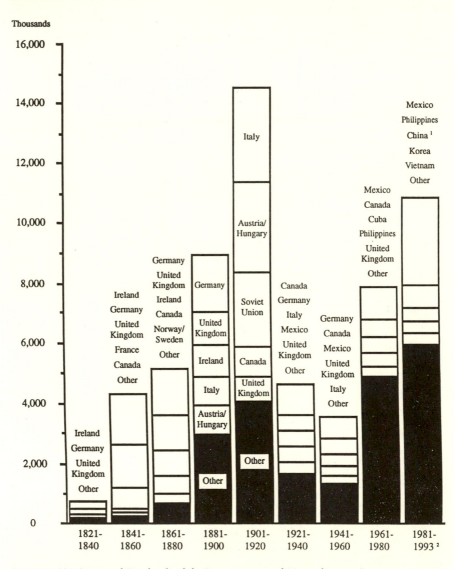

*Source: 1993 Statistical Yearbook of the Immigration and Naturalization Service.*

1. China includes Mainland China and Taiwan.
2. Thirteen-year period.

Figure 1.6
Estimated Illegal Immigrant Population in the United States, by State: October 1992

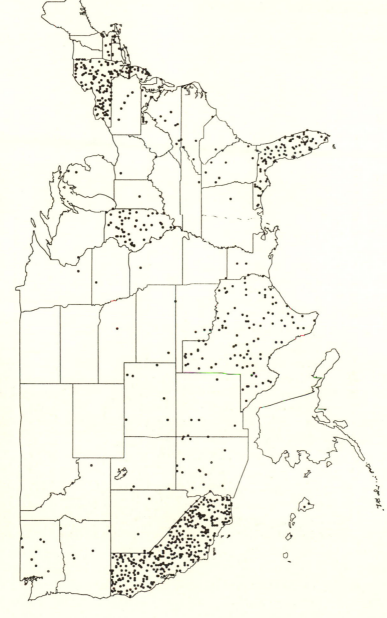

*Source: 1993 Statistical Yearbook of the Immigration and Naturalization Service.*

Note: Each dot represents 3,500 illegal aliens residing in the United States. Dots are distributed randomly within each
state.

Income (SSI), Medicaid, and food stamps, and many did so. For example between 1982 and 1994, the number of aged immigrants (over 65 years old) receiving SSI payments increased 500 percent, from 91,000 to 440,000, as did their proportion of the total number of recipients, which went from 6 percent to 30 percent. Most of those recipients were from Mexico, followed by the former Soviet Union, China, Philippines, Cuba, South Korea, Vietnam, India, the Dominican Republic, and Iran. A subsequent Census Bureau study found that contrary to pre-1970 immigrants, those coming after 1990 are more likely to receive public assistance than native-born Americans (5.7 percent and 2.9 percent, respectively).[19]

While there are no official records of how many people leave America permanently, it is generally agreed that relatively few do, native- or foreign-born. For example, 38 million immigrants were admitted between 1900 and 1990, while 12 million foreign-born residents left. It is not known how many native-born Americans leave, though census officials estimate that in recent years about 160,000 citizens and aliens left each year. Nor is it known how many political refugees return home, though it is obvious that relatively few do, even after political conditions back home improved, as in the case of Haiti and El Salvador (which reportedly does not want its former citizens to return because their remittances to their families total about $1 billion a year, which almost equals El Salvador's yearly export income).[20]

Generally, what an (Asian) Indian American wrote to his group readers holds true for other groups as well:

First thing is to understand and accept the eternal truth that all of us are going to live our lives in this country. The ridiculous idea of going back to India after saving a packet should be deeply buried away and replaced by the reality of continued living in America as there is no other country on this earth which provides us with comparable opportunities for living with dignity, growth and upward advancement under most favorable conditions.[21]

With the increasing diversity of people came the diversity of religions, places of residence, schools, and languages. By 1900, the once feared and hated Catholics had become the largest single denominational group, followed by the once widely disliked Baptists. No longer was America described in basically Protestant terms (as was the case in the eighteenth and nineteenth centuries), but rather in terms of Protestants, Catholics, and Jews (as became popular in the 1950s and 1960s). However, in recent years even the use of "Judeo-Christian" to describe America is fading as other religions establish sizable presences—such as Greek Orthodoxy, Islam, Buddhism, Hinduism, and Bahaism. For example, though Hindus and Muslims represented less than one-half of 1 percent each of the national population in 1993, Hindus had some 412 houses of worship across the country, Buddhists 1,515, and Muslims 1,139, with predictions that within a decade or so, the total Muslim population would exceed that of Presbyterians and Jews. Already, in order to meet the spiritual needs of the U.S. Army's Muslim population of 2,500, an Islamic army chaplain, the first ever, was appointed in late 1993.[22]

Contrary to the belief that the more religious options, the less the commitment, religion in America is alive and well, though attendance at religious centers is not as high as the clergy might wish. Polls generally show that Americans still consider themselves a religious people—with 95 percent believing in God, 92 percent affirming a religious preference, 90 percent believing there is a heaven, 68 percent belonging to a church or synagogue, 56 percent saying religion is "very important" in their lives, 40 percent attending religious services in a given week, and 42 percent of adults in 1994 saying they were saved, converted, and motivated by the Gospel. Nonbelievers or antibelievers are relatively few. In a 1989–90 poll, a mere 7.5 percent reported having "no religion," while 0.7 percent said they were humanists, and 1.7 percent said they were agnostics.[23]

Within denominations, however, dramatic changes in composition are evident. Instead of being far-off missionary targets, Africans, Asians, and South Americans are elbow-to-elbow worshippers, though not necessarily next-door neighbors. Just as ethnic differences existed among prior generations of immigrants of the same faith (such as between Irish, Italian, French and German Catholics, as well as between eastern and western European Jews), so today differences exist between American and immigrant Vietnamese Catholics, American and immigrant Korean Protestants, American and immigrant Syrian Jews, and American and immigrant Muslims from Africa, Asia, and the Middle East.

Also, as in the past, some religious believers of different nationalities are holding separate religious services, either in the same or separate building. For example, in the borough of Queens in New York City, a United Methodist church holds separate and simultaneous Sunday services in four different languages—English, Spanish, Korean, and Chinese. In Boston, the number of churches in 1993, particularly small immigrant ones, had increased 50 percent over a twenty-five-year period to 459, attracting members from 106 countries and holding services in thirty-three different languages, at such places as the Iglesia Pentecostal Cristo El Rey, l'Eglise de Dieu Haitienne de Boston, and the Indonesian Full Gospel Fellowship.[24]

Parallel changes are also taking place in the nation's schools, which, as in the early twentieth century, have large numbers of immigrant non–English-speaking children. Though representing some 145 languages, most immigrant children speak Spanish. Whereas in 1972, some 21 percent of students three to seventeen years old were African American, Hispanic, Asian, or a group other than white, by 1990, the number was 31 percent. The larger the urban school system, the greater the diversity: While almost

71 percent of all the nation's schools primarily were white in 1990–91, in forty-four of the nation's largest urban school systems the number was only 25 percent, with African Americans having 42.1 percent, Hispanics 26.5 percent, Asians or Pacific Islanders 5.9 percent, and Native Americans or others 0.5 percent. Contributing to the increasing percentages of immigrant offspring are the relative youth and high fertility rate of their parents. In California, for example, though Hispanics, Asians, and other minorities comprised less than 30 percent of the 1990 population, their children accounted for more than 50 percent of the elementary school population. New York City schools had students from almost 200 countries, speaking about 100 different languages.[25]

In some areas—Hawaii, New Mexico, and the District of Columbia— more than 50 percent of the high school graduates in 1989 were Hispanic, black, and Asian or Pacific Islander. Here, too, projections for the future indicate still larger percentages of one or another minority group and a decrease in the number of whites. For example, while from 1985 to 1994 the percentage of elementary and secondary school Asians and Pacific Islanders was expected to increase by 70 percent (from 940,000 to 1.6 million), and Hispanic enrollment by 54 percent (from 3.3 million to 5.1 million), overall white enrollment was expected to decrease from 71 percent to 66 percent. In many large inner cities, schools that were ordered to desegregate have been de facto resegregated, so that in Boston in 1990, 77.8 percent of public school enrollment was minority, in contrast to 1980 when it was 64 percent.[26]

Of course, the changes in religious institutional and public school populations often reflect the choices or necessities of where immigrants settle, work, rent, or buy homes. As in colonial times, geographical patterns of residence clearly exist, which are influenced by a variety of factors: where friends or family already live, where jobs are available, port of arrival, similarity of climate or proximity to the country of origin, the financial resources immigrants bring with them, familiarity with the country, and, recently, the ease with which state or federal aid could be obtained.

For example, Minnesota has the most Norwegians, Massachusetts the most French Canadians, Pennsylvania the most Slovaks, Texas the most Czechs, and Ohio the most Hungarians. In addition to having attracted more legal immigrants than any other state for the fiscal years 1983–92, as well as 75 percent of the million or so illegal immigrants in 1992, California leads all states in the number of German, Irish, English, French, Dutch, Scotch-Irish, Scottish, Swedish, Welsh, Danish, Portuguese, British, and Swiss; in addition, Los Angeles has the country's largest Gypsy (Roma) population, some 50,000. New York has the largest number of Italians, Poles, Russians, and Greeks. Asian and Pacific Islanders live mostly in the West, as do more than 50 percent of all Armenians and

Iranians. While one-half of American Indians live in the South, more of them live in Los Angeles County than in any other city or reservation, an estimated 60,000 to 80,000. West Indian groups are concentrated in the Northeast, as are Israelis. Hispanics vary in location, according to their nationality. Dominicans, Puerto Ricans, and Ecuadorans are found mainly in the Northeast, Cubans in the Southeast, Salvadorans and Guatemalans in the West, and Mexicans in the Southwest.[27]

In spite of such concentrations, Americans continue to be on the move. In the ten-month period prior to the census of 1990, more than two out of ten households had relocated, particularly young unmarried males. Within many states, minorities increasingly moved to the suburbs, with the black population in suburban areas growing by 34.4 percent from 1980 to 1990, the Hispanic population by 69.3 percent, and the Asian population by 125.9 percent. Minority suburbanization occurred "both as the black middle class came into its own and as more assimilated Latinos and Asians translated their moves up the socioeconomic ladder into a suburban life style," said University of Michigan demographer William H. Frey.[28]

In some other areas, whites are, or are becoming, a minority. According to 1990 census figures, in 186 counties and 1,930 places, Hispanics, blacks, Asians, Pacific Islanders, American Indians, Eskimos and Aleuts, by themselves or in combination, constitute more than 50 percent of the total population, and in one-fourth of the counties, they represent more than 75 percent.[29]

Within a generation or two, the group characteristics and ratios of entire cities changed dramatically. While in the 1920s, people of European descent constituted 95 percent of the population of our twelve largest cities, today they are largely a minority. Monterey Park, California, changed from being a "new Beverly Hills" for wealthy whites in 1916, to a "Mexican Beverly Hills" in the 1980s when Hispanics became the largest group, to now being termed a "Chinese Beverly Hills" because of its 56 percent Asian population. According to 1990 census figures, 85 percent of the black population lived in metropolitan areas, and in some large northern and southern cities constituted more than 50 percent of the population, such as 75.7 percent in Detroit, 67.1 percent in Atlanta, 65.8 percent in Washington, D.C., 63.3 percent in Birmingham, 61.9 percent in New Orleans, 59.2 percent in Baltimore, and 58.5 percent in Newark. Elsewhere, Hispanics have become a majority, as in Miami, Florida; El Paso, Texas; and Santa Ana, California; while in major cities like Los Angeles, San Francisco, Pasadena, Houston, Phoenix, and San Antonio they outnumber blacks.[30]

Illegal immigrants tend to be concentrated in a few states and in cities where they are least detected. In 1992, California had the most illegals (1,283,000), New York (490,000), Florida (345,000), Texas (319,000), Illinois (172,000), New Jersey (128,000), Massachusetts (48,000), Arizona (47,000), Virginia (37,000) and Georgia (28,000), with the bulk speaking Spanish. Not all states attract equal types and proportions of illegals. For example, in New York, a 1993 study found that 80 percent of its almost one-half million illegal residents lived in New York City, and that, contrary to the national pattern of some other states, the five largest groups were Ecuadorans (27,100), Italians (26,800), Poles (25,800), Dominicans (25,600), and Colombians (24,500). By way of contrast, New Jersey's top five were Portuguese (14,200), Colombians (10,400), Poles (10,100), Italians (8,300), and Filipinos (7,000).[31]

While English linguistically continues to prevail, more and more foreign languages are heard in the streets, workplaces, schools, and government. Here, too, certain patterns are obvious. Spanish is the most used foreign language in thirty-nine states and the District of Columbia; French most used in Louisiana, Maine, New Hampshire, and Vermont; German in Montana, Minnesota, and the Dakotas; Portuguese in Rhode Island; Yupik in Alaska; and Japanese in Hawaii.[32]

Such developments provoke deep public concern, particularly during economic recessions and close elections, when reputable and disreputable calls are made for immigration restriction; exclusion or expulsion; stringent policing of American borders; denial of automatic citizenship to infants of illegal immigrant mothers; an English fluency requirement for citizenship; the ending of dual citizenship; the restructuring of immigration and naturalization bureaucracy; stoppage of state and federal social benefits to immigrants; and a ban on the use of foreign languages in government agencies and public documents.

For example, in 1993 a Gallup poll found that the number of Americans who believed immigration should be reduced had doubled in the prior three decades, rising to 65 percent, while a *CNN/USA Today* poll found that 76 percent wanted immigration stopped or reduced until the economy improved. Resentment is especially high in states with large numbers of illegals, such as Florida, California, Texas, and Arizona, which want reimbursement from the government for expenses incurred in jailing, educating, or providing of health care services to illegal immigrants. In 1994, Californians by a 59 to 41 percent vote passed Proposition 187, which called for the cutting off of education, social services, and nonemergency health care to illegals and their children, as well as requiring teachers, doctors, and social workers to report all illegal aliens to government immigration officials. Resentment has also been brewing over foreign language usage, with some nineteen states as of mid-1994 passing legislation declaring English their official language.[33]

Across the country, to one degree or another, economic, political, religious, humanitarian, and moral arguments simmer over whether immigration—legal and illegal—is:

—exceeding governmental power to regulate and control

—hastening national overpopulation

—abusing our historic humanitarian and Judeo-Christian principles of welcoming the stranger and providing refuge to the persecuted

—causing wages to be lowered for native-born Americans or, worse, their losing jobs

—impeding modernization of industry because employers prefer cheap labor to long-term production investments

—provoking conflicts among immigrant groups and between them and native-born American workers

—straining social services, educational facilities, and welfare rolls

—weakening the financial resources of city, state, and federal governments, and thereby increasing the need for new taxes

—worsening inner-city health and living conditions

—threatening the primacy of English and its unifying ability

—undermining traditional American and Western European cultural values

—and contributing to the balkanization of the American population

It is also argued that recent immigrants, particularly illegal ones, are largely less skilled and educated than pre-1980 arrivals or today's American-born residents, and that they are coming at a time when there is less need for such workers and a much greater one for those literate in English and technology. The absence of these skills, it is argued, will confine recent immigrants to poverty and reliance on welfare. For example, recent studies show that as of 1990 the typical immigrant had 11.9 years of schooling compared to 13.2 years for native-born Americans, that immigrant men not fluent in English earned about half as much as those who were fluent, and that immigrants who had arrived since 1980 had a higher percentage of below-poverty incomes. A 1994 census study found that, paradoxically, while some recent immigrants 25 years and older were more likely to be college graduates than either native-born Americans or prior immigrants, some were also less likely than natives to have graduated from high school.[34]

Defenders of continued immigration consider such charges untrue, if not bigoted, saying that America was always a nation of immigrants, and that contrary to all nativist and xenophobic doomsayers, immigrants—whether eighteenth-century Quakers or Germans, nineteenth-century Irish Catholics and Chinese, or early twentieth-century Jews and Italians—became loyal, law-abiding citizens, who often took or created jobs that native American citizens would not or could not do. Immigrants, and particularly their children, readily defended American democracy, from the Revolutionary War to the Persian Gulf War. No field of the arts, sciences, professions, or politics is without multiple examples of immigrants' outstanding achievements, even though when they first arrived their group was undoubtedly accused of being unsuited, unmotivated, uneducable, and unadaptable to the American and Protestant work ethic.

Though large numbers of recent immigrants are un- or undereducated, many are more highly educated than prior immigrants or resident Americans. For example, a comparison of U.S.–born and foreign-born Americans aged 25 or older shows that 24 percent of those who immigrated in 1980 or later had a bachelor's degree or higher, compared to 20 percent of American-born citizens and 19 percent of pre-1980 immigrants. Among Iranian-born immigrants, 43 percent in the mid-1980s were college graduates. Children of immigrants are also distinguishing themselves educationally—representing one-third to one-half of the annual high school winners in the Westinghouse Science Talent Search.[35]

In spite of all the anti-immigrant concerns, criticisms, and even prejudice, the longer immigrants live in the United States, the more they don't want to return to their homelands. A 1995 Gallup poll found an overwhelming majority preferring to live out their lives in America—ranging from 53 percent of those here ten years or less to 83 percent of those here twenty-one or more years. Also, more than 80 percent felt welcomed when they first arrived and still feel welcomed. Though 38 to 48 percent agree that America "is a racist country," 92 to 95 percent believe that people in America "who work hard to better themselves can get ahead."[36]

While debate continues over how many and which immigrants should be admitted, what measures should be taken to restrict immigration and expel illegal immigrants, and whether the federal or state government is responsible for the welfare and educational costs of legal and illegal immigrants, intergroup differences have also surfaced over government policies that allegedly or actually favor one or another group, such as Cubans rather than Mexicans, Russian Jews rather than Haitians, Europeans rather than blacks, Hispanics rather than Europeans, men rather than women, and "straights" rather than gays or lesbians.

In summary, from our very beginnings as a nation, Americans have undergone changes in where they came from and why, where they settled, and how they practiced their religion. The result has been tension and often conflict between change and continuity, which will most likely intensify if present patterns of immigration and minority-group relations continue.

Governmental immigration policies likewise have undergone changes, fluctuating between openness, restriction, and exclusion—depending on the race, religion, and nationality of the groups involved, the national economy, the domestic political scene, and the government's relations with the homelands of would-be immigrants. Frequently, people fleeing governments the United States politically opposed were readily admitted, particularly during the cold war decades, while those from friendly countries were told to remain at home and apply for admission, which could take years. Contrary to most expectations, the easing of restrictive immigration policies in recent decades failed to slow the number of legal and illegal immigrants wanting to enter, while it hastened a decline in the country's historic European and Anglo-Saxon Protestant bases.

Whether immigrant or American-born, each generation has to decide how to define itself, its relation to members of the same group, to people of other groups, to its ancestral homeland, and to America as a whole. To better understand the problems involved, a closer look will now be taken at the dynamics of group identity.

## NOTES

1. *Detailed Ancestry Groups for States, 1990* CP-2-1-2 (Washington, D.C.: U.S. Department of Commerce, 1992), 111–1.

2. Ibid., 111-1 to 111-3; U.S. Department of Commerce *News,* Bureau of the Census, Washington, D.C., 17 December 1992, 1–2 and 28 April 1993, 1.

3. *Boston Globe,* 14 December 1993, 22; Tim Weiner, "U.S. to Charge Immigrants a Fee," *New York Times,* 17 February 1994, D22; Sam Howe Verhovek, "In a Shift, U.S. Grants Asylum to 55 Mexicans," *New York Times,* 1 December 1995, A1; Ashley Dunn, "U.S. to Accept Asylum Pleas For Sex Abuse," *New York Times,* 27 June 1995, 1.

4. Roberto Suro, "U.S. Attempting to Deter Fraud in Asylum Bids," *Boston Globe,* 30 March 1994, 3; Amy Kaslow and George Moffett, "Refugees Without a Refuge: U.S. Starts to Pull Up Drawbridge," *Christian Science Monitor,* 1 March 1995, 11.

5. Kenneth Macgowan and Joseph A. Hester, Jr., *Early Man in the New World* (Garden City, N.Y.: Anchor Books, 1962), 5, 26; Ian K. Steele, *Warpaths: Invasions of North America* (New York: Oxford University Press, 1994), 3.

6. Louis B. Wright, *The Cultural Life of the American Colonies* (New York: Harper Torchbooks, 1962), 46.

7. Ibid.; Constantine Panunzio, *Immigration Crossroads* (New York: Macmillan, 1927), 15; Steele, *Warpaths,* 4.

8. Philip Martin and Elizabeth Midgley, "Immigration to the United States: Journey to an Uncertain Destination," *Population Bulletin* 49, no. 2 (Washington, D.C.: Population Reference Bureau, September 1994): 19, 23.

9. Philip Perlmutter, *Divided We Fall: A History of Ethnic, Religious, and Racial Prejudice in America* (Ames: Iowa State University Press, 1992), 252–56; Martin and Midgley, "Immigration to the United States: Journey to an Uncertain Destination," 11–14; Lawrence Auster, *The Path to National Suicide* (Monterey, Va.: American Immigration Control Foundation, 1991), 12.

10. *Population Bulletin* 37, no. 2, June 1982; Martin and Midgley, "Immigration to the United States: Journey to an Uncertain Destination," 21.

11. Barry Edmonston and Jeffrey S. Passel, "U.S. Immigration and Ethnicity in the 21st Century," *Population Today* (October 1992): 6–7; Martin and Midgley,

"Immigration to the United States: Journey to an Uncertain Destination," 5; Morton D. Winsberg, "America's Foreign Born," *Population Today* (October 1993): 4; "U.S. Immigrant Count Climbs to 8.7 Percent," *Boston Globe,* 29 August 1995, 3.

12. Edmonston and Passel, "U.S. Immigration and Ethnicity in the 21st Century," 6–7; Susan Kalish, "Multiculturalism Grows, but Segregation Lingers," *Population Today* (July/August 1992): 3; *New York Times,* 7 December 1992, B1; United States Department of Commerce *News,* Bureau of the Census, 29 September 1993, 3 and 4 December 1992, 3; Peter Brimelow and Joseph E. Fallon, "Controlling our Demographic Destiny," *National Review,* 21 February 1994, 42; *Statistical Yearbook of the Immigration and Naturalization Service, 1993* (Washington, D.C.: U.S. Government Printing Office, 1994), 155–56.

13. Deborah Sontag, "Study Sees Illegal Aliens in New Light," *New York Times,* 2 September 1993, B1, 8; Joyce C. Vialet, "Illegal Immigration: Facts and Issues," in *CRS Report for Congress* (Washington, D.C.: The Library of Congress, 23 September 1993), 1–4.

14. *New York Times,* 5 July 1987, A16 and 23 August 1993, A1; Raymond Bonner, "New Road to West for Illegal Migrants," *New York Times,* 14 June 1995, A12; Deborah Sontag, "U.S. Arrests 3 in Immigration Marriage Fraud," *New York Times,* 22 July 1994, A1; Ashley Dunn, "Greeted at Nation's Front Door, Many Visitors Stay on Illegally," *New York Times,* 3 January 1995, A1; N. R. Kleinfield, "Five Accused of Running Brothel That Held Thai Women Captive," *New York Times,* 5 January 1995, B1.

15. Stephen Engelberg, "In Immigration Labyrinth, Corruption Comes Easily," *New York Times,* 12 September 1994, A1; Philip Gourevitch, ". . . But It Does Not Forgive," *New York Times,* 29 April 1995, 23; Seth Mydans, "Once Lost in Vietnam, Now Lost in America," *New York Times,* 7 July 1995, A12.

16. Joel Brinkley, "California's Woes on Aliens Appear Largely Self-Inflicted," *New York Times,* 15 October 1994, 1.

17. *National Review,* 23 August 1993, 34; Michael T. Lempres, "Getting Serious about Illegal Immigration," *National Review,* 21 February 1994, 53.

18. Michael J. Mandel, "It's Really Two Immigrant Economies," *Business Week,* 20 June 1994, 74–78; Martin and Midgley, "Immigration to the United States: Journey to an Uncertain Destination," 33.

19. Vialet, "Illegal Immigration: Facts and Issues," 10–15; Jennifer Dixon, "Benefits of Legal Immigrants Targeted," *Boston Globe,* 22 November 1994, 3; Kristin A. Hansen and Amara Bachu, "The Foreign-Born Population: 1994," *Current Population Reports* (Washington, D.C.: U.S. Department of Commerce, August 1995), 3.

20. Martin and Midgley, "Immigration to the United States: Journey to an Uncertain Destination," 4, 12; *Statistical Yearbook of the Immigration and Naturalization Service,* 181; *The American Experiment,* quarterly publication of The Center for the New American Community (Winter 1995): 7.

21. G. S. Sandhu, "Indian-Americans Are Industrious, Resourceful and Prudent," *India Worldwide,* North American Edition (January 1995): 18.

22. Jay P. Dolan, *The Immigrant Church* (Baltimore: Johns Hopkins University Press, 1975), 2; Richard Bernstein, "A Growing Islamic Presence: Balancing Sacred and Secular," *New York Times,* 2 May 1993, 1, 26; Peter Steinfels, "Despite Role

on World Stage, Muslims Turn to the Personal," *New York Times,* 7 May 1993, A1; Richard N. Ostling, "One Nation Under Gods," *Time, Special Issue* (Fall 1993): 62; "Gallup Poll," *The Jewish Advocate,* 11–17 March 1994, 5; *Boston Globe,* 3 December 1993, 29.

23. James R. Kelly, review of *Religion in Contemporary Society,* by Barry A. Kosmin and Seymour P. Lachman, *Commonweal* (11 March 1994): 25; George Gallup, Jr., and Jim Castelli, *The People's Religion* (New York: Macmillan, 1989), 16; *Boston Globe,* 12 September 1994, 20; James L. Franklin, "Quietly, America's Faith in Religion is Born Again," *Boston Globe,* 3 April 1994, 1.

24. James L. Franklin, "Storefront Religion," *Boston Globe,* 24 December 1993, 1; Ari L. Goldman, "Enter the New 4-in-1 Multilingual Church," *New York Times,* 23 November 1989, A1.

25. Rosalie Pedalino Porter, *Forked Tongue* (New York: Basic Books, 1990), 5; Robert Kominski and Andrea Adams, *School Enrollment: Social and Economic Characteristics of Students: October 1991* (Washington, D.C.: U.S. Department of Commerce, 1993), xii; *National Urban Education Goals: Baseline Indicators, 1990–91* (Washington, D.C.: The Council of the Great City Schools, 1992), xvi; Martin and Midgley, "Immigration to the United States: Journey to an Uncertain Destination," 8; *Rand Research Review* (Fall 1993):8.

26. *New York Times,* 13 September 1991, A14.

27. *Detailed Ancestry Groups for States,* 111–2 to 111–3; Zena Pearlstone, *Ethnic L.A.* (Beverly Hills: Hillcrest Press, 1990), 100; Susan Moffat, "Urban Indians Seek a Higher Profile," *Los Angeles Times,* 10 June 1994, B1; Robert Reinhold, "A Welcome for Immigrants Turns to Resentment," *New York Times,* 25 August 1993, A12.

28. Sam Roberts, "U.S. Census Study Reveals A Nation of Rolling Stones," *New York Times,* 12 December 1994, A14; Karen De Witt, "Wave of Suburban Growth Is Being Fed by Minorities," *New York Times,* 15 August 1994, A1.

29. United States Department of Commerce *News,* Bureau of the Census, 9 June 1993, 1.

30. Thomas Muller, *Immigrants and the American City* (New York: New York University Press, 1993), 8; Price, "Vote Heats Up a California Melting Pot," *Boston Globe,* 11 April 1994, 3; Claudette E. Bennett, *The Black Population in the United States: March 1992* (Washington, D.C.: U.S. Department of Commerce, 1993), 2; Sam Roberts, "Hispanic Population Outnumbers Blacks in Four Cities as Nation's Demographics Shift," *New York Times,* 9 October 1994, 34.

31. Ronald Brownstein and Richard Simon, "Hospitality Turns Into Hostility," *Los Angeles Times,* 14 November 1993, A6; Sontag, "Study Sees Illegal Aliens in New Light," B1, B4; *CRS Report for Congress,* Table 3.

32. United States Department of Commerce *News,* 28 April 1993, 1–2.

33. Richard L. Berke, "Politicians Discovering An Issue: Immigration," *New York Times,* 8 March 1994; David Aikman and David S. Jackson, "Not Quite So Welcome Anymore," *Time, Special Issue* (Fall 1993): 12; Roy Beck, "Right of Silence?" *National Review,* 11 July 1994, 32; *Boston Globe,* 30 April 1994, 6, and 3 May 1994, 10; Jane Meredith Adams, "California Voters Reject Most of Clinton's Agenda," *New York Times,* 10 November 1994, 21; Deborah Sontag, "New York's Politicians Treat Illegal Immigration Carefully," *New York Times,* 10 June 1994, A1.

34. Martin and Midgley, "Immigration to the United States: Journey to an Uncertain Destination," 32, 38; George J. Borjas, "Nine Immigration Myths—Know The Flow," *National Review,* 17 April 1995, 44; Hansen and Bachu, "The Foreign-Born Population: 1994," 3.

35. Martin and Midgley, "Immigration to the United States: Journey to an Uncertain Destination," 41; Ron K. Unz, "Value Added," *National Review,* 7 November 1994, 57; Marshall F. Stevenson, Jr., review of *Rethinking Today's Minorities,* ed. Vincent N. Parillo, *Journal of American Ethnic History* (Summer 1994): 90.

36. *The American Enterprise* (November/December 1995): 102.

# 2

# Patterns, Processes, and Problems of Group Life

Here [in these States] at last is something in the doings of man that corresponds with the broadest doings of the day and night. Here is not merely a nation but a teeming nation of nations.

—Walt Whitman,
*Leaves of Grass*

As with individual identities, ambiguities and contradictions exist in groups as well. All groups are alike, and yet unlike, in some or many recognizable ways. Most obvious, of course, are the similarities and dissimilarities based on color, sex, and language.

Whether to stress similarities or dissimilarities, and to what extent, is a perennial problem for those inside and outside a group. Still more controversial, if not daunting, is the making of value judgments about group behaviors—or normatively comparing the behaviors of one group to those of another. In either case, all groups and their behaviors are subject to change, though differentially so, depending on the time, place, and generation. "The America of freedom has been an America of sacrifice," wrote historian Thomas Wheeler. "For every freedom won, a tradition lost. For every second generation assimilated, a first generation in one way or another spurned. For the gains of goods and services, an identity lost, an uncertainty found." [1]

For example, in complaining about the erosion of German Lutheran identity in the early nineteenth century, particularly among children attending English-speaking schools, one observer said:

First evangelical teaching gradually disappears, and our children grow up without hymns, without prayer, without catechism, and therefore without religious instruction. . . . Next we gradually lose our German customs, diligence, and thrift, replacing them with English styles which frequently degenerate into pride, laziness, and extravagance. . . . And finally, through neglect of our mother tongue, we lose our majestic hymns, prayerbooks, and edifying literature—an unspeakable loss![2]

More recently, the chairman of the 38th Annual Meeting of the Assyrian American Federation delivered a speech with the dual theme of "United We Stand, Divided We Fall" and "When We Don't Respect our Assyrian Heritage, Others Won't Respect It Either." In the speech, he said:

How many of us weaken our heritage every day, literally wash it away, by self-depreciation? How quick our associates are to value us at our own estimate! If we belittle our heritage, how can we expect others to respect it? We shouldn't be such fools as to think less of our Assyrian heritage than it really is. The strategy for raising above the practice of Assyrian depreciation is to express actively Assyrian appreciation to the world. This will make us a strong and UNITED people.[3]

A number of sociological and psychological phases or stages are involved in the acculturation and assimilation process. Andrew Greeley noted six phases: First is "Culture Shock," when the immigrant's old pattern of behavior is jolted by the basic need to survive upon arriving in the United States. During the second phase of "Organization and Emerging Self-consciousness," communal, fraternal, religious and political groups and leaders are formed. The next phase involves the "Assimilation of the Elite," wherein some individuals break out of their group boundaries to enter society's mainstream, though they do so with some ambivalence. The fourth phase is the "Militancy" of middle- and even upper–middle-class members, who simultaneously warn others of the dangers of associating with the larger society and yet urge them to excel in everything the larger society values. Fifth is "Self-hatred and Anti-militancy," wherein a substantial number of upper–middle-class and professional people become uneasy or critical of their group's past history and provincialism. Last, with "Emerging Adjustment," those who are securely upper-middle class display no shame or aggressiveness about their group origins, and begin making trips to the old country, though more out of curiosity than to see family or friends. "It is about this time that members of an ethnic group . . . begin to wonder why other groups, which have not moved as far along, are so noisy, raucus and militant."[4]

Generally, some groups acculturate with relative ease within a generation or two, while others take longer, particularly those who socially, religiously, and/or geographically want to avoid contact with other groups. Immigrants coming from a land where they were part of the majority quickly discover that here they are a minority and that if they are to succeed socioeconomically, they must learn how to speak a foreign language—English—and how to interact with people of other groups, about whom they may know or care little. Immigrants who were a minority back home, particularly one discriminated against, similarly have to adapt, but happily find they are not as targeted as they were back home and that there are other groups more or less discriminated against. Third, immigrants, and particularly their children, find they have opportunities and freedoms in America that were unavailable in their ancestral lands or, if they were, were sometimes specifically denied them.

With few exceptions, survival as group members requires adjustments and compromises, particularly on how and to what degree ancestral language, dress, eating habits, values, modes of worship, and trades and skills should be maintained. "Here in America," said a recent Saudi Arabian immigrant, "you are constantly forced to question the things we took for granted back home. Here, you need to really understand your values and get the children to feel close to their culture while still letting them assimilate." [5]

The challenge is all the greater for non–English-speaking adults and those coming with children. "An immigrant almost loses his identity in just the 3½-hour flight from the Azores," said one Portuguese immigrant in Fall River, Massachusetts, in 1978. "A child looks up to his parents, his father as master of the house and all of a sudden the father is completely inadequate. He can't ask for a glass of water or where the toilet is. The kids learn English, and the parents depend on the child." Those unable to understand English often intuit what many native Americans feel about them. "We know they do not like us. We don't understand the words," said a Guatemalan immigrant in Palisades Park, New Jersey, pointing to his head, and then added, touching his heart, "We know what they mean." [6]

In such a setting, family and intergroup conflicts are unavoidable. Some examples follow:

—Writing on the state of religion in America in 1785, Father John Carroll noted a decline in the piety of newcomers because of "unavoidable intercourse with non-Catholics, and the examples thense derived: namely more free intercourse between young people of opposite sexes than is compatible with chastity of mind and body; too great fondness for dances and similar amusements; and an incredible eagerness, especially in girls, for reading love stories which are brought over in great quantities from Europe." [7]

—"It is a gala time for everyone but the young people," wrote an observer of a Swedish-American celebration in North Dakota, in the 1930s. "They must listen to foreign languages as though they understood. Old folk songs with unfamiliar music are supposed to inspire them. They cannot dance with the gusto of the older people. They do not know the old

games. They are out of color in their collegiate American clothes. Grand-
mother and her circle are a bit ashamed of their ignorance." [8]

—The Finnish-American novelist, Willfred J. Jokinen told how just before making a downtown shopping trip, a daughter asked her immigrant
mother not to speak Finnish in public, saying, "All those who have come
from Europe are so uncivilized and stupid. They even got their first decent
meal in this country. And our school books say that Finns are Mongolians.
I don't want to be a slant-eyed Mongolian. Everyone in school began to
laugh and looked at me when we read that . . . so don't speak to me in
town." [9]

For many immigrant offspring, serving in American wars abroad has
hastened their acculturation. This was particularly true of World War II.
Prior to the war, said one Slovak Lutheran minister, no English was spoken
in his church, but after the war, "the young people coming back demanded
that English be adopted as a separate service. The effect of the war was to
put people of all different backgrounds together, and the common language there was English . . . so that when they got home after the war,
their native towns and churches were like a foreign country." [10]

Though not formulated with immigrants in mind, psychologist Abraham Maslow's hierarchy of needs offers an excellent backdrop for understanding what immigrants must overcome in moving from uncertain to
surefooted citizens. Maslow believes that people have inborn behavioral
needs and tendencies that must be fulfilled in order to live life to its fullest.
The needs are hierarchical, with the highest achievable only after those
below are satisfied.[11]

The basic physiological and survival needs include shelter, clothing,
food, and sex. Except for some few highly trained or wealthy immigrants
in recent decades, most are not immune from these needs, even those coming as families or welcomed by family or friends. The next stage upward
includes needs for safety, security, orderliness, and protective rules, which
immigrants meet by living in ethnic neighborhoods, obtaining jobs, learning English, and so forth. As individuals become secure, their "belong-
ingness" needs are more easily met—making friends, joining organizations,
spending time with families, and venturing beyond their immediate environment. Once socially secure, they are also able to confront ego-status
needs: achieving social and professional recognition, esteem, and power.
The highest need is that of self-actualization, wherein the individual, relatively secure in identity, risks engaging in creative and educational activities beyond those necessary for earning a survival living.

Recent psychological and psychiatric studies of immigrants substantiate
much of Maslow's insights. For example, modern-day immigrants have
profound problems in resettling and adapting, even after three or four
years in the country, particularly if they come from wartorn or rebellion-
ridden lands where family and possessions remain and to which they have

little hope of soon returning or visiting. The anguish of adaptation is reflected in a poem by a Korean immigrant, who had been a teacher in his native land, but because of language difficulty was a janitor in America: "I do not see, although I have eyes. Then, have I become blind? No, I have not. I do not hear, although I have ears. Then, I have become deaf? No, I have not. I do not speak, although I have a mouth. Then, have I lost my speech? No, I have not. I have become an old stranger who wants to raise a young tree (to educate his child) in this wealthy land." [12]

Some groups are more ethnic or religious than others, or, conversely, less so, and this precedes immigration. When the National Opinion Research Center asked how important ethnic background was, 76 percent of the Jewish respondents, 43 percent of the Italians, and 32 percent of the Irish answered, "extremely important or quite important." Such identity is known to develop early in life, with many five-year-old children able to classify themselves or others along racial, ethnic, gender, and age lines. [13]

The depth of group identity was well noted by John Adams as early as 1775:

There is in the human breast a social affection which extends to our whole species, faintly indeed, but in some degree. The nation, kingdom, or community to which we belong is embraced by it more vigorously. It is stronger still towards the province to which we belong, and in which we had our birth. It is stronger and stronger as we descend to the country, town parish, neighborhood and family, we call our own. And here we find it often so powerful as to become partial, to blind our eyes, to darken our understanding and pervert our wills. [14]

Whether genetically or historically rooted, self-grouping also involves Freud's concept of narcissistic identification, wherein people associate with others because of shared features (such as physical attributes, material possessions, professional training, societal beliefs, ethnic heritage); or because they seek some goal that others also want (such as higher wages, better health care, cleaner air, or a stop sign on a street corner); or because they want to be respected for their group roots.

And yet, as noted at the start of this chapter, there are also many intergroup differences in such areas, for example, as "fertility rates, alcohol consumption, performance and behavior in school, suicide rates, and output per man-hour . . . standards of sanitation, incidences of crime and violence, proneness to become a charge upon the state." Within relatively homogeneous groups, too, differences persist or begin to erode. Thus, though Baltic people in America have few religious differences, Lithuanian, Latvian, and Estonian Roman Catholics are highly conscious of their ethnic differences, which are evidenced at weddings, in dietary preferences, in namings, and at celebrations of local saints. In contrast, regional and linguistic differences have been diminishing among Basques, who according to the census of 1990 were more prone to identify simply as "Basques" rather than as in previous times as "French Basques" or "Spanish Basques."[15]

Differential patterns of group attitudes toward doctors, health care, personal hygiene, social services, and the role of religion in cures are common, particularly among first generation immigrants. Researchers found that Japanese and Mexicans view mental illness as something to hide, deny, or rationalize. Estonians believed it degrading to have mental health problems. Ukrainians would rather starve than seek help, preferring first to consult a priest. In problems of child care, aging, and finances, working-class Poles and Italians relied on help from family, church, and, to a lesser extent, on voluntary organizations. Latino families were much less likely to use preschool and child care centers than other ethnic groups. Rather than see regular doctors, many Bahamians, Cubans, Haitians, Puerto Ricans and southern blacks in Miami, respectively, use Obeah, Santeria, Vodum, Espiritismo, and Rootwork. As one Asian psychotherapist explained, before Vietnamese immigrated to the United States they would "go to a fortune-teller . . . read poetry . . . go to the pagoda to meditate or . . . walk downtown to the market . . . see a friend or an elder in the family." Immigrant use of folk healers and their remedies for serious illnesses like cancer have proven useless, and sometimes fatal; in California, in 1994, state officials identified more than 700 products that were being illegally sold by various immigrant stores as cures for pain, colds, heart problems, insomnia, arthritis, anemia and kidney infections.[16]

The recent influx of different cultural groups has led many health providers to change their traditional ways of thinking and functioning. "The doctor must communicate respect to the patient," said Edward Poliandro, a hospital director of diversity training. "When patients are respected they will cooperate with the care." As a result, some hospitals, upon request, return the placenta to Filipino mothers so that they can bury it with books and thereby, they feel, make their baby more intelligent; allow Hindu families to sprinkle rose petals around a patient who died; permit Middle Eastern families to bless newborn babies by pouring oil on their heads; avoid scheduling tests or operations for Orthodox Jews on Saturdays (unless the patient's life is at risk); and expand maternity rooms and visiting hours for Hispanic patients, whose extended families like to visit for longer hours than usually allowed. A recent study of group attitudes toward dying found that almost twice as many African Americans and Euro-Americans as Korean Americans and one-and-a-half times as Mexican Americans, believed patients should be told of their metastatic cancer diagnosis and terminal prognosis, as well as decide on the use of life-support systems.[17]

Though to a lesser degree than in past decades, many urban and regional group differences continue. In spite of all the Woolworth stores,

McDonald's restaurants, and suburban shopping malls, one can feel, see, and hear the differences between Little Italies, Chinatowns, barrios and black sections of town, just as one can between many cities and countries. Santa Fe remains as different from Portland as New Orleans is from Chicago; and Italy, China, France, and Kenya cannot be confused with each other. Also, in spite of many linguistic and physical similarities, there are clear differences between America's many little ethnic colonies and their greater overseas homelands. As one modern-day Irish immigrant compared Boston to Ireland, "It's a lot less Irish than I thought it would be. Before I left, people in Ireland said, 'Oh, you're going home; Boston is just like here.' This is not like home. And people here are out of touch with Ireland." [18]

Demographic patterns are also obvious in terms of religion. Roman Catholicism pervades the New England states, which are also home to the Christian Science religion and Unitarianism, with a strong Congregational, Baptist and Episcopalian base; Methodism is particularly strong throughout the middle Atlantic states to the Rocky Mountains; Lutheranism and Catholicism permeate the upper Midwest; Baptists and Methodists are the two largest groups from Virginia to Texas; Mormons dominate Utah, southern Idaho, eastern Nevada and northern Arizona; and Spanish Catholics are strong in Texas, Arizona, California, and New Mexico. [19]

Helping to preserve regional differences, as well as group identity, are the huge numbers of new immigrants, who settle among or near their ethnic kinsmen. For example, by maintaining social, cultural, psychological, and linguistic contact with their homeland communities, immigrants from northern Mexico have been credited with slowing the erosion of Spanish culture in the Southwest. In contrast, the decline of the Yiddish press, theater, and cultural institutions in America started with the immigration restrictions on Eastern Europeans in the 1920s, which prevented any expansion in the group of Yiddish speakers and consumers. [20]

How is the tenacity of group identity explained? Social psychologist Simon Herman notes that groups use a "time perspective" of past, present, and future to describe or justify their existence. The more cohesive the group, the more time elements, whose overall presence or absence helps determine the group's sense of interdependence and mutual responsibility. [21]

The time elements can be subdivided into:

Scope: how large or small a time period is perceived by an ethnic group member

Structuralization: how the past, present, and future are organized and given a unifying significance

Continuity and Differentiation: how the past, present, and future are interrelated and divided into recognizable parts

Selectivity of Attitudes: what time periods ethnic groups seek out to enhance their
     past and adapt to the present

Probability of Locomotion: the attainability, timewise, of the group's goals


An additional way of trying to understand group identity is by looking
at the degree to which it penetrates the lives and thoughts of its members,
the degree to which members participate in group affairs, the degree to
which they are encouraged or pressured to comply with the group's customs and traditions, and the degree of consensus on group goals, teachings, and activities.[22]

Even after such analyses, this topic remains complex and contradictory,
with many second- and third-generation members affirming, highlighting,
downplaying, or denying their group identity. Simply put, the more generations in America, the greater is a group's acculturation and the less its
replication of parental and "old country" values and behaviors. For example, a study of Polish immigrants in 1970 found that 79 percent identified
themselves as "primarily Polish," 13 percent "primarily Americans," and
a fraction as "Polish Americans." However, eighteen years later, another
study found that only 42 percent considered themselves primarily "Polish," 44 percent "Polish Americans," and 11 percent "Americans," and
that with the change of identity went an adoption of American values,
such as independence, achievement, tolerance, pragmatism, and materi-
alism.[23]

Of course, the first to change are children. Writing in 1908, a Hungarian
visitor observed that while adult immigrants were having problems of acculturation, their children were "as American as if their parents had arrived with the first pilgrims. They are Yankees through and through, with
all the exuberance of American youth." The same can be seen in changes
in menus and eating habits. The Atlantic restaurant in the Norwegian section of Brooklyn has become "WeeKee's," which boasts of a "Chinese-
Norwegian-American" menu. Or, as one ten-year-old girl born in Laos,
raised in a refugee camp in Thailand, and now living in Kansas near immigrants from Mexico said, her favorite "American" food was tacos.[24]

At times, members of one group believe they have more in common
with those of other groups, though no reciprocity may exist. For example,
a 1993 Louis Harris poll found that blacks felt most in common with
Hispanics and least in common with whites and Asian Americans; Hispanics, however, felt most in common with whites and least in common with
blacks; Asians felt most in common with whites and least in common with
blacks; and whites felt most in common with blacks and least in common
with Asians. However, to solve pressing community problems, large majorities in each group said they would be willing to work together.[25]

For people of mixed racial, religious, or ethnic marriages, the problem of identity is especially complex. As one white Georgia mother whose husband is black recently explained, "My child has been white on the United States census, black at school, and multiracial at home—all at the same time." Equally perplexing is the case of a female law professor born of an African-Cuban mother and Australian-Irish father who some black and Hispanic students criticized for not asserting a specific identity. "I really don't spend a lot of time defining myself; other people do," she said. "These kinds of inquiries are racist and impolite in the extreme."[26]

Meanwhile, the number of multiracial births has been increasing, going from about 63,700 in 1978 to 133,200 in 1992. More specifically, where one parent was white and another black, the number went from 21,438 to 55,890; for Asian and white parents, from 21,013 to 42,033; for Native American and white, from 12,860 to 21,819; for Asian and black, from 1,669 to 4,051; for Native American and black, from 557 to 1,454; and for Native American and Asian, from 379 to 789.[27]

Many offspring of mixed backgrounds say they are half of one and the other; and in race, say they are biracial or multiracial, insisting that public and private forms seeking racial information not be limited to white, black, or other. By 1995, a number of states—Florida, Georgia, Illinois, Indiana, Michigan, and North Carolina—had adopted usage of "biracial" or "multiracial."[28]

How people identify themselves can also be influenced by a variety of other conditions. In Hawaii, for example, where nearly forty different racial and ethnic groups live, if a resident is asked by another resident "What are you?" the typical answer includes all of the respondent's racial and ethnic roots, but if a tourist asks the same question, the answer usually is simple, "local." Many Arab Americans are unhappy with the census of 1990 classifying them as "white, non-European," which inaccurately suggests "a common basis for a group that includes Egyptians, Sudanese, Iranians, and Norwegians." With the advent of affirmative action programs, some identities assumed greater economic importance. As one British-born immigrant, whose wife was a citizen of China, described the dilemma in 1994 for his American-born daughter:

When the time comes to fill out a Census form, which box do we check for her? Are we allowed to check both "white" and "Asian"? Or what? American friends tell us that most universities here operate quota systems against Asians so our daughter's future may be adversely affected by an "Asian" classification. On the other hand, there are . . . certain jobs in which Asians are underrepresented (police, mail carriers), so an "Asian" classification will benefit her if she decides to pursue one of these careers.[29]

Sometimes the root feelings of "group identity," "commonality," "interdependence," or "mutual responsibility" exist in broader settings. By stressing commonality of being and needs, many immigrants believe more can be accomplished for everyone. Thus on many American campuses, various panethnic, panracial, and pansexual student groups were formed, unlike among their parents or counterparts abroad where hostilities exist between such groups as Chinese and Japanese, Hmong and Chinese, Filipinos and Japanese, Vietnamese and Cambodians, and Hindus and Moslems. Since the race revolution, "Asian American" increasingly replaced "yellow" and "Oriental" as a collective self-description. At Boston College in 1979, the term *minority* was officially replaced by the acronym *AHANA,* meaning African-American, Hispanic, Asian and Native American. Also, some people prefer defining themselves primarily—at least in public—as athletes, writers, musicians, soldiers, scholars, and so forth, rather than by their race, religion, ethnicity, or sex. And for still a few others, specificity is avoided. As one young Japanese American said, "What I hate . . . is going into groups of people that all look the same," where "everybody has the same haircut, the same style." [30]

Whatever the group, there is always tension between a member's particular and universal identity. For example, in describing his teaching experience at a Lutheran seminary, a Reform rabbi noted that he had a greater kinship with his Christian students than with Orthodox rabbinical colleagues, "who refuse to meet as a body with non-Orthodox rabbis, and who deny that any religious expression other than their own has the right to call itself Jewish. . . . With Christians who affirm the validity and importance of Judaism, I feel accepted as a person and respected for my beliefs. With certain Orthodox Jews, I feel neither of these things." Similarly, a gay Republican state legislator recently said that while party colleagues "may disagree with me and not be too happy with the fact that I'm gay . . . there's a willingness to work with me, whereas in the gay community, people looked at me for a while as the Jew working for the Nazis." There are also "American Indians," "Native Americans," and "Indigenous People" who reject those generic terms, preferring to be known by their tribal name. [31]

Gender and sexual preferences, whether male, female, gay, lesbian, bisexual, or transgender, are also numerous. With the advent of women's liberation and equal rights legislation, opportunities opened to large numbers of women in fields long closed to them, and, like members of other groups, they confronted problems in deciding which of their identities is more important, sex, religion, race, ethnicity, profession, or class. Certainly, not all women agree on such issues as abortion, divorce, and sex education for children or on affirmative action programs that favor them.

More complex are the identity problems of people who are lesbian, gay, bisexual, or transgender. No one label can adequately define them, said William J. Mann, a white gay writer. "Neither 'gay' nor 'lesbian' allows for differences of politics, race, sexual perspective, spirituality or class."

Categorizing people as hetero- or homosexual demonizes them, wrote Marjorie Garber, author of *Vice Versa: Bisexuality and the Eroticism of Everyday Life,* who prefers using "bisexual" as an adjective rather than as a noun. Only after much heated debate did the planners of the 1995 city-wide gay parade change their name to the San Francisco Lesbian, Gay, Bisexual, Transgender Pride Celebration Committee. In New York City, however, a small group, the Lesbian Avengers, decided to hold their own parade a day before a much larger lesbian and gay one, because the latter was dominated by gay men. While Asians and racial minorities can closet their sexual identity, they cannot hide their physical appearance. "You can't stop being one," said a gay rights black activist. "We've done that too long. Saying, 'I'm going to be black when I go to the N.A.A.C.P. meeting, so I'll stop being gay right now.' Or, 'I'm going to sit in on the Gay Pride community meeting, so I'm going to stop being black.' "[32]

Of course, there are always minority individuals who won't join multigroup coalitions, either because they feel more comfortable associating with people of their own kind, believe others don't like them, think their group can gain more by working alone, don't like other groups, or are convinced that group pride and self-respect requires maintaining one's uniqueness and independence.

In the case of African-American identity, searing historical experiences with white society strongly influenced how blacks defined themselves and how they were defined by others. Unlike other groups, coming to America did not mean expanding opportunities, but restrictive subjugation to a continual process and institutionalization of slavery, in which skin color was used to justify how they were treated. Even after slavery was officially abolished in the nineteenth century and equal rights instituted, blacks were not free of white definitions, debasements, and exclusions, or of frustration and anger at how they and their ancestors had suffered.

In the early days of American slavery, black was frequently the designation, then African (as in the African Methodist Episcopal Zion Church), and a little later, Africo-American. A few early nineteenth-century freedmen scorned the terms *Negro, colored,* and *African,* and identified themselves as "oppressed Americans," believing that their people's plight would be solved when all people were uplifted "without distinction as to clime, country, or complexion."[33]

In midcentury, the editor of *The Colored American* preferred his paper's name because "We are written about, preached to, and prayed for, as Negroes, Africans, and blacks, all of which have been stereotyped, as terms of reproach, and on that account, if no other, are unacceptable." There were even suggestions that racemen, Anglo-African, or Negrosaxon be used. To others, black was the preferred term, and the use of Negroes, Colored people and African race was criticized.[34]

After the Civil War, freedman came into use, to be succeeded by Afro-

American and even Aframerican, and then Negro and Colored. Many emancipated slaves adopted the last names of American heroes, such as Washington, Jefferson, Jackson, Lincoln, and Clay. "Centuries of residence, centuries of toil, centuries of suffering have made us Americans," explained an 1874 black high school principal. With the civil rights movement of the 1960s, the term *black* became increasingly popular. Congress in 1963 ordered the changing or deletion of "nigger" in all geographic names, so that Nigger Run in New Jersey became Negro Run. A 1969 survey revealed that 38 percent most liked Negro, 20 percent Colored, 19 percent black, and 11 percent Afro-American. Clement E. Vontross, of George Washington University, told a 1970 interracial academic conference that blacks are psychologically together and "no longer hate themselves because of their black skin, kinky hair or previous servitude," in contrast to "Negroes . . . who are still dedicated to the possibility of integration" and "colored people . . . who continue to . . . feel inferior."[35]

In spite of the use of black throughout the 1970s, the NAACP refused to abandon the use of colored in its name, and Supreme Court Justice Marshall used Negro in his opinion in the 1978 *Bakke* case. To Boston's black weekly, *Bay State Banner,* "It seems quite inappropriate that Afro-Americans who are 30 million strong and have achieved so much despite adversity should be happy to refer to themselves merely as 'Blacks'. . . . Someone has to remind Afro-Americans that we are going through a process of self-identification. Just as the term 'Negro' has been rejected, so too will 'Black' one day become archaic."[36]

And, indeed, such began occurring in late 1988, when the Reverend Jesse Jackson and a group of prominent colleagues rejected black and advocated African American. To be so called, said Jackson, has cultural integrity. "It puts us in our proper historical context. Every ethnic group in this country has a reference to some land base, some historical cultural base. African Americans have hit that level of cultural maturity." However, his recommendation was not immediately accepted. In the following year, Justice Marshall used Afro-American for the first time in a Supreme Court decision, saying he preferred it to African American because it was in the dictionary and the latter was not. Major organizations, however, refused to change their historic names, such as the United Negro College Fund. Dramatic changes finally started occurring in the 1990s, when the percentage of people preferring to be identified as black declined from 72 percent in 1991 to 36 percent in 1994, and those preferring African American rose from 15 percent to 53 percent, according to a Time/CNN poll.[37]

Differences over how to identify oneself racially grew as more intergroup marriages and births occurred and as more people of color from different countries immigrated to the United States. As of the census of 1990, some 4.8 percent of the total black population were foreign-born, having come mostly from the Caribbean. To S. Allen Counter, director of the Harvard University Foundation, African American did not adequately reflect the "mixture of African, Native American Indian, and European bloodlines" and proposed Afrindeur-American as being more precise. Some others, like Professor Roy Simon Bryce-Laporte, who was born in Panama of Caribbean ancestry, refer to Spanish-, Portuguese- and French-speaking blacks of various backgrounds as Afro-Latinos. At a 1994 federal hearing, Teja Arboleda related that his maternal grandparents are European; his father's mother African American, his father's father the offspring of a Filipino and a Chinese; and he himself is listed as white on his birth certificate. Yet, when he refused to state his background on the census form in 1990, he was identified as "Hispanic."[38]

Whether in America or abroad, distinctions based on color of complexion and class are not new. The early peninsular Spanish in America created special social and legal terms—*criollas, mestizos, mulattos, zambos* (African-Indian offspring), and *castas* (Spanish-Indian-African descent). In Puerto Rico, a variety of terms are used socially or officially to describe a person's race or color, such as *trigueno* (for people neither all white or black), *grifo* (for people with kinky, African-like hair, but lighter skinned), and *Indio* (for people with Indian features). In Haiti, complexion and class are synonymous in the 1 percent of light-skinned elite controlling most of the wealth. And in Mexico, which officially takes pride in its Aztec roots, ethnic and racial discrimination is directed at those with Indian or dark complexions, many of whom use skin lighteners, hair dyes, and blue or green contact lenses to look more white European.[39]

There are also many dark-skinned Caribbean islanders, Brazilians, and Cape Verdeans in America who simply do not want to be identified with American blacks, preferring a British, French, or Portuguese identity in keeping with the country from where they came. Similarly, many Spanish blacks from Puerto Rico, Cuba, the Dominican Republic, and Panama prefer identifying with their white ethnic compatriots rather than with American blacks. The desire for status and avoidance of racism are integral in the self-identity process. For example, an early Cuban immigrant in Tampa, Florida, recalled, "If the crackers really wanted to make us Latins mad they'd call us Cuban niggers." Despite their geographical proximity, "Dominicans regard Haiti as a country more African than Latin American, and therefore inferior," said one diplomat who had worked in both lands. "Haitians, in turn, tend to think of Dominicans as a people unable to come to terms with their own blackness and harboring unreasonable pretensions to European grandeur." On continental America, some West Indian black immigrants don't want to be identified as African Americans, whom they consider "lazy, disorganized, obsessed with racial slights and barriers, with a disorganized and *laissez faire* attitude toward family life and child raising."[40]

At the same time, tensions between African Americans and Hispanics increased as the latter grew in number and demanded their proportional share of political and economic power, only to find black leaders opposing or not supporting them as they wished. To many Hispanics, wrote Charles Kamasaki and Raul Yzaguirre of the National Council of La Raza, "Blacks are perceived to be *culturally* more like whites than Hispanics are. . . . Many blacks frequently see Hispanics as yet another 'white' immigrant group that has come in at the bottom of the social and economic ladder and then overtaken them." In New York City, in 1993, West Indians began organizing themselves politically because they felt American black leaders did not adequately reflect their needs, such as more equitable immigration policies, local voting rights for noncitizens, and the influencing of American policy toward their homelands.[41]

Race and socioeconomic class aside, differences also abound among those of Spanish descent over nomenclature, though they share a common language, culture, and surnames. Do they or should they be called Spanish, Latinos, Spanish-speaking, Hispanics, or Latin Americans? Or do they or should they be identified by their specific country of origin in South America, Central America, or the Caribbean? Who within or outside of the group should decide, and how many members will agree?

No unanimity exists in the Southwest over which term to use: Mexican, Latin, Mexican American, Latin American, Latino, Hispano, Mejicano, Spanish, Spanish American, Raza, Chicano. In California, the pre-1848 Spanish-speaking residents preferred calling themselves Californios, but by the twentieth century they preferred Mexican Americans or simply Mexicans. For the young and more militant in the 1960s and 1970s, Chicano became the preferred term, though with the recent increasing immigration from South and Central America, Latino is gaining favor. What to call the offspring of intergroup marriages or unions remains unresolved, such as the 8.5 percent of American Indians, the 5.8 percent of whites of Hispanic origin, the earlier-noted 2.6 percent of blacks, and the small number of offspring with mainly Punjabi fathers and Mexican mothers whom outsiders call Mexican-Hindus, Mexidus, or half and halves.[42]

For many new Spanish-speaking immigrants, nationality is the preferred identification. Author Piri Thomas said that Puerto Ricans and others who speak Spanish as their first language do not like being "thrown into invisible masses of language," but want to be known by what they are, "and in our case, we are Puerto Rican." In southern Florida, a recent study of eighth and ninth graders found that almost two-thirds considered themselves Cuban or Cuban American, with very few thinking of themselves as Hispanic, which Nicaraguan students used almost as much as Nicaraguan.[43]

Not surprisingly, Spanish-speaking immigrants settled in areas on the basis of country of origin and in the process created separate organizations, restaurants, soccer teams, political clubs—and disagreements. For example, Cubans in Florida largely vote Republican, while Puerto Ricans in New York vote Democratic. In Washington, D.C., where some 250,000 Spanish-speaking people from twenty-three Caribbean and South and Central American countries lived in 1988, a Colombian immigrant businessman noted, "We speak the same language, but we don't understand each other." In Los Angeles, in 1989, Mexican Americans protested that two national Spanish-language television networks were too Cuban in values. "It seems that what you have . . . is a preference for the lighter complexioned Cubans who you'd swear are from England or Germany. Here in L.A., it's mostly blue-collar working folks, darker folks."[44]

Adding further to the complexity of inter-Hispanic relations are transplanted and/or American-spawned educational, economic, and class distinctions. For example, according to the 1990 Census, while the average poverty rate for all Hispanics was about 22 percent, for Paraguayans it was only 7 percent and for Dominicans 33 percent. Educationally, too, intra-Hispanic differences exist. Nineteen percent of those of South American origin had bachelor's degrees or postgraduate education in contrast to 16 percent for Cubans and 6 percent for Mexicans. As in non-Hispanic groups, some members prefer socializing or living among people of the same socioeconomic standing. For example, in Latin America, recalled one young immigrant attending Cornell University, "the upper class won't even speak to the lower class. The Hispanic kids come here with an 'us versus them' mentality; I had it when I came here."[45]

Sometimes there is shame at the belated recognition of one's group background. For others, their newly asserted identity is a reaction to the public and political attention given other groups. A few feel confused between their recently enhanced particularistic identity and their previous universalistic outlook. At other times, there is an uneasy acceptance of group uniqueness, whether as a badge of pride or as a sanctuary from the hurts inflicted by nongroup members. For still others, group identity has become a way of building political power and obtaining government benefits and positions. For most, group awareness provides a sense of strength:

—Upon returning to her native Hawaii after a decade's absence, Hunani Trask explained that she had originally left because she wanted to get as far away as possible from everything Hawaiian. "So I went to the University of Wisconsin. Now that I'm back, I feel like I want to get away from everything haole (Caucasian). I'm a Hawaiian."[46]

—Eugene Boe recalled that to speak Norwegian in his childhood "meant you were going to speak English with a Norwegian accent, and that would be fatal. To speak with an accent of any kind was to invite the mockery and abuse of one's peers—and a punishment far outweighing all possible benefits. . . . But the neglected opportunity to learn the language of my forebears now seems like such a high price to have paid for a silly conformity."[47]

—It was while on his first trip to Syria with a relative who had left fifty years earlier that Gregory Orfalea discovered "the blood bond that was previously invisible. Sometimes it is tight and sometimes it is loose. But it is there." [48]

Obviously, the tension between one's psychological particularity and universality, and between one's inherited ethnicity and land of birth, influences how one perceives and relates to members of other groups. This is all the more acute for group members whose racial, religious, ethnic, and sexual appearances or beliefs differ sharply from those of the society about them. As third or fourth generation Americans, Chinese and Japanese can still be asked by strangers, "Where were you born?" or be told, "You speak English well." People of color at a white party or get-together still evoke curiosity as to why and how they are there. In discussing Chinese-American life, Dr. Chung Shu Yang, a medical professor, said that "we are often considered 'foreigners' by others and, unfortunately, sometimes even by ourselves. . . . Thus, by referring to ourselves as 'Zhong Guo Ren' (Chinese) and others as 'Mei Guo Ren' (Americans) we promote the 'foreigner' image." To church historian Martin E. Marty, by becoming a Methodist, a follower of Billy Graham, or a speaker in tongues, "I may remain in the human family and the one, holy, catholic Church. But my identity is based on a separate tradition, and I use its distinct mode of looking at reality in order to keep claims of others at a distance." [49]

Some academics have criticized the sharp growth of ethnic pride in recent decades. The Swedish sociologist Gunnar Myrdal said the new ethnicity consisted merely of beliefs articulated by third-generation intellectuals, who made few if any serious attempts to help common people in search of historical identity. In their book *The Ethnic Imperative*, Howard F. Stein and Robert F. Hill describe it as a form of nativism where in-group rage and hostility are displaced "onto a stereotyped outgroup (the WASP), who now bears all the opprobrium of what was formerly self-hatred." Historian Arthur Mann faulted the new ethnicity for not grasping America's common heritage and how national unity was achieved. To sociologist Orlando Patterson, it was socially divisive, obscuring profound social problems, stressing trivial genetic and human differences, and representing a retreat from America's commitment to the ideal of equality. [50]

Psychologist Arthur Jensen emphasized that a person is not identical with his or her race or group, and that the chances of an individual's reproduction genotypically is less than 1 in 73 trillion! Those confusing the distinction between racism and social elitism fall victim to the two because they "ignore individuality in favor of group characteristics; they emphasize pride in group characteristics, not individual accomplishment; they are more concerned with who belongs to what, and with head-counting and percentages and quotas than with respecting the characteristics of individuals in their own right." [51]

Whether one agrees or disagrees with such criticisms, the rise in ethnic awareness continues and brings much pleasure, pride, and benefit to many group members (as shall be explored in a later chapter).

In summary, each generation of Americans—immigrant or native-born—struggles with the problems of group change and continuity. Depending on the time, place and generation, all groups experience changes, though differentially so. A variety of psychosocial stages are involved in both the maintenance and the change of group identity. The processes and problems involved are complex and never without strain, pain, or conflict. Some years ago, Robert Payne wrote that America had become Europe with all the walls down.[52] Today, with rising Asian, Hispanic, and African immigration, and with increasing politicization of group identity, America is becoming the world with all the walls down, and, unfortunately, vulnerable to the kinds of intragroup and intergroup problems encountered abroad.

## NOTES

1. Thomas Wheeler, *The Immigrant Experience* (Baltimore: Penguin Books, 1971), 1.

2. Clifford E. Nelson, *The Lutherans in North America* (Philadelphia: Fortress Press, 1980), 97.

3. *Yearbook, 38th Annual Assyrian American Federation Convention*, September 2–6, 1971.

4. Andrew M. Greeley, *Why Can't They Be Like Us?* (New York: Institute of Human Relations, 1969), 32.

5. *New York Times*, 8 November 1993, B9.

6. *Boston Globe*, 18 May 1978, 1; Iver Peterson, "Our Towns," *New York Times*, 30 July 1993, B5.

7. John Tracy Ellis, *Documents of American Catholic History*, Vol. 1 (Chicago: Henry Regnery Company, 1967), 149.

8. Charles H. Anderson, *White Protestant Americans* (Englewood Cliffs, N.J.: Prentice-Hall, 1970), 50.

9. Ibid., 74.

10. Howard F. Stein and Robert F. Hill, *The Ethnic Imperative* (University Park: Pennsylvania State University Press, 1977), 35.

11. *Psychology '73–'74* (Guilford, Conn.: Dushkin Publishing Group, 1973), 461–462.

12. Bon-Youn Choy, *Koreans in America* (Chicago: Nelson-Hall, 1979), 248.

13. Arthur Mann, *The One and the Many* (Chicago: University of Chicago Press, 1979), 170.

14. Michael Kammen, "A Nation of Nations," in *American Issues*, ed. William T. Alderson (Nashville: American Association for State and Local History, 1976), 8.

15. Thomas Sowell, *Race and Culture* (New York: Basic Books, 1994), 3, 42; Martin E. Marty, *A Nation of Believers* (Chicago: University of Chicago Press,

1976), 171; William A. Douglass, "Re-counting Basques," The Basque Studies Program *Newsletter,* April 1993, 8.

16. Joseph Giordano and Grace Pineiro Giordano, *The Ethno-Cultural Factor in Mental Health* (New York: American Jewish Committee, 1977), 9–10; Victoria Benning, "Study Finds Few Latinos Use Outside Child Care," *Boston Globe,* 8 April 1994, 31; *Washington Post,* 6 January 1985, B4; Sam Enriquez and Jeanette Regaldo, "Death Punctuates Poor's Growing Use of Folk Healers," *Los Angeles Times,* 13 April 1994, B3.

17. Monique P. Yazigi, "Curing Sick Stereotypes," *New York Times Educational Life,* 10 April 1994, 8; Renee Tawa, "Multicultural Medicine," *Los Angeles Times,* 27 January 1994, 10–12; Seth Mydans, "Should Dying Patients Be Told? Ethnic Pitfall Is Found," *New York Times,* 13 September 1995, D24.

18. Philip Bennett, "On Boston's Fringe," *Boston Globe,* 27 October 1993, 8.

19. Samuel S. Hill, "Religion and Region in America," *Annals of the American Academy of Political and Social Science* (July 1985): 135.

20. Rudolph O. De La Garza, "Mexican Americans in the United States: The Evolution of a Relationship," in *Case Studies on Human Rights and Fundamental Freedoms,* Vol. 5 (The Hague: Foundation for the Study of Plural Societies, 1976), 262–63; Henry L. Feingold, "Was There Communal Failure? Thoughts on the American Jewish Response to the Holocaust," *American Jewish History* (Autumn 1993): 63–64.

21. Simon N. Herman, *Israelis and Jews: The Continuity of an Identity* (New York: Random House, 1970), 22–24.

22. Boyd C. Shafer, *Faces of Nationalism* (New York: Harcourt Brace Jovanovich, 1972), 12–13.

23. Danuta Mostwin, "The Unknown Polish Immigrant," *Migration World* 17, no. 2 (1989): 28–29.

24. Vay de Vaya & Luskod, *The Inner Life of the United States* (New York: E. P. Dutton and Company, 1900), 20; Andrew L. Yarrow, "In Brooklyn, Wontons, Not Lapskaus," *New York Times,* 17 March 1991, 36; Deborah Sontag, "New Immigrants Test Nation's Heartland," *New York Times,* 18 October 1993, B7.

25. *Taking America's Pulse, A Summary Report of the National Conference Survey on Inter-Group Relations* (New York: National Conference of Christians and Jews, n.d.), 10.

26. Lawrence Wright, "One Drop of Blood," *The New Yorker,* 25 July 1994, 47; Rohan Preston, "Battle to Keep Black Professor Leaves Bruised Egos and Reputations," *New York Times,* 8 March 1995, B8.

27. Susan Kalish, "Multiracial Births Increase as U.S. Ponders Racial Definitions," *Population Today* (April 1995): 1, 2.

28. Peggy Gillespie, "Portraits of Multiracial Families," *The Boston Globe Magazine,* 24 April 1994, 26; Michael K. Frisby, "Multiracial Debate," *Emerge* (December/January 1996): 54.

29. Glen Grant and Dennis M. Ogawa, "Living Proof: Is Hawaii the Answer?" *Annals of the American Academy of Political and Social Science* (November 1993): 151; Steven A. Holmes, "Federal Government Is Rethinking Its System of Racial Classification," 8 July 1994, A18; John Derbyshire, Letter to the Editor, *New York Times,* 17 July 1994, 16E.

30. Donald Brown, "Labels Can Give Students a Sense of Belonging or Alien-

ation," *Blacks in Higher Education*, 13 April 1989, 20; Jan Breslauer, "Not-So-Clueless," *The New Republic*, 4 September 1995, 25.

31. Stephen Fuchs, "Teaching Judaism to Lutheran Seminarians," *The Christian Century* (30 April 1980): 486; David W. Dunlap, "For Gay Republicans, the Ideological Sniping Comes From Both Camps," *New York Times*, 4 October 1995, A9.

32. William J. Mann, "NoHopride," Supplement of *Boston Phoenix* (May 1995), 17; Joseph P. Kahn, "The New Book on Bisexuality," *Boston Globe*, 6 September 1995, 75, 80; Trip Gabriel, "A New Generation Seems Ready to Give Bisexuality a Place in the Spectrum," *New York Times*, 12 June 1995, A12; David W. Dunlap, "At Fifth Avenue Parade, Thousands Celebrate Gay Pride," *New York Times*, 26 June 1995, B4; Dana Y. Takagi, "Maiden Voyage: Excursion into Sexuality and Identity Politics in Asian America," *Amerasia Journal* 20, no. 1 (1994), 4; Lena Williams, "Blacks Reject Gay Rights Fight as Equal to Theirs," *New York Times*, 28 June 1993, A12.

33. H. L. Mencken, *The American Language* (New York: Alfred A. Knopf, 1963), 380–81; August Meier and Elliott Rudwick, *From Plantation to Ghetto* (New York: Hill and Wang, 1970), 111.

34. Mencken, *The American Language*, 380–81; Derrick Z. Jackson, "Please Don't Call Me Black," *Boston Globe*, 15 January 1989, A26; George E. Walker, letter in *New York Times*, 6 January 1989, A30.

35. Milton L. Barron, "Recent Developments in Minority and Race Relations," *Annals of the American Academy of Political and Social Science* (July 1975):142–43; Jon Nordheimer, "A Creek, Negro Run Is the Source of Debate," *New York Times*, 3 November 1994, B6; Harry J. Crockett and Jerome L. Schulman, *Achievement Among Minority Americans* (Cambridge: Schenkman Publishing Company, 1973), 37–38.

36. *Bay State Banner*, editorial, 11 November 1982, 4.

37. *New York Times*, 12 December 1988, A16; 17 October 1989, A21; and 29 January 1991, A19; *Time*, 4 April 1994, 12.

38. Mary C. Waters, "Ethnic and Racial Identities of Second-Generation Black Immigrants in New York City," *International Migration Review* (Winter 1994):796; *Boston Globe*, letter, 22 January 1989, A30; Roy Simon Bryce-Laporte, "Voluntary Immigration and Continuing Encounters between Blacks: The Post-Quincentenary Challenge," *Annals of the American Academy of Political and Social Science* (November 1993):38; Steven A. Holmes, "Federal Government Is Rethinking Its System of Racial Classification," *New York Times*, 8 July 1994, A18.

39. Joseph Fitzpatrick, *Puerto Rican Americans* (Englewood Cliffs, N.J.: Prentice-Hall, 1971), 102; Rick Bragg, "Haiti's Light-Skinned Elite: The Tiny Minority Behind Aristide's Ouster," *New York Times*, 28 August 1994, 14; Anthony DePalma, "Racism? Mexico's in Denial," *New York Times*, 11 June 1995, 4E.

40. Larry Rohter, "As Hispanic Presence Grows, So Does Black Anger," *New York Times*, 20 June 1993, 27 and "On a Divided Island, Two Estranged Peoples," *New York Times*, 14 November 1993, 18E; Nancy Raquel Mirabel, "The Afro-Cuban Community in Ybor City and Tampa, 1886–1910," *Magazine of History* (Summer 1993): 19, 22; Waters, "Ethnic and Racial Identities of Second-Generation Black Immigrants in New York City," 797.

41. Charles Kamasaki and Raul Yzaguirre, "Black-Hispanic Tensions: One Perspective," *Journal of Intergroup Relations* (Winter 1994–1995):19; Garry Pierre-

Pierre, "West Indians Adding Clout at Ballot Box," *New York Times,* 6 September 1993, 17.

42. Roger Daniels, *Coming to America: A History of Immigration and Ethnicity in American Life* (New York: Harper Perennial, 1990), 313; Juanita Tamayo Lott, "Do United States Racial/Ethnic Categories Still Fit?" *Population Today* (January 1993):7; David E. Hayes-Bautista and Gregory Rodriguez, "The Chicano Movement: More Nostalgia Than Reality," *Los Angeles Times,* 17 September 1995, M6; Crockett and Schulman, *Achievement Among Minority Americans,* 59; Stephan Thernstrom, *Harvard Encyclopedia of American Ethnic Groups* (Cambridge: Harvard University Press, 1980), 298; Lon Kurashige, review of *Making Ethnic Choices: California's Punjabi-Mexican Americans,* by Karen Isaksen Leonard, *Amerasia Journal* 19, no. 2 (1993): 200; Karen Leonard, "Historical Constructions of Ethnicity: Research on Punjabi Immigrants in California," *Journal of American Ethnic History* (Summer 1993): 7.

43. Piri Thomas, "Puerto Ricans in the Promised Land," *Civil Rights Digest* 6, no. 2 (1975): 12–13; Alejandro Portes and Min Zhou, "Should Immigrants Assimilate?" *Public Interest* (Summer 1994): 31–32.

44. *Washington Post,* 23 October 1988, B1; *New York Times,* 15 November 1983, 29 and 21 July 1989, C16.

45. United States Department of Commerce *News,* Washington D.C., Bureau of Census, 13 January 1994, 2; Patrick Welsh, "Our Classroom Barrios," *Network News and Views* (October 1991):37.

46. Jon Stewart, "Making Waves—The New Hawaiian," *Equal Opportunity Forum* (October 1980), 40.

47. Wheeler, *The Immigrant Experience,* 82.

48. Gregory Orfalea, *Before the Flames: A Quest for the History of Arab Americans* (Austin: University of Texas Press, 1988), 4.

49. Chung Shu Yang, "Bias," *Asian Week,* 23 January 1987, 2; Marty, *A Nation of Believers,* 180.

50. Gunnar Myrdal, "The Case Against Romantic Ethnicity," *The Center Magazine* 7 (July/August 1974): 28; Stein and Hill, *The Ethnic Imperative,* 161; Mann, *The One and the Many,* 44; Orlando Patterson, "Hidden Dangers in the Ethnic Revival," *New York Times,* 20 February 1978, 17.

51. Arthur R. Jensen, *Educability & Group Differences* (New York: Harper & Row, 1973), 9–10.

52. Max Lerner, "The Idea of American Civilization," in *The Character of Americans,* ed. Michael McGiffert (Homewood, Ill.: Dorsey Press, 1964), 11.

# 3

# Intragroup and Intergroup Differences

Let us not be blind to our differences—but let us also direct attention to our common interests and the means by which those differences can be resolved. And if we cannot end now our differences, at least we can help make the world safe for diversity.

—John F. Kennedy,
Address, American University,
Washington, D.C., 1963

Just as various groups of animals differ and fight among themselves over food, territory, mates, status and power, so it is with humans, who do so for more varied reasons and with greater sophistication, often in larger numbers and among more varieties of beings.

Both intragroup and intergroup differences involve a host of psychological, social, economic, political, religious, and institutional factors, which in turn are influenced by family, friends, schools, the media, popular culture, and governmental policies. More specifically, bigotry and violence result from some or many of the following human characteristics:

—pride in one's own group, wherein distance, separation, or disdain for others is defended in the name of group security, survival, or purity

—desire to excel or prove a group's inherent superiority to others, whether in government, religion, industry, sports, the arts, or war

—suspicion or hatred of those who are, appear, or want to be different—culturally, religiously, racially, physically, linguistically

—ignorance of or indifference to the cultural traditions, yearnings, and history of other groups

—resentment and demonization of people, groups, or countries competing for profits, land, jobs, status, political power, or government aid

—envy of those who have—or have more—wealth, political power, social status, education, professional achievement, or even sexual appeal

—nostalgia for bygone times and group achievements or bitter remembrances of past persecutions

—anger at being demeaned or discriminated against, together with desire for revenge or compensation

—susceptibility to political and religious demagoguery

—readiness to conform with values and behavioral patterns of major private and public institutions

—a predisposition, if not instinct, to demean or harm other humans

While the dynamics of such intergroup differences and violence are well known, those of intragroup relations are less so, and are the thrust of this chapter. As with group identity, little and big differences exist over other matters as well as between parents and offspring, traditionalists and modernists, separatists and integrationists, religious reformers and conservatives, newcomers and oldtimers, and those with different political views or from different regions of a given homeland.

Whether in large or small organizations, group leaders usually oppose publicly airing internal problems, believing it will reveal group weakness, undermine the group's public image, lead to fragmentation, threaten group survival, and help their critics and enemies. Strong dissent and change are feared, and those advocating them are viewed as mavericks, ingrates, sinners, renegades, apostates, traitors and/or self-haters, particularly if they move away from the community's neighborhoods, refuse to contribute to a group's major organizations or politicians, join groups believed unfriendly, intermarry, or somehow bring shame on the group. For example, in the 1920s Japanese-American leaders in a California community warned chronic gamblers that if they did not change their way of life, their activities would be reported to their home villages, where their families would be shamed. More extreme and contemporary are the views of the leader of the Aryan Nations, a paramilitary hate group headquartered in Utah, who labeled all whites denying their racial superiority "traitors who are white outside, black inside and have Jewish minds."[1] Also resented are minority reporters, authors, and artists who either criticize what is occurring in their own group or who do not highlight its virtues.

Historically, punishment for violating a group's religious beliefs ranged from reprimand to burning at the stake. In America, Roger Williams and Anne Hutchinson were expelled from the Massachusetts Bay Colony for their dissenting Protestant views, and some colonists disrespectful of clergy were forced to stand on a block, with a placard on their chest saying, "An Open and Obstinate Contemner of God's Holy Ordinances."[2]

More recently, in 1993, the Mormon Church excommunicated five members for questioning official church history and disfellowshipped (denied certain sacramental privileges) a sixth member for advocating that women be allowed to become priests. From a racial perspective, Juan Williams of the *Washington Post* wrote, "Most of the questions I get from the black community suggest that a black writer's sole mission should be to speak for all black people—as if all black people were of one mind—and to hail anyone claiming to be a black hero, reflect whatever politically proper opinions the loudest black voices are shouting, and defend against all claims of problems inside the black community." Gay-bashing by other gays is increasing, wrote Stephen Miller, who says he was purged from his position in a gay and lesbian organization simply because he had challenged its "left-wing politically correct mantras."[3]

To some extent, the guardians of group unity, purity, and pride are correct in that internal differences can lead to defection of members, organizational fracturing, public embarrassment, loss of political power or the opportunity to gain it, and even total breakup.

Intragroup differences are also facilitated, if not exacerbated, by America's historic opposition to centralized government and church-state alliance, as well as by its openness to dissent and change, wherein individuals have more freedom to create, join, or quit organizations than in the lands from which they or forebears originated. Some examples are:

American Jews built Orthodox, Conservative, and Reform synagogues, which until recent decades were often constructed along ethnic lines wherein people from Russia, Poland, Germany, Spain, and so forth, prayed, socialized, and married only those of their own kind. From their earliest days in America, a pecking order of social status was evident. Eighteenth-century Spanish and Portuguese Jews considered themselves to be better than later arriving German Jews, whom they derisively called "tedescos" (the German boors). In turn, the latter looked down on late nineteenth-century Eastern European Jewish immigrants as illiterate, tribalistic, and lacking in social graces.[4]

Within and between each denomination, differences arose over traditions and to what extent they should be surrendered. With post–World War II generations, and particularly after the establishment of the State of Israel, ethnic, class, and social differences began declining, as did the knowledge of Yiddish. Interfaith marriages began to increase. Sharp differences remained over "Who is a Jew?" particularly in relation to children of interfaith marriages and non-Orthodox conversions of Christians. However, as Israel entered into peace negotiations with the Palestine Liberation Organization, public recriminations erupted between established Israeli government leaders and some American Jews. The former claimed the Americans had no right to interfere in their peace efforts, while the latter accused the Israelis of endangering Israel's security. At the same time, a small but growing number of politically conservative and Republican American Jews began challenging the overwhelming political support by Jews of the Democratic Party (which dated back to the Roosevelt years).

Among Catholics, too, differences arose between various European groups. Irish Catholics, who had arrived earliest, had the most clergy, spoke English, and had built many of the first churches in America. Nineteenth-century French, German, and Italian Catholics, however, preferred having their own organizations, clergy and churches, where services could be held in their native language and children educated in old-country culture and history.

In New England, interethnic Catholic conflicts at times led to French refusal to attend Mass or to contribute to building parochial schools that did not teach French. In New York, German and Irish parishioners clashed over control of churches and cemeteries, and in Philadelphia, separate hospitals were created—St. Joseph's for Irish and St. Mary's for Germans. New Italian immigrants were sometimes consigned to holding services in the basements of Irish churches, prompting one Italian priest in Minnesota to complain how embarrassing it was "to meet under the feet of a different people which looks down at us from above with contempt." [5]

Such differences were also reflected in the nineteenth-century American Catholic press, where "readers too often were first Irish or German or Slovak, then Catholic and, almost in afterthought, American" and where readers and papers were "absorbed in Old World causes and attitudes that spilled over into competitions, jealousies, and frictions in the New." [6]

In spite of differences in the Polish community between the working class, the middle class, and the clergy, all sides resented the Irish hierarchy's indifference to their language and to their cultural needs. Many Polish priests wanted bishops of their own nationality and the Church to be organized along ethnic rather than territorial lines—with "Polyglot Bishops for Polyglot Dioceses." When such desires proved futile, some twenty-four parishes founded a Polish National Catholic Church at the turn of the century, which today numbers more than 300,000 worshippers. With the elevation of Pope John Paul II, who was born in Poland, reconciliation discussions began. Another Slavic group resentful of Irish Catholic insensitivity were Ukrainian eastern-rite Catholics, whose 163 parishes with over 200,000 members switched by 1916 to the Russian Orthodox Church. [7]

To a lesser extent, anti-Irish sentiments and intra-Catholic tensions have surfaced among newer immigrant groups. Hispanics resent holding services in church basements in cities like San Francisco, New York, and Boston, where one Hispanic diocesan official said, "The Anglos are still shoving us into the basement." In Monterey, California, where Catholic Asians have begun to exceed Hispanic ones, tensions between the two groups grew when church officials decided to turn a mostly Spanish church into a Chinese one and to replace a Spanish-speaking priest with two Chinese-speaking ones. Lebanese Maronites, who are Catholics, feel uncomfortable and/or unwelcome in many immigrant Italian, Irish, and French-Canadian Catholic churches because of differing religious customs, such as not being allowed to say their prayers in Aramaic. In 1986, Vietnamese Catholics in San Jose, California, rented facilities in a high school to hold services because the local bishop refused their appeal to create a separate parish.[8]

Ethnicity aside, creedal differences also prevail between liberal and conservative Catholics in America, and between those in the Vatican hierarchy and among American bishops, some of whom feel the former are too controlling over matters other than faith and morals. As the late nineteenth-century Archbishop John Ireland once said, "Americans have no longing for a Church with a foreign accent." Much more recently, Mitch Finley, a Catholic News Service columnist, wrote: "For right-wing Catholics you're a bad Catholic unless you believe that the Pope is God's older brother. For left-wing Catholics you're not a good Catholic unless you ignore the Vatican, throw blood on nuclear bombs, sell all you have and go live in a South American slum."[9]

America's freedom of belief and principles of church-state separation facilitated divisions among old religious groups and the creations of new ones, such as Mormons and Jehovah's Witnesses. Recent immigrants from older, established religious groups often found themselves uncomfortable with the Americanized religious practices of their kinsmen, and once they became socially and economically secure, started churches more in keeping with their old world traditions. "The accommodation of the older immigrant group to the new civilization," wrote Richard Niebuhr, "the adoption of the native language and of native forms of church life, the rise also of this older immigration in economic position, make the two generations of immigrants essentially alien to each other."[10]

Thus, a little more than two centuries after the Dutch Reformed Church was organized in 1628, newer immigrants from the Netherlands, unhappy with the abandonment of some ancient church practices, organized the True Dutch Reformed Church. With other immigrant groups, too, as new waves arrived, religious differences and splits took place, spawning a variety of sects and churches, such as the Armenian Orthodox Church in America, the Assyrian Jacobite Apostolic Church, the Free Magyar Reform Church of America, thirteen varieties of Mennonites, three of German Dunkers, and nine of Eastern Orthodoxy.[11]

At times, immigrants from the same country differed in socioeconomic origins, reasons for coming to America, and the success, or lack of it, that they and their children had in adapting to their new surroundings. For example, early nineteenth-century Germans, who were largely farmers, laborers, craftsmen, and religious conservatives, resented the more intellectual, freethinking, and political German refugees who started coming in 1848; the earlier immigrant group became known as the "greys" in contrast to the "greens," who the earlier group thought were good only at showing how smart they were, making speeches, and criticizing American institutions. Similarly, Italians from northern Italy looked down on the more numerous arrivals from southern Italy. In 1872, some northerners in New York City's Italian Society accused the Italian government of deliberately sending the lowest and meanest of residents here, making the city "a penal colony for the refuse of Italy." A *New York Times* reporter, in 1875, wrote that unlike northern Italians, those from Sicily were "miserably poor . . . resort to theft and robbery. . . . It would be unjust, however, to permit them to cast reproach upon the industrious and orderly Italians of Northern Italy." [12]

Even among American-born minority groups like Indians and African Americans, differences existed before and after contact with whites. Through much of American history, Indian tribes not only fought each other, such as the Apalachee and Timucua in Florida, Iroquois and Hurons in the northeast, and the Comanches and Apaches in the western plains, but they often sought whites as allies in fighting each other or other whites—European or American. As early as 1642, a Narrangansett chief vainly urged intertribal unity against the English, because "we are all Indians as the English are, and say brother to one another; so must we be one as they are, otherwise we shall all be gone shortly." [13] In the American Revolution, the War of 1812, and the Civil War, Indians fought on both sides, as did other ethnic and religious groups.

Though generally without the extensive violence of prior centuries, some intertribal rivalries and hostilities still exist, as between the Hopi and Navajo Indians over territorial claims. Vine Deloria, Jr., likened National Indian leadership meetings to a Tower of Babel, where "the first Indian will announce that he lives in a one-room shack. He will be rebutted by an Indian educator who has lost his identity between two cultures. Another will agree about the two cultures and will immediately be refuted by an old timer fighting for his treaty rights who is simultaneously challenged because he doesn't speak for all the Indians." [14]

More extensive are the intratribal differences between full bloods and half bloods, modernists and traditionalists, radicals and conservatives, and supporters and opponents of the Bureau of Indian Affairs. In recent years, bitter differences over the advisibility of opening gambling casinos erupted among the Mohawks straddling New York and Canada, the Oneidas in central New York, and the Wampanoags in Massachusetts. Elsewhere, some tribes began competing with each other over who would first deal with nontribal investment and management companies, as in the case of the Ak-Chin Indians and Gila River Indians in Arizona.[15]

Just as inter-Indian conflicts existed before contact with white Europeans, the same can be seen with black Africans, whose wars, raids, kidnappings, and enslavement of other blacks were facilitated and often encouraged by whites and their weapons, bribery, and greed, particularly in the expansion of the slave trade and the partitioning of Africa. Without the cooperation of many black African leaders and traders, Europeans and Arabs could not have purchased and transported so many millions of slaves, who were the only group brought to America against their will (other than relatively small numbers of white European prisoners), denied the right to return home, excluded from schooling, prevented from practicing their tribal, linguistic and cultural traditions, and forced to conform with the class and color values of white society.[16]

In America, as elsewhere, while white racism ignored African tribal or social distinctions, it did make them based on lightness of complexion, which some African Americans adopted. For example, antebellum free persons of color, particularly prosperous ones in cities like Charleston and New Orleans, viewed the Civil War's emancipated slaves with ambivalence and often avoided social contact with them; later, in the North, many longtime resident blacks behaved likewise when southern blacks migrated to their areas.[17]

As in many other groups, differences rooted in socioeconomics, geographic origins, and especially politics occurred. In the early twentieth century, Booker T. Washington praised gradualism, self-help and industrial education, while William Monroe Trotter and W. E. B. Du Bois urged political agitation for immediate racial equality. In the 1920s, A. Philip Randolph denounced growing black factionalism, saying that the masses continued to suffer because of "the vanities, foibles, indiscretions and vaulting ambitions . . . of various leaderships." Reciprocal resentments developed between West Indian black immigrants and American-born blacks. Not until the civil rights movement did many black social organizations and colleges stop favoring light-skinned blacks for membership or admission, respectively. Though the 1960s were a highpoint of black-white, black-Jewish, and interblack cooperation, Martin Luther King, Jr., and Malcolm X differed sharply over goals and tactics. After their assassinations, younger, more militant black leaders insisted upon immediate black empowerment rather than relying on the more time-consuming, coalitional strategy of societal change. By 1989, King's widow, Coretta Scott King, regretfully noted, "we have more of what we fought for. More African American elected officials, more educational opportunities, more access to public accommodations, yet we have less unity than we had during the civil rights movement."[18]

The rising prominence of Minister Louis Farrakhan as leader of the Nation of Islam further strained relations among established black organizations and between them and other human rights organizations, especially Jewish groups. In 1994, when some black leaders refused to attend a national black conference convened by the NAACP, the latter's then chief executive, the Reverend Benjamin F. Chavis, Jr., angrily declared, "The last time I checked my back, it was someone of African descent that put the dagger in and twisted it."[19]

Shortly afterward, the NAACP itself was rent with a series of policy and administrative differences. Chavis was removed from office because of alleged mismanagement and the use of organizational funds to settle a sexual harassment complaint against him. Continuing internal differences resulted in the ouster of board chairman Dr. William Gibson by a narrow vote of thirty to twenty-nine and his replacement by Myrlie Evers-Williams, the widow of slain civil rights leader Medgar Evers. Some months later, former NAACP head Benjamin Chavis announced the formation of the National African American Leadership Summit, whose goal is to unite black political and religious leaders. Intrablack differences manifested themselves in 1995 with Farrakhan's Million Man March in Washington, D.C., which, in spite of its unprecedented turnout of African-American males, lacked the support of many prominent blacks and such organizations as the NAACP and the Urban League.[20]

Among Koreans, there are differences between new and old immigrants, and between acculturationists and traditionalists. For example, at one West Coast high school, assimilated Korean students teased new immigrants as FOBs ("fresh off the boat"). Afghans who immigrated to the United States before the Soviet Union entered their war-ridden homeland looked down upon those who came after the Soviets withdrew in the late 1980s as having "no education, no cultural ties, sometimes even no religious ties and no moral ties." As in Somalia, political differences surfaced along clan lines in 1993 among the some 2,000 immigrants in America, who either opposed or supported the warlord General Mohamed Farrah Aidid.[21]

With the increase in Chinese immigrants after 1965, communal divisions multiplied: native-born versus foreign-born, Cantonese-speaking versus Mandarin-speaking, and those politically promainland China versus pronationalist China in Taiwan. In addressing a Chinese-American convention in 1981, Anna Chennault humorously said, "You get three Chinese together and you get three different organizations." In the early 1990s, with the decline of communist economics, differences between Chinese American prodemocracy activists and business leaders escalated, wherein the former opposed America's granting most-favored-nation trading status to mainland China until it changed its repressive human rights policies, while the latter favored such status, believing, "You have to continue communicating with people if you are to help them to change." Then, in 1994, New York City's Chinatown officially held a parade celebrating the founding of the mainland People's Republic of China, much to the unhappiness of the neighborhood's traditional anti-Communist leadership.[22]

Haitian immigrants brought their status and linguistic differences with them. On the island, knowledge of French is associated with power, position and education, while Creole is considered the language of the poor and illiterate. In Harlem, where many early Haitian immigrants settled, blacks called them "French fries." Because of their dark complexion and also because of white racism against African Americans, some adult Haitians took to speaking only French in public, hoping to exploit white American respect for that language. However, in recent years, as young Haitians attended school with large numbers of blacks, some adopted the latter's body language, speech patterns, and social behavior. Some Haitians in Miami claimed that their refugees were not treated as well as others. "The problem is that we Haitians don't speak with one voice so we don't get the respect the Cubans do here." For most Haitian immigrants, however, the Creole language and their island origin connote authenticity and serve as unifying forces, particularly in the Little Haiti communities in New York City and Miami.[23]

As in the Middle East, differences are many between American Arab Christians and Moslems, in addition to those between early twentieth-century immigrants and the recent ones from dozens of different countries in Asia, Africa, and Europe. In Washington, D.C., in 1985, reciprocal hostility flared among Iranian Shiite immigrants over the late Ayatollah Khomeini. As a result of Iraq's invasion of Kuwait in 1990 and America's sending troops to defend it and American oil interests, tensions erupted not only between immigrants from those countries in America, but among Arab Americans generally. As former Congresswoman Mary Oakar, an Arab American, once said, "One of the problems of our own people [is] that they do not agree on all issues. If I went to three different churches in my hometown and asked what they will do about Lebanon, each will have a different position."[24]

In summary, no family, group, community, or nation is free of some differences, whose intensities and causes vary and involve a constellation of psychological, social, economic, political, and religious factors. Just how much unity should exist, and how much dissension should be tolerated, are perpetual problems, which each generation confronts and defines.

Whether on a microlevel (family, clan, tribe, association) or on a macrolevel (nation-state and international alliances), multiple options are always present for strengthening or destroying relations between group members or groups themselves. While splits and divisions take place, gradual change rather than sudden revolution characterizes most of American group life. Fortunately, the violence that did take place within and between some groups progressively declined, in contrast to life in many multicultural countries abroad. That doesn't mean, as we shall later see, that such relative calm will continue.

A closer look will now be taken at the relationship between national and group identity.

## NOTES

1. Eiichiro Azuma, "Interethnic Conflict under Racial Subordination: Japanese Immigrants and Their Asian Neighbors in Walnut Grove, California 1908–1941," *Amerasia Journal* 20, no. 2 (1994): 32; Michael Janofsky, "For Aryan Congress, Stridency and Scrutiny," *New York Times,* 23 July 1995, 14.

2. Leo Pfeffer, *Church, State, and Freedom* (Boston: Beacon Press, 1953), 66–67.

3. Juan Williams, "Being Black, Being Fair," *Washington Post,* 16 July 1989, B1; Dirk Johnson, "As Mormon Church Grows," *New York Times,* 2 October 1993, 7; Stephen Miller, "Gay-Bashing by Homosexuals," *Heterodoxy* (November-December 1994): 4.

4. Naomi W. Cohen, *Encounter with Emancipation* (Philadelphia: Jewish Publication Society of America, 1984), 13.

5. Jacques Portes, "The Emergence of the 'Franco-Americans,' " *Boston Globe,* 21 February 1982, A2; Jay P. Dolan, *The Immigrant Church* (Baltimore: Johns Hopkins University Press, 1975), 89–96; Jay P. Dolan, *The American Catholic Experience* (Garden City, N.Y.: Doubleday & Company, 1985), 175; *New York Times,* 26 December 1986, A29; Alan M. Kraut, *Silent Travelers: Germs, Genes, and the "Immigrant Menace"* (New York: Basic Books, 1994), 46.

6. John G. Deedy, Jr., "The Catholic Press," in *The Religious Press in America,* ed. Marty E. Martin, John G. Deedy, Jr., David W. Silverman, and Robert Lekachman (New York: Holt, Rinehart and Winston, 1963), 70–71.

7. Edward R. Kantowicz, "Polish Chicago: Survival Through Solidarity," in *The Ethnic Frontier,* ed. Melvin G. Holli and Peter d'A. Jones (Grand Rapids, Mich.: Wm. B. Eerdmans Publishing Co., 1977), 119; Dolan, *The American Catholic Experience,* 188.

8. Leila Prelec, " 'Basement' Catholics," *The Newton Tab,* 13 April 1993, 24; Mark Kendall, "Ethnic Feuding May Threaten Parish's Future," *Pasadena Star News,* 30 May 1994, A1; George T. Labaki, "Struggle of the Maronite," *Migration World,* 67, no. 1 (1989): 25; Eric J. Hooglund, "From the Near East to Down East," in *Crossing the Waters: Arabic-Speaking Immigrants to the United States before 1940,* ed. Eric J. Hooglund (Washington, D.C.: Smithsonian Institution Press, 1987), 97; *New York Times,* 26 December 1986, A29; Niko Price, "Vote Heats Up a California Melting Pot," *Boston Globe,* 11 April 1994, 3.

9. Mitch Finley, "When Catholics Disagree," *The Pilot,* 25 November 1994, 13; Mark J. Hurley, *The Unholy Ghost: Anti-Catholicism in the American Experience* (Huntington, Ind.: Our Sunday Visitor Publishing Division, 1992), 45.

10. Richard H. Niebuhr, *The Social Sources of Denominationalism* (New York: Meridian Books, 1959), 213–14.

11. Ibid., 214; Carl N. Degler, *Out of Our Past* (New York: Harper & Row, 1962), 292.

12. Salvatore J. LaGumina, *WOP!* (San Francisco: Straight Arrow Books, 1973), 24, 26; Frederic C. Luebke, *Germans in the New World* (Urbana: University of Illinois Press, 1990), 10–11; Christian Goldenboog, "Germans in the American Civil War: Revolutionaries and Laborers Fought for 'A New Birth of Freedom,' " *Germany/Deutschland, Magazine of Politics, Culture, Business, and Science* (no. 1 September/October 1993): 41.

13. Ian K. Steele, *Warpaths: Invasions of North America,* (New York: Oxford University Press, 1994), 94.

14. Vine Deloria, Jr., *Custer Died for Your Sins* (New York: Anchor Books, 1975), 211.

15. Barry Meier, "Casinos Putting Tribes at Odds," *New York Times,* 13 January 1994, D1; Lynda Gorov, "Wampanoags Pin Revival on Casino Dream," *Boston Globe,* 15 May 1994, 22; *New York Times,* 28 April 1990, 28 and 11 March 1993, B1.

16. Patrick Manning, *Slavery and African Life* (New York: Cambridge University Press, 1993), 88.

17. Thomas Sowell, *Race and Economics* (New York: David McKay Company, 1975), 121.

18. August Meier and Elliott Rudwick, *From Plantation to Ghetto* (New York: Hill and Wang, 1970), 251; Peter Applebome, "Lawsuit Raises Issue of Color Bias Between Blacks," *New York Times,* 23 May 1989, A1; Stephen L. Carter, *Reflections of an Affirmative Action Baby* (New York: Basic Books, 1991), 139.

19. Sylvester Monroe, "The Risky Association," *Time,* 27 June 1994, 39.

20. Sam Fulwood, "NAACP Faces Wider Sex Bias Lawsuit," *Boston Globe,* 28 March 1995, 3; *New York Times,* 12 June 1995, B7.

21. Jodi Wilgoren, "High-Pressure High," *Los Angeles Times,* 4 December 1994, 3; Richard Perez-Pena, "From Afghanistan to the Bronx," *New York Times,* 29 November 1993, B3; Colum Lynch, "Somalis in US Spar on Policy," *Boston Globe,* 10 October 1993, 18.

22. Betty Lee Sung, *Transplanted Chinese Children* (New York: The City College of New York, 1979), 32; *Bay State Banner,* 14 May 1981, 2; Denise Hamilton, "Many Chinese in U.S. Back Trade Privileges," *New York Times,* 3 June 1994, B4; *New York Times,* 26 September 1994, B2.

23. Susan Heulsebusch Buchanan, "Language and Identity: Haitians in New York City," *International Migration Review* 13 (Summer 1979): 298–310; Pamela Constable, "Fla. Hotel is Host to a Refugee Crisis," *Boston Globe,* 24 August 1994, 2; Deborah Sontag, "Haitian Migrants Settle In, Looking Back," *New York Times,* 3 June 1994, B4.

24. *Action,* 11 May 1981, 8.

# 4

## Group Identity versus National Identity

> What then is the American, this new man? He is either an European, or the descendant of an European, hence that strange mixture of blood, which you will find in no other country. I could point out to you a family whose grandfather was an Englishman, whose wife was Dutch, whose son married a French woman, and whose present four sons have now four wives of different nations. He is an American, who, leaving behind him all his ancient prejudices and manners, receives new ones from the new mode of life he has embraced, the new government he obeys, and the new rank he holds.
>
> —J. Hector St. John de Crevecoeur,
> *Letters from an American Farmer*

Just as tensions, ambiguities, and conflicts exist between individual and group identity, so it is with national identity. Rarely are all three congruent, though in the course of history various people, from demagogues to idealists, wished it so. The last of the learned identities is that of nationality, simply because it is not as immediately or intimately experienced as those of family, religion, or neighborhood.

From our very beginnings as a nation, ambiguities existed on what it meant to be an American. Though of the same color, language, and religion (but not denomination), early immigrants from the British Isles differed over how they viewed themselves. The Scots, Scotch-Irish, Irish, and Welsh brought bitter memories of how the English had mistreated them or their forebears. Those of English, Anglican descent took pride in their roots, with Benjamin Franklin rejoicing in England's conquest of Canada during the French and Indian War "not merely as I am a colonist but as I am a Briton." Likewise, while white colonists viewed all blacks as Africans and all indigenous natives as Indians, these two groups saw themselves as members of various African tribes, such as Akan, Ibo, Wolof, Yoruba, or of any one of the hundreds of existing original tribes.[1]

By the time of the American Revolution, joint identities were common among longtime eighteenth-century white colonists, who considered themselves Anglo-Americans, loyal both to their particular area of residence and to their British heritage. In fact, up to a few months before writing the Declaration of Independence, the Continental Congress said its intention was not "to dissolve that union which has so long and so happily subsisted between" the colonies and England; and two months after the Battle of Bunker Hill, Thomas Jefferson wrote that he looked "with fondness towards a reconciliation with Great Britain."[2]

Also, just as many nineteenth-century immigrants defined themselves in terms of their village or region, so it was with many American revolutionaries. For instance, John Adams called both Massachusetts and the United States "my country," as did James Madison and Thomas Jefferson refer to Virginia and the United States. Joseph Calloway told the first Continental Congress, "I know of no American Constitution. A Virginia Constitution, A Pennsylvania Constitution We have. We are totally independent of each other."[3]

Such seemingly contradictory attitudes are not surprising, since most colonists were of English descent and lived in areas long under English law and protection, which since 1740 allowed practically all foreign residents to become English subjects, except for Catholics.[4] Not until the Civil Rights Act of 1866 and the Fourteenth Amendment two years later did the federal government clearly assert its primacy over the states in defining and protecting citizenship:

All persons born or naturalized in the United States, and subject to the jurisdiction thereof, are citizens of the United States and of the State wherein they reside. No State shall make or enforce any law which shall abridge the privileges or immunities of citizens of the United States; nor shall any State deprive any person of life, liberty, or property, without due process of law, nor deny to any person within its jurisdiction the equal protection of the laws.

Giving up geographic and ancestral attachments was not easily done, as evidenced by colonists who fought on both sides of the Revolutionary War, by the divisiveness of the Civil War, and by immigrant groups that found it easier to discard their clothes than their memories, language, or customs. For example, many English immigrants identified themselves primarily as Yorkshiremen or Cornishmen, Irish as Dubliners or Kerrymen, and Germans as Bavarians or Westphalians. Likewise with nineteenth-century Chinese, Japanese, or Korean immigrants, who didn't think of themselves by nationality or as Asians, but rather as people from a same district, prefecture, or region who spoke the same dialect or language. Not until the latter nineteenth century did the united countries of Italy and Germany come into being, with large numbers of people beginning to identify themselves by the name of the country rather than by the village in which they were born.[5]

With the Balkan Wars, World War I, and the breakdown of the Ottoman and Austro-Hungarian empires, new nation-states were created, such as Yugoslavia, Czechoslovakia, Poland, Latvia, Lithuania and Estonia, though other groups were denied national self-determination, such as Ukrainians, Kurds, Armenians, and Jews. Similar developments took place in the Middle East, where only after the breakup of the Ottoman Empire did immigrants begin identifying themselves nationally as Lebanese, Syrian, Jordanian, or Palestinian. In Africa, European powers established countries without regard to tribal identities, boundaries, or alliances. Whether they came voluntarily or in chains, many newcomers arrived when their birthlands had not, or had just, gained national independence, and Americans generally knew little about them.

When asked from whence they came, many a nineteenth- and early twentieth-century immigrant found it expedient to identify with the old country as a whole. "I usually say I'm Russian," said one. "If you say you're Ukrainian, the guy tells you, 'Jesus Christ, what's that?' and you have to go into the whole history of Ukraine and explain to the guy what you mean. It is easier to just say that you are Russian."[6]

Generally, western European immigrants came with a relatively clear national identity. Among many Asians, identity was more linguistic than national, as with Chinese immigrants who went to the West Coast from Hawaii and the Philippines and expressed little allegiance to their former homeland. Enslaved black Africans had their tribal, linguistic, and geographic identities destroyed in America, though with the ending of European colonialism in Africa and the rise of black political power in America, American blacks increasingly adopted a pan-African pride, which manifested itself in African names, hairstyles, clothing, and celebrations.

For some white immigrant groups, coming to America allowed them to freely express a group identity that had been denied back home either because they had been discriminated against as minorities or because they were part of a majority group dominated by a foreign power. Thus, the historical irony evolved that many immigrants assumed a proud homeland identity in America, where they could freely practice the language, religion and/or customs prohibited back home, as happened, for example, with Poles from Prussia, Slovaks from Hungary, Armenians from Turkey, and, most recently, Tibetans from China-occupied Tibet.

The first Lithuanian newspaper is said to have been published in America, the revival of Erse begun, and the political campaign directed for World War I Czechoslovakian national independence. Denied a homeland in Russia, late nineteenth-century Ukrainian immigrants in America and Canada developed a strong sense of nationalism and community organization. What came to be Africa's first republic, Liberia, was primarily created by American black colonists and white supporters. Booker T. Washington's strategy for racial progress was adopted by the early leaders of the African National Congress in South Africa. Many Haitian immigrants who fled the island's poverty or tyrannical rule by President Jean-Claude Duvalier were ashamed of being associated with voodoo and illegal "boat people," but in South Florida, where some 300,000 lived in 1990, their sense of national pride grew with their improved economic standing.[7]

While settling in America and living among different people stimulates some immigrants to abandon their old-country ways and values, it encourages others to learn more about their culture and history, even to the extent, as Thomas Sowell noted, of becoming the abandoned culture's "most strident apostles." Kinsmen in America are "ten times more Welsh than they were at home . . . and will travel hundreds of miles to hear anything Welsh," wrote an early twentieth-century Welsh immigrant. "Only by being thousands of miles away did I set out to learn my own past," said Marion W. Roydhouse, a recent immigrant from New Zealand. "Coming from a nation whose surnames were almost all only British or Maori, it struck me as amazing that people (in America) I met would identify someone immediately as 'Polish' or 'Jewish.' I had never expected the depth of the divisions created by racial, cultural and ethnic diversity." Bora Pervane, a Turkish-born Muslim immigrant, said he became more devout in America because, "I had to set an example for my kids."[8]

Wars, revolutions, and national liberation movements abroad always galvanize American ethnic and racial groups. As an early twentieth-century observer described American Bulgarians helping their homeland gain freedom from the Ottoman Empire: "10,000 of these people were in the habit of assembling on Sundays in Granite City, Illinois, to discuss the affairs of their native land, to pass resolutions in behalf of freedom, and subscribe aid to the cause they loved." To the German-American newspaper *Abendpost* in Chicago, the outbreak of World War I wonderfully "revived the loyalty and patriotism of German-Americans of the second and third generations." Japanese aggression against Manchuria in 1931 and full-scale war against China five years later triggered aid and propaganda efforts by their respective ex-patriots in America. When Japan occupied Manchuria in 1931 and then launched all-out war against China five years later, their respective emigrees in America organized aid and propaganda efforts on their behalf. Similarly, during World War II, more than 200 organizations, not including small local or state societies, engaged in a wide variety of activities on behalf of their ancestral homelands.[9]

American and foreign religious, lay, and political leaders often play a major role in building or maintaining such connections. "Polish leaders indoctrinate their people with Polish enthusiasm and hopes for a future free Poland . . . the Slovak is taught . . . to interest himself in the struggle for national existence in Hungary," wrote Emily Greene Balch in 1910, in the same way that "the Irish, and later the Syrians, Armenians and other oppressed and burdened peoples have found in America, where liberty and prosperity give them room, a national recruiting ground for patriots." Visiting foreign dignitaries regularly appealed to the pride and prejudices of their former nationals and descendants to vacation in the old homeland, send money to relatives, serve in the military, help sustain religious and cultural institutions, and/or help lobby Congress. Doing so, they were also told, would also gain them the respect of their American neighbors. As one Irish leader in 1880 admonished his Irish-American listeners, if you "want to be honored among the elements that constitute this nation, as a people not coming from a paupered land; and in order that no sneers be cast on you when you stand for any position . . . aid us in Ireland to remove the stain of degradation from your birth."[10]

In recent decades, examples include Premier Rene Levesque's invitation to Franco-Americans from New England and Louisiana to participate, in 1978, in Quebec's 370th founding anniversary. Two years later, the Iraqi government reportedly pledged close to $2 million to Detroit's Chaldean churches and related organizations, as well as free trips to Baghdad for community leaders. While seeking to reestablish relations with America, Vietnamese officials urged former nationals to return for a visit and send money to their families. Though a democratic government was restored in Nicaragua, its president, Violeta Chamorro, urged President Clinton in 1994 to allow earlier political refugees to remain in America because "the economy of my country is still fragile and couldn't take a massive return of our citizens." El Salvador established counseling services in America to help former nationals file claims for political asylum here, thereby insuring their ability to send remittances back home. Other governments have funded a variety of language and cultural programs in America, such as France, Germany, and Japan. A few foreign extremist Islamic groups not only sought to raise money from former nationals but also to recruit members.[11]

Various governments regularly encourage expatriot involvement in homeland elections. For example, during the 1987 Korean presidential elections, seven candidates established committees in America to raise contributions, with the hope expatriots would also contact friends and family back home to vote for them. Mexican officials and politicians regularly visit southern California to muster support from former nationals and their descendants. In 1994, South African emigres in America were allowed to vote in the election that led to Nelson Mandela's victory.[12]

Also contributing to group pride and political power in recent decades is the arrival of large numbers of new immigrants, such as Chinese, Lebanese, Koreans, Russian Jews, Vietnamese, and Spanish, who moved into old, or formed new, neighborhoods, businesses, restaurants, and newspapers, often shaming their predecessors into relearning their ancestral language. In addition, the growth of affirmative action and multicultural programming, as well as the media's and politicians' favorable treatment of them, encouraged many minority members to project rather than downplay their group identity.

As post–World War II foreign problems developed in other parts of the world, both new and old immigrant groups spoke up. In reaction to escalating interethnic bloodshed in Yugoslavia, a 79-year-old Serbian American said, "everybody has a right to protect his own nation. . . . I am not a Serbian if I remain neutral." Likewise, Tibetan Americans demonstrated against China's continued occupation of Tibet. Azerbaijani Americans defended their homeland's retention of the mainly Armenian region of Nagorno-Karabakh. When Governor Michael Dukakis of Massachusetts ran for the presidency against George Bush in 1988, American Turks expressed concern about his objectivity toward Turkey because his parents were born in Greece.[13]

Though lacking linguistic fluency, personal recollections, or known family connections with the specific country or region from which their ancestors were brought here in slavery, many American blacks, especially after the rise of black independent African nations and the civil rights movement in America, adopted a pan-African pride, which manifested itself in assuming African names, hair-styles, clothes, and advocacy for congressional foreign aid to their ancestral continent.

As never before, American and African blacks established cultural and business contacts. While in Africa, Black Muslim leader Louis Farrakhan urged countries there to grant American blacks dual citizenship because "we don't know where we came from." In 1995, a conference in Senegal promoting cultural and economic relations attracted 1,000 American participants, "the largest number of blacks to return to Africa since the end of slavery," said the Reverend Leon Sullivan, who enjoined them to help Africa the way American Poles and American Jews help Poland and Israel, respectively. Some American black leaders and organizations, as well as African emigres, are also beginning to speak out against black injustices in Nigeria, Kenya, Ethiopia, Zaire, and Angola. "The fact that you are in the United States of America, the most powerful nation on earth, gives you all the tools to influence what happens in Nigeria," said the chairman of the Nigerian Democratic Awareness Committee to a gathering in 1995 of American and African black leaders.[14]

To gain public and political support for their ancestral homeland, some American ethnic groups purchase newspaper advertising space to gain public attention and support. For example, in a *New York Times* ad, The Kashmiri-American Foundation denounced India's "genocide in Kashmir" and called upon America to help the Kashmiri people gain self-determination. The group Exile Latvians demanded that "not only the Russian military but also its civilian foot soldiers (colonists) must leave Latvia." In vain, "Concerned Greek Americans," in a 1993 *Boston Globe* ad, opposed President Clinton's recognition of the newly formed country of Macedonia, because its name had long belonged to Greece, and it had been home to historical figures such as Aristotle and Alexander the Great. In 1991, after Croatia declared its independence, the Croatian Democratic Union of America and the United Croatian Youth of America published "an open letter to the President, Congress, and our fellow Americans" urging their support of the new government. After President Clinton barred trade and investment in 1995 with Iran, the Iranian American Society of New York placed a full-page open letter to him in the *New York Times* protesting his executive order forbidding trade and investment with Iran and his insinuating that Iranians have a behavior problem, wherein they do "not hesitate to commit acts of violence." [15]

More ambiguous is the relationship between mainland and island Puerto Ricans. In 1993, Puerto Rican islanders decided to hold a plebiscite on whether the island should become independent, remain a commonwealth, or apply for American statehood. Almost immediately, a group of American Puerto Ricans, mainly in New York City, decided to hold a similar vote, much to the opposition of island political leaders. To Jose Luis Rodriguez, an activist for the plebiscite in America, island political leadership always looked down on kinsmen in America as "poor, dark-skinned hillbillies who moved to the mainland," but who "conveniently establish relations with us when they feel their interests are at stake." The vote to remain a commonwealth won out with 48.4 percent, in contrast to 46.2 percent of the vote favoring statehood. [16]

For some groups, homeland events are a source of shame and a cause for national redefinition. When first arriving in the nineteenth century, many Luxembourgers called themselves Germans or Luxembourger Germans, but after the Franco-Prussian War and both World Wars, they increasingly asserted a distinctly Luxembourger identity. While pre–World War I immigrants from Belgium considered themselves either Flemish or Walloon, the wartime suffering of their kinsmen prompted many to identify as Belgians and to form Belgium cultural associations. [17] Prior to Cape Verde Independence in 1975, immigrants viewed themselves as Portuguese Americans, but after independence, as Cape Verdean Americans.

For many American Germans and Italians, identification with their homelands was at first respectively enhanced by Germany's victory in the

Franco-Prussian War and reunification after 1870, and by Mussolini's rebuilding and rearming of Italy. However, when those countries and Japan were at war with America, former nationals and their offspring repudiated, disassociated, or suppressed such identification, while many Americans denounced them as treacherous and unpatriotic. Many American Arabs reacted similarly during the Persian Gulf War. More complex are American Serb reactions to the war in Bosnia, which many supported. They criticized the American media for focusing only on the brutalities of their kinsmen, while other American Serbs had mixed or critical feelings, but feared to express them lest they be deemed traitors.[18]

Politics aside, not all immigrants look homeward with fondness. Many willingly and, at times, eagerly leave lands where there is little or no hope for work, professional advancement, artistic expression, or surcease of suffering or oppression. "I could claim no nationality and no flag," wrote Abraham M. Rihbany, a Christian Arab immigrant from the Ottoman Empire in the early 1900s. "The rule of the Turk . . . was painfully repressive. . . . We left our 'mother country' with nothing but curses for her Government on our lips." More recently, Seiji Ozawa, conductor of the Boston Symphony, said that the reason large numbers of talented soloists, pianists, and musicians leave Japan each year and do not return is that "they don't think they will get the musical satisfaction" there that they can elsewhere.[19]

Some immigrants are irreconcilable in their anger at their government for what they or their forebears experienced, including some native-born Americans. For example, after the American Revolution, 50,000 American supporters of the British fled to Canada, where some of their descendants still feel that "George Washington and his crowd were the traitors, not the loyalists." During the Vietnam War, an estimated 20,000 American draft dodgers and 12,000 military deserters also fled to Canada.[20]

Other immigrants seek to assimilate totally to their new surroundings. One of the earliest examples involves sixteenth-century conquistadores who "went native," preferring Indian tribal life to that of the *hidalgo* (nobleman). In refusing to rejoin Spanish forces, Gonzalo Guerrero explained, "I am married and have three children, and they look on me as a Cacique here, and a captain in time of war. . . . (M)y face is tattooed and my ears are pierced. What would the Spaniards say if they saw me like this?" Later, some other Europeans taken captive and adopted by Indians refused to rejoin their ethnic kinsmen when they had an opportunity to do so. Mid–eighteenth-century American Jews, particularly the younger ones, were described at the time as being unlike their coreligionists in Europe, because they "dressed like other citizens, get shaved regularly, and also eat pork. . . . The women also go about with curled hair and in French finery such as is worn by the ladies of other religions."[21]

When Stephan Graham asked Russian immigrants in 1913, "Which do you prefer? Are you Americans now or Russians?," nearly all replied "Americans," because in America they could obtain money and power to buy land, some luxuries, and a trip home or to another country. However, for a short while after the Russian Revolution, many Russian immigrants did boast of their motherland. "If in America he was considered an inferior," wrote Jerome Davis in 1922, "at least his own country and his own people had been the first to lead the world in a workers' commonwealth." [22] Even after the destruction of the Iron Curtain and the dissolution of the Union of Soviet Socialist Republics, there is scant pride among Russian Americans in the new or old Russian government.

Criminals, draft dodgers, and political refugees, of course, dare not return home, at least not as long as those from whom they fled are still in power. Occasionally some young men who had fled foreign military service do return, but only after becoming American citizens in the belief that that would exempt them from being drafted. Few of the intellectuals who left Nazi Germany or Nazi-dominated Europe returned after World War II ended. Similarly, in 1993, Professor Nestor Castellanos and his wife fled Cuba with "just the clothes on our backs," explaining that "when an enormous apparatus is trying to crush you, finally the pressure becomes unbearable." [23]

Still, separation does not necessarily mean divorce. For example, after a visitor criticized Danish Americans in 1915 for having lost their culture, not being able to adjust to American society, and always longing for Denmark, an American Danish newspaper invited reader reactions. Nearly all replies noted: "We don't love Denmark less, but America more" and "We will not forget Denmark . . . but our longing is that of a longing for childhood." Likewise, a Nicaraguan who became an American citizen in 1986 said, "I adore this country. . . . Even though I'll do everything possible to help Nicaragua with money, I can never go back." [24]

Some immigrants in recent years started exploiting business opportunities in their former homelands, often to the resentment of fellow immigrants, as in the case of some Cuban, Chinese, Russian, Polish, and Asian businessmen or officials. For example, before America reestablished diplomatic relations with Vietnam in 1995, those Vietnamese Americans urging such a policy were often threatened, firebombed, or killed by other Vietnamese; when some businessmen from a California "Little Vietnam" planned to visit their homeland, opponents created street banners proclaiming, "To foster Communism for dollars is a crime against humanity." In Miami, when a group of Cubans returned to their island homeland to attend a conference, they were denounced as dogs, whores, and spies for Cuba. Among Korean immigrants, it was largely economic opportunity in 1995 that prompted about one in two to return home, in contrast to one in ten in 1987. [25]

At times, immigrants or their offspring who return home to vacation, visit family, work, retire, or show their American-born children their roots, experience a variety of feelings. Some discover that in America they had become more nationalistic than the friends or family they had left. "I never realized that I was an Albanian until my brother came from America," where he "belonged to an Albanian society," recalled one immigrant. Conversely, Robert C. Christopher, in his book on America's power elite, tells how as a youngster he had felt "some special if imprecise tie to the people of Great Britain," but during World War II, while assigned to a military unit with many British personnel, found them to be foreigners and "much less congenial on the whole than fellow Americans with whom I had previously thought I had little in common." To Dr. Michael Shadid, in 1928, taking his daughter to visit Lebanon thirty years after he had left proved a failure. She "was visibly shocked and frightened" seeing the miserable living conditions in the region and before even seeing her father's homeland asked "if we couldn't return to the United States at once."[26]

Much to their dismay, others returning home discover that they, or their children, are viewed with suspicion by the native residents or are pejoratively labelled Americans. Because of their accent, attitude, dress, behavior, and lack of knowledge of old-country ways, they become oddities, if not strangers.

Some examples:

—Though the number of black Americans visiting Africa increased in recent years, some resident Africans criticized them for their superficial knowledge of the countries and noninvolvement in their political and economic problems. "Black Americans make noise about Haiti," said Kwame Karikari, of the University of Ghana, in 1994, "but they come here and stay silent while they hobnob with political elites that often have blood on their hands."[27]

—Returning Puerto Ricans confronted problems of language, adjustment, and rejection. Some were denigrated as "Newyoricans," because they could not speak island Spanish well, and were told, "Well, why don't you go back to where you belong?" Language problems for children raised in America were so intense that Puerto Rico established bilingual classes to help them speak, read, and write Spanish.[28]

—Japanese born or raised abroad found themselves viewed with suspicion and even subjected to social prejudice upon returning home. Some of their reactions were: "Native Japanese expect me to be more Japanese since I look like them. They often ask, 'Why can't you speak Japanese?' " "When they see me talking in English, they think, 'What gives her the right to speak English?' " "People look at me with a dirty look when I'm talking with a Hakujin (white American)."[29]

In America, some longtime immigrants, especially their children and grandchildren, are accused by newly arrived kinsmen of having foresaken their group heritage. Punjabi-Americans in rural California were viewed by new immigrants as unnatural because of their intermarriages with Mexican women and abandonment of ancestral language, religion, and names. Eighteen-year-old Martha Florence Vedrine found that, though her Haitian parents had taught her to love the island and speak Creole, new immigrant Haitians viewed her differently:

> To them I am an intruder, a foreigner. To them, because I have yet to feel the soil of the Haitian countryside beneath my feet, because I have yet to breathe the air of the mountains of Haiti, because I have yet to see the bays of Port-au-Prince and the beauty of Jacmel, to them I am not Haitian. Automatically, I am set aside by them because I can speak English and because I speak Creole, "their" native tongue, with an accent. To the people whom my life revolves around, I am American.[30]

Generally, with each generation there is a decline in attachment to the old country, though there are always some members and groups who are more concerned with their country and their kinsmen abroad than others, believing themselves to be in a diaspora, in exile, on a sojourn, or even to be threatened. For example, though highly acculturated, today's American Jews, Armenians, and Greeks are more concerned about their ancestral homelands and kinsmen than are today's American Irish, Italians, or Germans, just as today's newest Hispanic immigrant groups are more concerned than the latter European groups, especially in their desire to retain ancestral language fluency.

Minority group life in America is not solely one of adaptation, acculturation, and assimilation, but for some, it means relocation, erosion, and even disappearance. No longer does Russia have settlements in Alaska, which was once called "Russian America," where colonists, traders, and fur hunters entered in 1741 and, like other European powers elsewhere on the continent, exploited the natives. After America purchased the territory in 1867, the Russians withdrew, leaving behind many Aleuts of mixed descent and with Russian names. Similarly, all that remains of the Greeks, Italians and Minorcans who established "New Smyrna" in eastern Florida, in 1768, are some of their descendants, who now live in St. Augustine.

The most short-lived of all groups were small utopian communities, whose exact numbers are unknown. Whether religious, ethnic, secular, or philosophic, they were conceived as ideal societies, self-contained and separated from other people. Of the dozens of well-known, religio-ethnic communities and utopian societies that once flourished, none exists today.[31]

Various groups of German, French, Italian, Finnish, Norwegian, Danish, Swiss, Swedish, English, Slovak, Belgian and Jewish immigrants tried to establish communities, with varying degrees of success. Ararat was conceived in the early nineteenth century as a city of refuge for Jews on Grand

Island outside of Buffalo, New York, but never gained Jewish support in America or abroad, and all that remains of the project is the cornerstone, which is in the Buffalo Historical Society.

Early nineteenth-century German intellectuals believed they could create "a new and free Germany in the great North American Republic," but to no avail. A Swedish settlement in Illinois with some 1,500 members failed because of a cholera epidemic, excessive land and business speculation, and the murder of its founder. In vain, the British Temperance Emigration Society tried to establish an alcohol-free community in Wisconsin. Various Norwegian groups failed to establish colonies in New York, Missouri, Texas, Iowa, Pennsylvania, as well as in Illinois, where Cleng Peerson hoped all Norwegians in America would settle and own land in common. In the mid-nineteenth century, the Belgian government encouraged Flemish paupers to immigrate to Algeria, Guatemala, Texas, Missouri and Pennsylvania, where a "New Flanders" actually lasted some ten years.[32]

Generally, groups with a religious basis were most successful, a phenomenon President Madison credited to "the united labors of many for the common object" and "a religious impulse in the members, and a religious authority in the head."[33] Such early communal societies were welcomed in America, and, unlike similarly idealistic ones established in recent decades, consisted of devout, practicing Christians, such as Seventh-Day Baptists who settled in Pennsylvania in 1732, Shakers who settled in New York in 1785, and Harmonites and Rappites who settled in Pennsylvania and Indiana a few decades later.

Continually persecuted by Catholics and Protestants in Europe, Mennonites and Amish eventually migrated to America and Canada. As Anabaptists, both groups rejected infant baptism and involvement in the larger society, even to the extent of refusing to serve in the armed forces. Hutterites also came to America in search of religious freedom, but most left during World War I to avoid government harassment for refusing to serve in the military or to help the war effort in any manner.[34]

Sociology rather than theology or ethnicity motivated the formation of many other utopian societies. Ralph Waldo Emerson noted in 1840 the existence of "numberless projects of collective ownership. Not a reading man has but a draft of a new Community in his waistcoat pocket." Robert Owen came from Scotland to establish New Harmony in Indiana, where he hoped to introduce "an entire new state of society, to change it from an ignorant, selfish system to an enlightened social system which shall gradually unite all interests into one and remove all causes for contest between individuals." He failed, as did Victor Considerant, who attempted to establish a Fourierist Phalanstery in Texas, proclaiming in 1854 that "the Promised Land is a reality." After trying to establish their Icaria in various states, French utopians gave up in 1856, when a majority of the group expelled their leader. Various nineteenth-century Bohemian groups considered or attempted to establish communities, with one Chicago group in 1876 hoping to do so in the Southwest where "The idea of freeing one's self from the yoke of capital and building one's own existence in the country is excellent. We recognized it to be the only feasible and practicable solution of the so-called workingmen's problems. . . ."[35]

Attempts were also made to form anarchistic utopias, such as Modern Times in Long Island, where the "sovereignty of the individual" would prevail, without marriage, and where people would live in peace through obeying only their consciences. Equally futile was the attempt to establish a colony—Runnymede—of rich English gentlemen in Kansas, where they could have fox hunts and play polo.[36]

Whether religious or not, communes and utopias failed because of a variety of reasons: economic problems, organizational differences, factionalism, corruption, lack of or the death of strong leaders, opposition by neighbors, failure to attract new members, or even success of belief, as in the case of the Shakers whose celibate practices precluded a second generation of endogenous members. In addition, as with individual ethnic or religious identity, some members found total separation from the larger society difficult, if not impossible, to maintain.

There are some small religio-ethnic groups, however, that succeeded in establishing colonies or communities for a number of generations before declining. Though fleeing religious persecution in France, seventeenth-century Huguenots in the English colonies replicated the occupations of those about them, whether in rural or urban areas, while continually abandoning their ancestral language and church. Socioeconomic success, plus an absence from abroad of additional immigrants and church leaders, further undermined their survival. Also bleak is the corporate future of nineteenth-century Wends (an ancient Slavic people from eastern Germany who settled mainly in Texas) and mid-twentieth-century Kalmuks (Russian Mongolian Buddhists who settled mainly in New Jersey and Pennsylvania). Their offspring, like those of the Huguenots, are progressively assimilating and losing command of their ancestral languages, without their numbers being added to by new immigrants.[37]

The Mormons are certainly the most successful and extraordinary of all the groups that formed their own community with no, or with a minimum of, contact with outsiders. After nearly two decades of persecution and migration, they settled in a desolate area and created their own Zion, free of and from Gentiles. Though blacks could become Mormons, they were specifically excluded from the church's priesthood until 1978, when Mormon leaders declared they had received a revelation whereby "all worthy male members of the Church may be ordained to the priesthood without regard for race or color." By 1990, of the more than 7 million Mormons worldwide, 4 million resided in the United States, almost one-half in Utah.

Though smaller in number, the deeply pious Jews known as Chassidim are equally successful. After World War II, several thousand survivors came from Europe and settled in various sections of Brooklyn, where they continue to practice their traditional ways, in spite of living among Hispanics, African Americans, and less religiously observant Jews. To date, defections have been few.[38]

In short, while group and national identity are not congruent, they do have a reciprocal relationship, wherein each influences the other, though with each succeeding generation to lesser degrees. As with individual identity, change and continuity characterize group and national identity, undermining most attempts for group self-segregation. With few exceptions, group members become Americans or at least hyphenated ones, speak English, and want the same respect, rights, and protection that members of other groups have. Whether that process of Americanization will continue as in the past is, as we shall see, open to debate, if not doubt.

## NOTES

1. Antonio McDaniel, "The Dynamic Racial Composition of the United States," *Daedalus* (Winter 1995): 181; Ian K. Steele, *Warpaths: Invasions of North America* (New York: Oxford University Press, 1994), 224.

2. Robert Kelley, *The Cultural Pattern in American Politics* (New York: Alfred A. Knopf, 1979), 34; Merle Curti, *The Roots of American Loyalty* (New York: Atheneum, 1968), 12–13.

3. Curti, *The Roots of American Loyalty,* 23; Carl Bridenbaugh, *The Spirit of '76* (New York: Oxford University Press, 1975), 3.

4. Stephan Thernstrom, *Harvard Encyclopedia of American Ethnic Groups* (Cambridge: Harvard University Press, 1980), 735, 739.

5. Maldwyn Allen Jones, *American Immigration* (Chicago: University of Chicago Press, 1960), 135–36; Yen Le Espiritu, *Asian American Panethnicity* (Philadelphia: Temple University Press, 1992), 19.

6. Myron Bohdon Kuropas, "Ukrainian Chicago: The Making of a Nationality Group in America," in *Ethnic Chicago,* ed. Peter d'A. Jones and Melvin G. Holli (Grand Rapids, Mich.: William B. Eerdmans, 1981), 145.

7. William Petersen, *Population* (New York: Macmillan, 1969), 119; Stephanie Bernardo, *The Ethnic Almanac* (Garden City, N.Y.: Dolphin Books, 1981), 93; Kuropas, "Ukrainian Chicago: The Making of a Nationality Group in America," 141; *New York Times,* 13 February 1986, A6; Thomas Sowell, *Race and Culture* (New York: Basic Books, 1994), 131; Joel Dreyfuss, "The Invisible Immigrants," *New York Times Magazine,* 23 May 1993, 21.

8. Sowell, *Race and Culture,* 28; *New Dimensions* (Philadelphia: The Balch Institute for Ethnic Studies, Fall 1988):6; Charles H. Anderson, *White Protestant Americans* (Englewood Cliffs, N.J.: Prentice-Hall, 1970), 30.

9. Peter Roberts, *The New Immigrants* (New York: Macmillan, 1912), 10; Melvin G. Holli, "The Great War Sinks Chicago's German *Kultur*," in *Ethnic Chicago,* ed. Peter d'A. Jones and Melvin G. Holli (Grand Rapids, Mich.: William B. Eerdmans, 1981), 279; Eiichiro Azuma, "Interethnic Conflict under Racial Subor-

dination: Japanese Immigrants and Their Asian Neighbors in Walnut Grove, California 1908–1941," *Amerasia Journal* 7, no. 2 (1994): 43–47; Louis L. Gerson, *The Hyphenate in Recent American Politics and Diplomacy* (Lawrence: University of Kansas Press, 1964), 134.

10. Gerson, *The Hyphenate in Recent American Politics and Diplomacy,* 8, 10.

11. Henry Giniger, "Americans Courted by Quebec Leaders," *New York Times,* 4 July 1978, 1 and 22 November 1987, 1; *The Assyrian Sentinel,* February 1981, 1; *Boston Globe,* 20 June 1993, 1, 14; Mireyo Navarro, "After Years in Exile in South Florida, Nicaraguans Feel the Tug of 2 Homes," *New York Times,* 21 March 1995, A14; Doreen Carvajal, "On L.I., El Salvador Helps Own Refugees Get Asylum," *New York Times,* 27 October 1995, A1; Alice Dembner, "A Language in Eclipse? 'Mais Non!' " *Boston Globe,* 11 July 1994, 1; Steven Emerson, "The Other Fundamentalists," *The New Republic* (12 June 1995): 21–30.

12. *Christian Science Monitor,* 23 November 1987, 9; Diego Ribadeneira, "Mexicans Consider Their Own in LA," *Boston Globe,* 24 April 1994, 14; Lisa Respers, "Campaign for Cherokee Chief Comes to L.A.," *Los Angeles Times,* 30 April 1995, B1.

13. James T. Madore and Cameron McWhirter, "Recent Turmoil Prompts Renewed Cries for 'China out of Tibet,' " *Christian Science Monitor,* 30 March 1988, 7; Mary Tabor, "Local Azerbaijanis Deplore Violence," *Boston Globe,* 21 January 1990, 8; Haldun Armagan, "Turks Wary of Greeks Seeking the White House," *WorldPaper,* October 1988, 13; Isabel Wilkerson, "Serb-Americans Feel Distant War," *New York Times,* 10 May 1993, A12.

14. Thomas J. Lueck, "A Little City Trolls for Trade," *New York Times,* 27 January 1994, B1; Jason B. Johnson, "ANC Official Taps Hub Leaders in U.S. Fund-raising Tour," *Boston Herald,* 4 February 1994, 3; *New York Times,* 27 May 1993, A10; Steven Greenhouse, "U.S. Blacks Urge to Aid African Lands," *New York Times,* 10 May 1995, A3; Karen De Witt, "Black Group Begins Protest Against Nigeria," *New York Times,* 17 March 1995, A10; Zachary R. Dowdy, "Local Nigerians Urge Ruler's Ouster," *Boston Globe,* 6 August 1995, 12.

15. *New York Times,* 28 October 1990, E19, 30 January 1994, 17, 28 June 1995, A15, and 10 May 1991, A31; *Boston Globe,* 27 January 1993, 19.

16. Raymond Hernandez, "New York Vote Plan Seeks to Gain Voice in Puerto Rico Status," *New York Times,* 26 July 1993, A1; David Gonzalez, "Conquering Divide on Puerto Rico," *New York Times,* 23 August 1993, B1; Larry Rohter, "Puerto Rico Votes to Retain Status as Commonwealth," *New York Times,* 15 November 1993, A1.

17. Thernstrom, *Harvard Encyclopedia of American Ethnic Groups,* 677–78.

18. Zachary R. Dowdy, "Protesters Demand US, UN Act to Save Bosnian 'Safe Zone,' " *Boston Globe,* 28 November 1994, 14; Randolph Ryan, "Many Serbs in America Besieged by Bosnia War," *Boston Globe,* 29 July 1995, 1, 6.

19. Michael W. Suleiman, "Early Arab-Americans," in *Crossing the Waters: Arabic-Speaking Immigrants to the United States before 1940,* ed. Eric J. Hooglund (Washington, D.C.: Smithsonian Institution Press, 1987), 47; Charles A. Radin and Mugi Hanao, "Ozawa Conducts Japan's Best," *Boston Globe,* 22 January 1995, 16.

20. Charles Hillinger, "That George and His Crowd!" *Boston Globe,* 23 August

1975, 1, 9; Clyde H. Farnsworth, "Canada Rebuffs Veterans of U.S. Forces in Vietnam," *New York Times,* 19 June 1994, 8.

21. Magnus Morner, *Race Mixture in the History of Latin America* (Boston: Little, Brown and Company, 1967), 29; Francis Jennings, *The Invasion of America* (New York: W. W. Norton & Company, 1975), 152; Eli Faber, "The Formative Era of American Jewish History," *American Jewish History* (Autumn 1993): 10.

22. Stephen Graham, *With Poor Immigrants to America* (New York: Macmillan, 1914), 135; Jerome Davis, *The Russian Immigrant* (New York: Macmillan, 1922), 172.

23. Karen Schniedewind, "Migrants Return to Bremen: Social Structure and Motivations, 1850 to 1914," *Journal of American Ethnic History* (Winter 1993): 48–51; Pamela Constable, "Disenchanted Professionals Flee Cuba in Rising Numbers," *Boston Globe,* 15 July 1993, 1.

24. Marion Marzolf, "The Danish-Language Press in America," *Norwegian-American Studies* 28 (Northfield, Minn.: The Norwegian-American Historical Association, 1979), 284; Navarro, "After Years in Exile in South Florida, Nicaraguans Feel the Tug of 2 Homes," A14.

25. Seth Mydans, "Former Refugees See Opportunity in Vietnam," *New York Times,* 5 December 1994, A8; idem, "For Many of Those Who Fled Vietnam, a Day of Sadness, Anger and Hope," *New York Times,* 12 July 1995, A9; idem, "California Vietnamese Seek Hanoi's Business," *New York Times,* 12 September 1994, A10; Mireya Navarro, "New Tolerance Sprouts Among Cuban Exiles," *New York Times,* 25 August 1995, A14; Pam Belluck, "Healthy Korean Economy Draws Immigrants Home," *New York Times,* 22 August 1995, A1, B4.

26. Richard Krickus, *Pursuing the American Dream* (Garden City, N.Y.: Anchor Books, 1976), 139; Robert C. Christopher, *Crashing the Gates* (New York: Simon and Schuster, 1989), 46; Suleiman, "Early Arab-Americans," 46.

27. Howard W. French, "On Slavery, Africans Say the Guilt Is Theirs, Too," *New York Times,* 27 December 1994, A5.

28. *New York Times,* 3 October 1975, 20.

29. Jiro Suzuki and Mickey Sakamoto, "Discrimination Against Foreigners of Japanese Descent in Japan," in *Case Studies on Human Rights and Fundamental Freedoms,* Vol. 2 (The Hague: The Foundation for the Study of Plural Societies, 1976), 263–64.

30. Karen Leonard, "Historical Constructions of Ethnicity: Research on Punjabi Immigrants in California," *Journal of American Ethnic History* (Summer 1993): 8, 13; Martha Florence Vedrine, "Who am I?" *The Boston Globe Magazine,* 6 February 1994, 14.

31. Calvin Wall Redekop, *The Old Colony Mennonites* (Baltimore: Johns Hopkins University Press, 1975), 1–2.

32. Samuel P. Orth, *Our Foreigners* (New Haven: Yale University Press, 1921), 135; Ronald G. Walters, *American Reformers 1815–1860* (New York: Hill and Wang, 1978), 44; Frank Thistlethwaite, *America and the Atlantic Community* (New York: Harper Torchbook, 1959), 191; Thernstrom, *Harvard Encyclopedia of American Ethnic Groups,* 753, 179.

33. Matthew Mellon, *Early American Views on Negro Slavery* (New York: Bergman Publishers, 1969), 139.

34. Eldon G. Ernst, *Without Help or Hindrance* (Philadelphia: Westminister

Press, 1977), 59; Halvdan Koht, *The American Spirit in Europe* (Philadelphia: University of Pennsylvania Press, 1949), 2–3; David Flint, *The Hutterites* (Toronto: Oxford University Press, 1975), 74.

35. M. J. Heale, *American Communism: Combatting the Enemy Within* (Baltimore: Johns Hopkins University Press, 1990), 8; Koht, *The American Spirit in Europe,* 61; Orth, *Our Foreigners,* 100; Thomas Capek, *The Cechs (Bohemians) in America* (Westport, Conn.: Greenwood Press, 1970), 107.

36. Walters, *American Reformers 1815–1860,* 73; Oscar O. Winther, "The English and Kansas, 1865–1890," in *The Frontier Challenge,* ed. John G. Clark (Lawrence: University Press of Kansas, 1971), 265–66.

37. Thernstrom, *Harvard Encyclopedia of American Ethnic Groups,* 599–600, 1,017–20; Sam Howe Verhovek, "Kalmuks in U.S. Facing Loss of Traditions," *New York Times,* 20 July 1987, B1; Jon Butler, *The Huguenots in America* (Cambridge: Harvard University Press, 1983), 199–215.

38. Israel Rubin, *Satmar: An Island in the City* (Chicago: Quadrangle Books, 1972), 232.

# 5

# Groups and Stereotypes

No lie is ever so fantastic that it does not muster its legion or legions of avid believers.

—Gustavus Myers,
*History of Bigotry in the United States*

Stereotyping is probably the most prevalent of intergroup malaises, wherein people are pejoratively characterized because of their group rather than individual identity. The worse the stereotype, the worse the treatment. The process allows no distinctions between some, many, or most members of a group. Nor does it acknowledge any similarities between the good or bad characteristics of those stereotyped and those doing the stereotyping. It is always "those" people and not "my" people who are the scoundrels.

Unlike common generalizations, stereotypes resist correction, are rooted more in fantasy than in fact, and appear in all areas of society: family, politics, schools, religious centers, private clubs, public restrooms, and print and electronic media. Wherever stereotypes appear, they are easily made and have a life before and beyond the moment expressed. The number of negative terms, phrases, and images that can be used are manifold, with one scholar identifying more than 1,000 derogatory terms, with hundreds of variations, for some fifty American groups.[1]

Colors, too, are used to stereotype people, with white signifying cleanliness, superiority, morality, and all other colors signifying varying degrees of baseness—black connoting dirtiness, evil, inferiority; red connoting rev-

olutionary, bomb thrower, wild; and yellow connoting cowardness, mean-
ness, sneakiness. Thus, throughout American history white people were
deemed superior to African Americans, Native Americans, and Asians.

Stereotypes are also conveyed by the way in which words are enunciated
and accompanied by facial or bodily gestures. For example, a person's
description of someone as a Catholic, a woman, or an Asian can be a
simple, value-free statement—but the same description with a change of
intonation, accent, or bodily movement can express criticism, contempt,
and/or outright bias. When Senator Alfonse D'Amato criticized Japanese-
American Judge Lance Ito in 1995 over how he was presiding at the O. J.
Simpson murder trial, a number of antidiscrimination groups immediately
accused him of bigotry—not for what he had said about Judge Ito, but the
mocking way in which he had said it—with an exaggerated Japanese accent reminiscent of old World War II movies.[2]

Though many favorable stereotypes exist (fighting Irish, smart Jews,
French lovers, brave Indians), the focus in this chapter is on those that
purposely or mindlessly reflect, rationalize, validate or perpetuate defamation of groups or individuals because of their group affiliation.

Stereotypes can:

—be generated and nurtured by ignorance or familiarity

—be utilized by people with low, normal, high or exceptional intelligence

—be rooted in past or present history

—be reflectors of bias or hostility within an individual, family, peer group, neighborhood, and/or society

—be created by majority and minority group members, particularly when competing for social, economic, or political position

—be used to assault, demean, or intimidate others—or to justify doing so

—be expressed defensively in order to preempt others making them or expressed
aggressively in retaliation for having been stereotyped

—be adopted as a way of maintaining social distance and status—and asserting
one's superiority

—be changed for the better or the worse—or disappear entirely

—be applied simultaneously or successively to more than one group

—be contrary to logic, as when negative and positive stereotypes are simultaneously applied to a group

—be a source of enjoyment for their users and pain for their referents

—be a preamble, concomitant, or consequence of more bigoted forms of behavior

Though stereotypes distort reality, they are not necessarily bereft of
some truths. Many groups clearly display some characteristics that distin-
guish them from other groups, or have certain characteristics to a greater

or lesser degree than other groups—whether they be in height, alcohol consumption, religious practices, work ethic, family size, education, criminal arrests, or joining the military. Simply put, it cannot be generally said that the Chinese are prominent in basketball, the Irish in grand opera, Mormons in alcohol consumption, or Native Americans in politics.

Saying so, however, does not mean that behaviors are genetically or socially fixed, that members of different groups do not have similar or identical behaviors, or that a group's having more or less of a given virtue or fault is true of every member. The line between a stereotype and a generalization can be thin, depending on the time, place, and setting of who is being described and who is doing the describing—and with what motivation and substantiation. Unlike the generalizer, the stereotyper is indifferent, if not hostile, to verification. However, the generalizer has to be careful, lest he or she be rightfully or wrongfully accused of stereotyping—or, worse, bigotry.

Unfortunately, all too often negative stereotyping exceeds objective generalizing, and no minority group can escape being targeted to some degree.

For most of their years in America, the Irish were subjected to a succession of negative stereotypes. Nineteenth-century cartoons portrayed them as rough and uncivilized, for example, as a "gorilla, stovepipe hat on his head, a shamrock in his lapel, a vast jug of liquor in one hand and a large club in the other. His face was a mask of simian brutality and stupidity." By the late nineteenth and early twentieth centuries, the Irishman began evolving into an endearing leprechaun, as well as being portrayed as lucky and adept at fighting. While Irish women were portrayed as stupid, they were felt to have less negative qualities than their male counterparts and were often portrayed as loving and lovable. Mexican Americans underwent a progression of negative stereotypes from 1890 to 1970, such as peasant Mexican, Pachuco or Zootsuiter (flashy clothes wearer), and Wetback (illegal alien who waded or swam across the Rio Grande river), all of whom had few redeeming qualities. They were often also portrayed as comic and incompetent bandits in movies and advertising.[3]

Polish-American stereotypes followed a circular pattern. A study of the first 100 years of Detroit's Polish community noted: "The brutish, antidemocratic ignoramus; the strikebreaking supplanter of honest American labor; the advance guard of anarchism and bolshevism; the mindless tool of the papal conspiracy was transformed by the 1940s into the kindly, gentle, slightly comic fellow who, waving his citizenship papers proudly, burbled heartwarming patriotic cliches in his broken nightschool English. Now, he is again transformed into the racist hard-hat."[4] Polish jokes proliferated, belittling Polish intelligence both in America and abroad. There was an easing off these jokes in the 1990s, but only after mounting protests by Polish-American organizations.

With some groups, negative stereotypes changed to the positive—or disappeared altogether. Peter Stuyvesant and his council once issued a decree criticizing Scottish merchants from abroad for their underselling other merchants and quickly returning to Europe with their profits. Today, being Scotch connotes being prudently frugal, with some businesses using an illustration of a kilted Scotchman or add "Mac" to their corporate name to indicate inexpensive or good value. For many years the word *Cajun* was used offensively in Louisiana to signify a rustic of French descent; now the term proudly appears on bumper stickers and in the name of the University of Southwestern Louisiana's athletic teams. Out west on the range in the mid-nineteenth century, the use of the word *cowboy* was an insult, signifying outlawry, banditry, or otherwise being uncivilized; the preferred description was *buckeroo,* an anglified form of the Spanish *vacquero.*[5]

In colonial days, a Yankee meant "swindler, weasel-keen at a trade, all opportunist, pious-spoken." The president of Georgetown described New England Yankees as "the most knavish and capable of the most ingenious impositions. The large volume of business that they carry on in all the other states, and the tricks they resort to for profits have fixed this conception on them." Early nineteenth-century Southerners were said at the time to "hate Yankees worse than snakes, because they have cheated them or speculated on their credulity with so many Connecticut clocks and New England notions." Almost as a counterpoise, stereotypes arose of Southern gentlemen and Southern belles. To many foreign observers also, Yankees were not nice. Listening to one, wrote Frances Trollope in 1832, "you might fancy him a god—though a tricky one. . . . In acuteness, cautiousness, industry, and perseverance, he resembles the Scotch; in habits of frugal neatness, he resembles the Dutch; in love of lucre he doth greatly resemble the sons of Abraham; but in frank admission, and superlative admiration of his own peculiarities, he is like nothing on earth but himself."[6] Only long after the Civil War did the term gradually become synonymous with patriotism, friendliness, and freedom loving, except in some foreign countries where extreme nationalists demanded that "Yankees Go Home."

Totally gone today are the late eighteenth- and early nineteenth-century negative stereotypes of Frenchmen and their supporters as being bloody revolutionaries, though some negative stereotypes exist of New England Franco-Americans as frog eaters or dumb frogs. Also gone are the negative stereotypes of Australians, who, during the California gold rush, were called Sydney ducks and whose crime-ridden neighborhoods were disparaged as Sydney Towns. No longer do public school textbooks contain vicious stereotypes, such as those depicting Spanish colonists as idle, ignorant and corrupt, Asians as luxurious, indolent, effeminate and servile, and

Catholics as deceitful, the Pope a son of perdition, and monasteries seats of voluptuousness.[7]

Probably the fastest reversal in stereotyping involves the Japanese, who before and during World War II were stereotyped as grinning, buck-toothed, slant-eyed, and treacherous. In his journal, President Truman described them as "savages, ruthless, merciless, and fanatic." However, a few decades later, they were described as exotic, graceful, picturesque, polite, industrious, and quality manufacturers of cars and cameras. By 1982, only 3 percent of Americans polled believed they were people who could not be trusted. Though still overwhelmingly viewed favorably, and often enviously so, a new negative stereotype began emerging in the 1990s of the Japanese as sinister businessmen trying to take over America.[8]

Stereotypes can alternate from the favorable to the unfavorable, depending on the time and place. Arabs were portrayed in motion pictures in the 1920s and 1930s as daring camel riders, good fighters, and exotic lovers, but with America's growing dependence on Arab oil and the rise of political and religious extremism in the Arab world in the late 1970s, they began being depicted as rich, sex-starved, treacherous, and murderous. Similarly, school textbooks frequently portrayed Muslims as if they were all desert-dwelling Arabs, given to terrorism. As late as 1993, the American Arab Anti-Discrimination Committee protested lyrics in the Disney film *Aladdin,* which described Arabs "in a faraway place. . . . Where they cut off your ear/If they don't like your face." Nineteenth-century Chinese were at first welcomed on the West Coast as "most orderly and industrious citizens," but as they increased in number and job competition with whites, they began being portrayed as dangerous, deceitful, vicious, and a threat to society. Similarly, Jews, Italians, and Greeks were enviously stereotyped as taking care of their own and sticking together, but when they improved their socioeconomic lot, they were denounced as being as pushy and aggressive.[9]

In Soldotna, Alaska, attitudes toward Russian neighbors across the Bering Sea changed with the ending of the cold war, or as it was referred to there, the lowering of the "Ice Curtain." Before then, many Alaskans felt the Russians were "just like us, we share the same kind of environment, and wouldn't it be great if they got rid of Communism." But when Russians began visiting Soldotna, Alaskans began saying, "They stink, they drink too much and they all want to buy guns," adding, honestly enough, that the same things could be said about Alaskans.[10]

At times, a stereotype can have a conflicting or contradictory meaning, wherein what is admired is also disliked, or vice versa. In colonial days, the Scotch-Irish were sarcastically said to not only keep the Sabbath, but also everything they put their hands on.[11] More than simple admiration is involved in describing a *good* Jewish lawyer, German scientist, or black athlete. The use of *good* in describing the Jewish lawyer can connote legal cunning; in the German scientist, heartless efficiency; and in the black athlete, primitive muscle. Conversely, what is disliked can also be desired—as with those who welcome having an Italian Mafia family protect them or avenge wrongs done to them. Likewise, acts disliked in some groups can be praised in others, as with Puerto Ricans or French Canadians being criticized for having large families, but not the large families of their critics, who are hailed for their togetherness.

Stereotypes, even well-intentioned ones, distort reality, as in the case of immigrant women depicted as illiterate and doting, though many Slovene, Lithuanian, Polish, Ukrainian, Lebanese, Syrian, Jewish, and other immigrant women successfully formed local, regional, and national charitable and educational organizations and became leaders and administrators of religious schools, hospitals, orphanages, and social service institutions.[12] The stereotypes invariably downplayed their constructive roles as wives and mothers in holding the family together, without the time or means to hire baby-sitters or maids or to supposedly fulfill themselves.

Some stereotypes are applied to more than one group, or to successive ones. In the former instance, as H. L. Mencken noted in *The American Language, squarehead* was used for either a German or a Scandinavian. Mid–nineteenth-century Germans and Dutch were both called *cabbageheads*. Hungarians and other neighboring Europeans were called *hunkies*. *Greaseballs* denoted Greeks and Italians. New England fishermen used the term *herring choker* to defame Scandinavians, Newfoundlanders, Nova Scotians, and Canadians in general. In California in the 1930s, Dust Bowl migrants from Arkansas, Oklahoma, Texas, and Missouri were derided as *Okies* and *Arkies,* accused of shiftlessness, lack of ambition, and of stealing jobs from local residents, and were subjected to the same kind of exploitation as were Afro-Americans and Asians.[13]

From our earliest history, some groups were stereotyped as filthy disease carriers and a menace to the health of society. Early nineteenth-century Irish were associated with cholera, late nineteenth-century Chinese with bubonic plague, early twentieth-century Italians with polio, and recent Haitians with AIDS. Abroad, Germans called syphilis the French disease; the French called it the Neapolitan disease; the Dutch, the Spanish disease; and the Japanese, the Chinese ulcer. Early converts to Mormonism were accused of bearing a pestilence or having inhaled the malaria of its founder Joseph Smith. At the same time, Mexicans in the Southwest were said to have habits "as filthy as their persons." Syrians, too, were deemed unclean, with Senator David Reed, in 1929, describing them as the "trash of the Mediterranean."[14]

Many a late nineteenth- and early twentieth-century academic claimed that unless immigration restrictions were imposed on south, central, and eastern Europeans, they would contaminate the gene pool of Americans and cause them to "rapidly become darker in pigmentation, smaller in stature, more mercurial . . . more given to crimes of larceny, kidnapping, assault, murder, rape and sex immorality . . . than were the original English settlers."[15]

At times a particular disease was blamed on different or successive groups. For example, yellow fever in colonial Philadelphia was blamed on Germans and called "the Palatine fever." Then it was blamed on immigrants from the Caribbean and termed the "Barbados distemper." White and black French refugees from late eighteenth-century, revolution-torn Haiti were blamed next, particularly by the Federalists, while a few other Americans blamed Englishmen for bringing the disease from the British West Indies. One New England editor suggested the disease might have come from his homeland of Ireland. More recently, in 1993, when federal health officials favored the name "Muerto Canyon Hantavirus" for a virus that had killed some forty people in New Mexico and Arizona, including many Native Americans, the Navajo Nation Council accused the media of provoking discrimination against its people by sensationalizing hantavirus as a Navajo disease.[16]

Just as ignorance can breed stereotypes, so can familiarity, particularly when it is experienced to a limited degree. The results are often simultaneous and contradictory stereotypes, which invariably enhance the self-image of their projectors. "We Americans," wrote Katharine Fullerton Gerould, "are apt either to despise the alien or to fawn on him—muddling all comparative values in either case."[17]

Some examples: When Europeans first met Indians, they viewed them as either noble savages living in primeval innocence or as cruel savages, little better than animals. The more the Europeans sought to expand their land base, the worse became their stereotypes of the Indians—and vice versa. Early seventeenth-century Indians in Massachusetts referred to the Pilgrims as Wotowquenange, meaning stabbers or cutthroats. In the early 1900s, American Basques in the West were praised by some for being solid citizens and yet damned by others as itinerant nomads. Slavs were demeaned as *hunkies,* who were brutishly strong, ignorant, violent and given to "beer like ducks to water"—and, yet, at the same time, they were respected for their manliness, self-sufficiency, law abidance, and willingness to do long and hard work. If young Eskimo women were friendly, sociable, and desirous of becoming part of a white settlement, whites labeled them loose, but if they were shy, remained at home, and generally avoided contact with whites, they were deemed to be nice, but stupid. The role of self-interest in such stereotypes is well captured by a Great Depression "Okie" who said: "When they need us they call us migrants. When we've picked their crop, we're bums and we got to get out."[18]

Countries, too, have been subjected to dual and contradictory stereotypes. Salvador de Madariaga, in his study of national character, pointed out that the English have been characterized as both hypocritical and practical, the French as clear thinking and licentious, the Germans as thorough and clumsy, the Spanish as dignified and cruel, and the Americans as vulgar and vital.[19]

At their simplest, stereotypes mirror prejudice, malice, aggression, or desire of the stereotypers for social distancing, power, or dominance. By stereotyping others, people consciously or unconsciously assert their perceived psychological or social superiority, while rationalizing away any need to learn more about other groups and justifying whatever aggression they initiate. The Abenaki Indians referred to the Iroquois as *Maguak,* meaning cowards; and, in return, the latter pejoratively referred to the Abenakis as *Adirondacks,* meaning bark-eaters. White settlers usually spoke of the Indian man as a buck and the Indian woman as a squaw, and by "a very natural and easy transition, from being spoken of as brutes, they came to be thought of as game to be shot, or as vermin to be destroyed," wrote a mid–nineteenth-century settler in the West.[20]

Even when not explicit, stereotypes are laden with memories and allusions, whose pain their targets know all too well. A swastika is not viewed the same way by Christians as by Jews, nor does a Confederate flag provoke the same emotions in blacks and whites, whether in the South or in the North. A protester in front of a Catholic church carrying the signs, "Fuck the church" and "Get over it, Mary," is not seen in the same way by Protestants, Jews, and nonbelievers as by Catholics.

"I can still recall the anger and pain I felt as my white classmates read aloud the word 'nigger,' " in *Huckleberry Finn,* wrote an Afro-American professor about his youth. "I wanted to sink into my seat. Some of the whites snickered, others giggled. . . . I only recall the sense of relief when I would flip ahead a few pages and see that the word 'nigger' would not be read that hour." Similarly, a columnist's use of the word *Chinaman* provoked May Seto to write the newspaper's editor that the word was as demeaning as *Chink* or *China Doll* and that as a Chinese American who had long heard such degrading descriptions, "I can attest to the anger, isolation, and psychological damage inflicted on the individual each time these words are heard."[21]

When challenged, stereotypers reply in a variety of ways, from outright defiance to delayed apology. Some insist that what they said is basically true and that individuals not conforming with the stereotype are exceptions to the rule or exceptions that prove the rule. A few deny having said what they were reported to have said, or claim their words were taken out of context, or accuse their critics of being too ready to complain, overly sensitive, lacking a sense of humor, or seeking to restrict their freedom of speech.

Most often, what stereotypers say is that they meant no harm. They claim they are simply teasing or using words or phrases heard from childhood on—such as Polack, Wop, Jap, Honkey, or Gringo. They may even cite friends in other groups who frequently call each other these names without complaint. A few claim they accidently misspoke, saying the opposite of what they really believe, which Rutgers University president Francis Lawrence claimed when he told a group of faculty members that blacks don't have the "genetic, hereditary background" to score better on standardized tests. A few admit having wanted to hurt the person stereotyped, but not all members of the person's group. "Maybe they thought the only way to hurt her was to insult her religion," said a high school student about some classmates who had sent a woman teacher a vulgar anti-Semitic note. "Maybe they knew that this was something that was important to her. They probably only wanted to get even with her."[22]

Politicians and public celebrities sometimes seem to be particularly given to engaging in stereotypes, and when criticized for doing so, particularly by the media, almost always apologize, saying they had meant no harm and that anyone familiar with their personal life knows they would never knowingly insult anyone. In contrast, some comedians and satirists regularly trade in demeaning and insulting stereotypes without any apology, except to say that they spare no one, not even members of their group or their immediate family.

And indeed, in some instances, any of the above responses may be accurate. There are individuals who use stereotypes and mean no harm, there are other people who see negative stereotypes where none exist, and there are stereotypical books, plays, paintings, and sculpture over whose merits reputable people can differ sharply. Who is to be the judge? The stereotyper or stereotyped? Which one is to be believed? Both cannot be completely correct, though both know that stereotypes hurt, demean, or ridicule. No less difficult is the problem of what should be done about stereotypes—ignore them, challenge their accuracy, or ban them by law or speech codes.

Painful as it may be, being stereotyped does not stop a group from stereotyping others. Just as majorities have vilified minorities, so have minorities defamed each other. For example, a 1985 *New York Times*/WCBS-TV poll showed that 57 percent of African Americans and 59 percent of Hispanics had friends who used racial slurs, with 23 percent and 22 percent, respectively, of those polled saying they themselves made racial slurs about other groups. The irony of various minorities using "WASP" to connote white, Protestant elitist, prudish, and tightly controlled emotions was noted by Edward Hoagland, who wrote, it is "O.K. to remark that John V. Lindsay, a former Mayor of New York City, 'was too WASPy,' but never, for instance, that Mayor Koch is 'too Jewy,' Pres. Reagan a 'Mick' or Gov. Cuomo a 'Dago.' "[23]

More extensive stereotyping was found in a Louis Harris 1993 poll of minority groups' attitudes toward the white majority and toward each other. While large majorities of African Americans, Hispanics, and Asians had negative views of whites, they often harbored greater percentages of prejudices against other minority groups than did whites. For example:

—46 percent of Hispanics and 42 percent of African Americans polled agreed with a description of Asians as "unscrupulous, crafty and devious in business"—in contrast to 27 percent of whites

—68 percent of Asians and 49 percent of African Americans agreed that Hispanics tend "to have bigger families than they are able to support"—in contrast to 50 percent of whites

—33 percent of Hispanics and 22 percent of Asians believed that African Americans, "Even if given a chance, aren't capable of getting ahead"—in contrast to 12 percent of whites

—54 percent of African Americans, 43 percent of Hispanics, and 35 percent of Asians agreed, "When it comes to choosing between people and money, Jews will choose money"—in contrast to 12 percent of non-Jewish whites

—58 percent of non-Catholic Hispanics, 57 percent of Asians, and 49 percent of African Americans believed that Catholics are "narrow-minded because they are too controlled by their church"—in contrast to 34 percent of non-Catholic whites

—48 percent of Hispanics, 39 percent of African Americans, and 30 percent of Asians believed that Muslims belong "to a religion that condones or supports terrorism"—to which, in contrast to the above, non-Muslim whites were largely in agreement by 41 percent.[24]

Sometimes minorities stereotype members of their own group, which if done by outsiders would be severely condemned, as if reaffirming the conventionally held truism that only a family member can legitimately beat up a relative. Thus, when criticized for describing Hollywood's "Jewish network" and its preference "to deal with other Jews," a British non-Jewish author replied that he had gotten his information from a book by one of his Jewish critics, noting the irony that while "it is acceptable for a Jewish writer . . . to use words like 'network' or 'reverse discrimination,' when a Brit uses similar phrases, he is publicly barbecued."[25]

Some minority group members are known to stereotype members of their own group in order to establish social distance or, conversely, to win acceptance. For example, during World War II, Hawaiian Japanese in the American army referred to mainland American Japanese as *Katonks,* meaning hollowheads, while the latter called their debasers *Buddahheads,* in ridicule of their island English and more traditional ways. Also, rather than being booed, Mayor Andrew Young of Atlanta, in 1984, evoked sympathetic laughter when he told an audience of Afro-American journalists, "I didn't know there were this many niggers that could write," adding that Walter Mondale's presidential advisers were "smart-assed white boys" who thought they knew it all. In recent years, the use of the word nigger has increased among black rap music entertainers, as in songs like "Straight Up Nigga" and "Nigger Vampire." In such cases, wrote *New York Times* reporter Kenneth Noble, the term nigger, like that of homeboy, is one of endearment.[26]

There are also minority group members who take issue with other members of their own group about the use of some stereotypes, saying that they are either true or largely so, or that they are said in jest and without malice. For example, in responding to a minister's criticism of a columnist's remarks about Episcopalians, another Episcopalian wrote that he found them humorous, that equally humorous ones exist in Episcopalian literature, and that he had "first heard from priests some of the best-known one-liners about Episcopalians' warmth (God's frozen people) and social habits (Where three or four Episcopalians are gathered, there will be a fifth)." Similarly, a Welsh American strongly disagreed with a fellow group member's objection to a reporter's use of the phrase "to welsh," saying that "I'm so Welsh in appearance that I was taken for a native when I visited Wales," that she herself uses the verb "on a regular basis," and that she is "more amused" by its survival than "its alleged knock against the country of my ancestors."[27]

Popular folk culture, humor, societal norms, and language standards are major repositories and purveyors of stereotypes. The famed lexicographer Noah Webster noted that a sure way of evoking scorn in strangers is to mock their accents—"small differences in pronunciation at first excite ridicule—a habit of laughing at the singularities of strangers is followed by disrespect—and without respect friendship is a name, and social intercourse a mere ceremony."[28]

The language of early vaudeville was rife with words such as coons, sheenies, dumb Swedes, Krauts, Shylock Jews, and so forth. Englishmen were caricatured as foppish, and amusingly drinking tea. Ethnic jokebooks and stage comics presented characters such as the Irish Pat and Mike, the Finnish Eino and Weino, the Cornish Jan and Bill, the Swedish Ole and Yon, and the Jewish Abie and Ikie. Asians were an upside-down people, exotic and bizarre; and circuses promoted wild men of Borneo, Chinese women with bound feet, and ring-necked Burmese women. In contemporary Hawaii, ethnic humor still refers to "the Portogee" as being stupid, talkative, and filled with himself. Males have long been demeaned by likening them to females. "You were either a faggot, a queer, or weak as a woman," testified a former cadet about the admission policy at an all-male military academy.[29]

In recent decades, too, as new immigrant groups have arrived, new stereotypes have come into being—*raghead* and *Indian boy* for Asian Indians, *rug rider* and *towel head* for Arabs, *pineapple* for Samoans, *Charlie* for Vietnamese, and *gook* for Koreans. Because of the media, today's stereotypes reach far larger audiences in much less time than in past decades. As with prior European immigrants, contemporary immigrants are accused of a wide range of sins, including the standard one that they take jobs away from native-born Americans. Asian Indians have been blamed for supporting Hare Krishna and causing a cockroach infestation; Vietnamese immigrants, of stealing and eating other people's pets; and American Arabs, of being terrorists.[30]

Some stereotypes are so tenacious that they evolve into norms of derogation, applicable to groups beyond those at whom they were originally directed, as with the words Indian, black, and Chinese, which were used singly or in combination. For example, to Cotton Mather, lazy, blasphemous, or disorderly English settlers were said "to Indianize, and by the Indian vices of lying, and Idleness, and sorcery, and a notorious want of all Family-Discipline, to become obnoxious." During the Whiskey Rebellion of 1794, Scotch-Irish whiskey makers in Pennsylvania were termed white Indians because of their fondness for the drink. Filipinos were no better than Indians, wrote one correspondent in *The Nation,* in 1899, and a senator said they were "as ignorant and savage as the aboriginal Indians." West Coast Armenians in the 1920s and 1930s were called Fresno Indians and not wanted as neighbors. Even today, slurs or comments are made about people being an Indian giver, drunker than an Indian, and wild as an Indian. However, the cruel adage that "the only good Indian is a dead Indian" is said to have been derived from the adage, "the only good wild Irishman is a dead wild Irishman."[31]

A group of late seventeenth-century Long Island Dutch settlers warned that unless a minister from Amsterdam were sent to the colony, the residents "may be turned into negroes, and become black and polluted." Nineteenth-century Protestant New Englanders referred to French Canadians as "the Chinese of the Eastern states" because of their alleged ignorance, poverty, nonassimilability, and readiness to work for low wages. Italians, too, were disparaged as the Chinese of Europe and as being just as bad as the Negroes. Prospective Welsh immigrants were warned that upon arriving they would be "exactly in the position of a nigger coolie." Early Sicilian immigrants in Louisiana were called black dagoes because they were the only whites willing to work in plantation fields and mills. Many early nineteenth-century white Texans viewed Mexicans as "greasers," "yaller niggers," "a mongrel breed of negroes, Indians and Spaniards of the baser sort," and white South Carolinians referred to Indians of racially mixed descent as yellow people, half-niggers, or half-Indians. Even the famed Karl Marx engaged in racial obscenities, calling Ferdinand Lassalle a "Nigger-Jew." Some mid–nineteenth-century blacks referred to the Irish as white niggers, because like them, they were doing menial and hard work. In recent years, Arabs have sometimes been labeled sand niggers.[32]

The invidious use of stereotypes is often legitimated by being included in standard English and reference books, as well as in newspaper stories, without noting their insulting and mean-spirited nature. Thus, the 1980 edition of *Roget's Thesaurus* listed Scotchman, Yorkshireman, and Yankee as synonyms for cunning; Jesuit and Pharisee for thief; Negro for servant; and Hibernicism and Irishman for absurdity. Only after the Anti-Defamation League complained to the publishers of the *Official Scrabble Players Dictionary* about their "literally playing games with hate" by including words like "nigger," "spic," and "dago" was it agreed that dozens of slurs and sexual references would be dropped from the 1994 edition.[33]

Popular culture is replete with derogatory ethnic verbs (Jew down), metaphors (Italian perfume for garlic), and jokes, which Irving Allen aptly said are "often blank checks in which the names of various groups are substituted according to the prejudices of the moment and of the company." Likewise, in his study of American jokebooks, Robert Secor noted that in ethnic humor, "everything is referenced to one's own group as the center of value, nourishing the group's own pride and vanity [and]. . . is a device of control, serving to keep the social value system intact."[34]

The very historical tenacity, media projection, popular usage, and reference book inclusion of stereotypes is reinforced by the psychological tendency of people to behave as they have been conditioned, taught, or expected to behave, presenting exceptions as generalizations or contriving generalizations that are untrue. Beliefs long nurtured are not easily altered or abandoned. A synergistic relationship of derogation exists between the stereotype and stereotyped, so that long before people meet an Armenian, a Frenchman, a Swede, a Greek, or an Italian, they may believe the stereotypes they had heard about them, namely that they are, respectively, wily, sexy, dumb, pederastic, or criminal, and therefore deserving of contempt or even physical attack. Conversely, being wily, sexy, dumb, pederastic, or criminal suggests that the person is Armenian, French, Swedish, Greek, or Italian.

For example, in 1993, in sentencing three Mafia members to life in prison, a federal district court judge expressed the hope that "a large part of the young Italo-American community" would be discouraged from going into crime, as if this were an accurate expectation of that community. Likewise, young black men and black repair servicemen shopping or making calls in white areas know they will be viewed with the suspicion, if not the fear, that they are robbers or muggers. Similarly, when the Oklahoma federal building was bombed in 1995, rumors and accusations multiplied in the media of Arab and Muslim extremists being responsible, all of which proved to be totally wrong.[35]

In summary, throughout American history, racial, religious, and ethnic groups were stereotyped, with the newest arrivals usually becoming the latest targets. Wittingly or unwittingly, stereotypes serve a variety of purposes, from the playful to the murderous. In the process, exceptions and fantasies are confused with generalizations and realities.

Over time, many stereotypes can change for the better or worse, or dis-

appear from current usage. Some, however, become standards of derogation. Though those targetted resent being stereotyped, some are not averse
to stereotyping others. As with prejudice generally, stereotyping remains
an integral component of individual, group, and societal life, and it is clear
from both history and psychology that wherever there is a will to demean,
harass, attack, or dominate people, a verbal way, and a rationale, will be
found to do so.

## NOTES

1. Irving Lewis Allen, *The Language of Ethnic Conflict* (New York: Columbia
University Press, 1983), 7.

2. Lawrence Van Gelder, "Gibe by D'Amato Sets Off Criticism," *New York
Times,* 6 April 1995, B1.

3. Andrew Greeley, *That Most Distressful Nation* (Chicago: Quadrangle
Books, 1972), 119; Hasia R. Diner, *Erin's Daughters in America* (Baltimore: Johns
Hopkins University Press, 1983), 70–72; Felix Gutierrez, "Making News—Media
Coverage of Chicano," *Agenda, A Journal of Hispanic Issues* (November/Decem-
ber 1978): 21.

4. Andrew Greeley, *Ethnicity in the United States* (New York: John Wiley &
Sons, 1974), 285.

5. Gustavus Myers, *History of Bigotry in the United States* (New York: Capricorn Books, 1960), 286; Stan Steiner, "The Waning of the West," *Natural History*
(June-July 1975): 52.

6. J. C. Furnas, *The Americans,* Vol. 1 (New York: Capricorn Books, 1969),
244; Peter C. Marzio, ed., *A Nation of Nations* (New York: Harper & Row,
1976), 142; Kenneth H. Winn, *Exiles in a Land of Liberty* (Chapel Hill: University
of North Carolina Press, 1989), 88; Robert Kelley, *The Shaping of the American
Past to 1877* (Englewood Cliffs, N.J.: Prentice-Hall, Inc., 1975), 364–65; Richard
A. Bartlett, *The New Country* (New York: Oxford University Press, 1979), 123.

7. Werner Levi, *American Australian Relations* (Minneapolis: University of
Minnesota Press, 1947), 39; Ruth Miller Elson, *Guardians of Tradition* (Lincoln:
University of Nebraska Press, 1964), 156, 161; Mark J. Hurley, *The Unholy
Ghost: Anti-Catholicism in the American Experience* (Huntington, Ind.: Our Sun-
day Visitor Publishing Division, 1992), 22.

8. William L. Neuman, *America Encounters Japan* (New York: Harper Colophon Books, 1965), 302–4; Bruce Loebs, "Hiroshima & Nagasaki," *Commonweal,* 18 August 1995, 15; Bill Hosokawa, "Accentuating the American in Japanese American," *Perspectives* (Fall 1982): 44; Stephen Schaefer, " 'Japan-bashing'
Charges Follow Novel to Screen," *Boston Herald,* 30 July 1993, S5–S7.

9. Jack G. Shaheen, "The Arab: TV's Most Popular Villain," *Christian Cen-
tury* (13 December 1978): 1,214; James Franklin, "Islamic Group Seeks Fair Por-
trayal in Textbooks," *Boston Globe,* 27 June 1993, 26; Editorial, "It's Racist, but
Hey, It's Disney," *New York Times,* 14 July 1993, A18; Stan Steiner, *Fusang: The
Chinese Who Built America* (New York: Harper Colophon Books, 1980), 108–9;
Cheng-Tsu Wu, ed., *"Chink!"* (New York: Meridian Press, 1972), 2–3.

10. Timothy Egan, "In Alaska, a Yearning for a New Ice Curtain," *New York
Times,* 13 May 1994, A12.

11. George Stimpson, *A Book about American History* (New York: Harper & Brothers, 1950), 77.

12. Maxine S. Seller "Beyond the Stereotype: A New Look at the Immigrant Woman, 1880–1924," *The Journal of Ethnic Studies* (Spring 1975): 66.

13. Anne Loftis, *California: Where the Twain Did Meet* (New York: Macmillan, 1973), 210; Lisa H. Lawson, "Scorned Outsiders of Another Era," *Los Angeles Times,* 28 December 1993, B7.

14. Alan M. Kraut, *Silent Travelers: Germs, Genes, and the "Immigrant Menace"* (New York: Basic Books, 1994), 4–27; Robin Marantz Henig, "The Lessons of Syphilis in the Age of AIDS," *Civilization* (December 1995): 40–41; Winn, *Exiles in a Land of Liberty,* 72–73; Aronoldo De Leon, *They Called Them Greasers* (Austin: University of Texas Press, 1994), 17; Raouf J. Halaby, "Dr. Shadid and the Debate Over Identity in the *Syrian World,*" in *Crossing the Waters,* ed. Eric J. Hoaglund (Washington, D.C.: Smithsonian Institution Press, 1987), 63.

15. Allan Chase, *The Legacy of Malthus* (Urbana: University of Illinois Press, 1980), 161.

16. Kraut, *Silent Travelers,* 4–27; *New York Times,* 24 April 1994, 21.

17. Katharine Fullerton Gerould, *The Aristocratic West* (New York: Harper & Brothers, 1925), 133.

18. William A. Douglass and Jon Bilbao, *Amerikanuak: Basques in the New World* (Reno: University of Nevada Press, 1975), 268; Karel D. Bicha, "Hunkies: Stereotyping and Slavic Immigrants, 1890–1920," *Journal of Ethnic History* (Fall 1982): 16–34; Hugh Brody, *The People's Land: Eskimos and Whites in the Eastern Arctic* (New York: Penguin Books, 1977), 85; Robert Glass Cleland, *From Wilderness to Empire: A History of California* (New York: Alfred A. Knopf, 1962), 372; Frank Chalk and Kurt Jonassohn, *The History and Sociology of Genocide* (New Haven: Yale University Press, 1990), 184.

19. Salvador de Madariaga, *Englishmen, Frenchmen, Spaniards* (New York: Hill and Wang, 1969), xi.

20. Stephen Laurent, "The Abenakis: Aborigines of Vermont: Part II," *Vermont History* (January 1956): 4; William Miller, *A New History of the United States* (New York: Dell Publishing Company, 1967), 269–70.

21. *New York Times,* 9 May 1982, E20; *Boston Globe,* 19 January 1983, 14.

22. Adam Tanner, "Why a Racial Remark at Rutgers University Stirs Such Emotion," *Christian Science Monitor,* 13 February 1995, 3; Raymond Hernandez, "Students Say Racial Slurs Go Beyond Hatred," *New York Times,* 26 June 1995, B2.

23. *New York Times,* 14 May 1985; Edward Hoagland, " 'WASP' Stings. It Isn't Amusing," *New York Times,* 16 September 1988, A35.

24. *New York Times,* 3 March 1994, B8; National Conference of Christians and Jews, *News Release,* 2 March 1994 and 21 March 1994, 1–8.

25. William Cash, "Hollywood Article Intended No Anti-Semitism," *New York Times,* Letters to the Editor, 18 November 1994, A34.

26. Ronald Smothers, "Japanese-Americans Recall War Service," *New York Times,* 19 June 1995, A8; *Boston Globe,* 18 August 1982, 5; *New York Times,* 24 January 1993, 1; Kenneth B. Noble, "One Hateful Word," *New York Times,* 19 March 1995, E4.

27. Michael M. Short, "Letters," *Boston Globe,* 5 March 1994, 18; Lisa Evans, "Letters," *Boston Globe,* 31 August 1995, 14.

28. Marzio, *A Nation of Nations,* 314.

29. Alain Locke and Bernhard J. Stern, eds., *When Peoples Meet: A Study in Race and Culture Contacts* (New York: Hinds, Hayden & Eldredge, 1946), 353–54; Richard M. Dorson, *American Folklore* (Chicago: University of Chicago Press, 1959), 138; Glen Grant and Dennis M. Ogawa, "Living Proof: Is Hawaii the Answer?" *Annals of the American Academy of Political and Social Science* (November 1993): 145; *Boston Globe,* 21 May 1994, 12.

30. *New York Times,* 2 August 1977 and 10 September 1983, 9.

31. Kathleen Joan Bragdon, "Crime and Punishment Among the Indians of Massachusetts, 1675–1750," *Ethnohistory* (Winter 1981): 28; Gerald Carson, "Watermelon Armies and Whiskey Boys," in *American Vistas, 1607–1877,* ed. Leonard Dinnerstein and Kenneth T. Jackson (New York: Oxford University Press, 1975), 121; Walter L. Williams, "United States Indian Policy and the Debate over Philippine Annexation: Implications for the Origins of American Imperialism," *Journal of American History* (March 1980): 825; Ara Baliozian, "Reflections of a Chauvinist," *The Armenian Weekly,* 2 February 1985, 9; Wolfgang Mieder, " 'The Only Good Indian Is a Dead Indian,' History and Meaning of a Proverbial Stereotype," *Journal of American Folklore* (Winter 1993): 48–49; Brian Jenkins, *Fenians and Anglo-American Relations During Reconstruction* (Ithaca: Cornell University Press, 1969), 3.

32. George L. Smith, *Religion and Trade in New Netherland* (Ithaca: Cornell University Press, 1973), 128; Iris Saunders Podea, "Quebec to 'Little Canada': The Coming of the French Canadians to New England in the Nineteenth Century," in *The Aliens: A History of Ethnic Minorities in America,* ed. Leonard Dinnerstein and Frederic Jaher (New York: Appleton-Century-Crofts, 1970), 205; Leonard Dinnerstein and David M. Reimers, *Ethnic Americans: A History of Immigration and Assimilation* (New York: Dodd, Mead & Company, 1975), 40; Alan Conway, "Welsh Emigration to the United States," in *Perspectives in American History,* Vol. 7, ed. Donald Fleming and Bernard Bailyn (Cambridge: Harvard University Press, 1974), 252; Richard Gambino, *Vendetta* (Garden City, N.Y.: Doubleday & Company, 1977), 56; Oscar Uribe, Jr., "Measuring the Degree of Discrimination," *Agenda, A Journal of Hispanic Issues* (July/August 1979): 14; Jack D. Forbes, "Mulattoes and People of Color in Anglo-North America: Implication for Black-Indian Relations," *Journal of Ethnic Studies* (Summer 1984): 39–40; De Leon, *They Called Them Greasers,* 13; Saul K. Padover, *The Letters of Karl Marx* (Englewood Cliffs, N.J.: Prentice-Hall, 1979), 411; Edward Wakin, *Enter the Irish-American* (New York: Thomas Y. Crowell, 1976), 53.

33. Michael Grunwald and David Arnold, "Scrabble's Dictionary to Purge Vulgarities," *Boston Globe,* 11 May 1994, 1.

34. Allen, *The Language of Ethnic Conflict,* 11; Carey Goldberg, "Welcome to New York, Capital of Profanities," *New York Times,* 19 June 1995, B1, B3; Robert Secor, "Ethnic Humor in Early American Jest Books," in *A Mixed Race,* ed. Frank Shuffelton (New York: Oxford University Press, 1993), 164.

35. Joseph P. Fried, "Judge's Advice to Young Italian-Americans: Avoid Mafia," *New York Times,* 25 May 1993, B3; Adrian Maher, "Black Tradesmen Face a Daily Wall of Suspicion," *Los Angeles Times,* 20 March 1995, A1.

# 6

# Minority and Majority Group Goals

> Injustice anywhere is a threat to justice everywhere. We are caught in an inescapable network of mutuality tied in a single garment of destiny. Whatever affects one directly affects all indirectly.
> —Martin Luther King, Jr.,
> Letter from Birmingham City Jail, 1963

Both minority and majority groups project goals for themselves and for the nation as a whole, which are not always congruent, formally articulated, free of ambiguity, supported by all members of the group, or immune to change. Each generation invariably redefines the contents and priorities they wish for themselves personally and for the group as a whole. The results are often varied and sometimes overlapping or conflicting.

Generally, the larger the group, the greater the opportunities for internal differences, which are influenced by the age of its members, the number of generations in America, socioeconomic standing, quality of leadership, vulnerability to discrimination, and the prevailing economic and political climate. Immigrants in particular not only must deal with the problems of surviving in a new environment, but as discussed in chapter 2 by Greeley and Maslow, must also deal with transforming their aspirations into realities. In the past, as in the present, most immigrants deemed America preferable to their land of birth:

—A French immigrant, in 1795, wrote her cousin in Paris that "it is easy for a worker to amass some savings. But the lazy, I warn you, would be worse off than in France."[1]

—A Welshman, in 1817, wrote, "Whoever has the heart and the resolution to come here will never be sorry after one once sets foot on the land. . . . I live better here now than I have ever lived before."[2]

—A German immigrant, in 1834, wrote, "Once this new country shall have become a new fatherland to us, we may indeed be able to fully value and appreciate all the benefits which a loving Creator has so lavishly bestowed upon the inhabitants of this fortunate continent."[3]

—A Hungarian visitor, in 1838, wrote that the "clergy and the army, the police and the judges, the scholars and bankers, these are common equal citizens. . . . There are no privileges, no nobility, no titles, no guilds, no secret police! How important all these issues are to the stranger!"[4]

—A Swiss immigrant assured his wife in 1848, "You will surely like St. Louis better than Basel. . . . Even if I only work as a journeyman here, I will earn so much money that I can support my family well, and even better once I am on my own."[5]

Of course, as today, there were immigrants who complained of loneliness, homesickness, learning English, unfriendly people, the rigors of frontier life, the difficulty of getting a job or the job itself, and encountering prejudice and discrimination. For example, an English immigrant in the 1830s warned that Americans were overly competitive—"You must either turn regular Yankee and do as they do, or you have no chance of getting on in this country." To a late nineteenth-century Hungarian Catholic priest, America was a "land which not only gives bread, but gravestones as well," and a Polish immigrant stated, "Where a dog does not want to sit, there the Pole is made to sit, and the poor wretch works because he wants to eat." An early twentieth-century Greek immigrant in Alabama recalled how native residents called him as well as Italians "dagos," and how "everybody would murmur if they wanted to speak to somebody in their native tongue."[6]

The relatively few immigrants who returned home were also motivated by a variety of factors: disappointment or anger with living or working conditions, homesickness, having achieved their goal of earning a certain amount of money, resuming responsibility for family matters or property, retirement, and, if dead or dying, burial with one's ancestors, or, as a contemporary illegal Mexican immigrant said, "I was tired of hiding, of feeling unwanted." Even in the seventeenth century, immigrant-laden ships arriving in New England were greeted at dockside by groups of prior immigrants waiting to return home; as did at least six of the original *Mayflower* passengers and an estimated one in six later immigrants.[7]

A variety of terms have been used to describe the goals of minorities, such as assimilation, acculturation, secession, separation, domination, fight, flight, millennialism, sojourn, and, most recently, proportional representation. Majority goals, too, vary, and can include assimilation, cultural pluralism, legal protection, separation and segregation, population transfer or deportation, invidious immigration policies, violence and mass murder, obviation, and proportional representation.

Whether many or few, living on farms or in large cities, or working in factories or mines, all minority group members have to learn how to relate to people of other religions, ethnicities, races, and languages. Government, too, has to learn how to relate to the continuously multivarying nature of the population, how to make all newcomers loyal Americans, and, in times of war or the threat of such, how to maintain national unity and support, particularly when the enemy country is one from which some citizens or their parents had emigrated.

In the Americanization process, intergroup suspicions, competition, and bigotry invariably surface, but differentially so. Historically, not only did white immigrants and white native-born residents dislike each other, but they both viewed blacks, Indians, Mexican Americans, and Asians as biologically and socially inferior. The result was a pecking order of derogation and reciprocal avoidance, which social practices and laws increasingly institutionalized. Just as old-timers wanted to live and relax with their own kind, so it was with newcomers, who formed their own communities and organizations.

Even then, within each group (particularly the first generation) and between each group, there are frequently differing interpretations over how groups or society should be governed, how social relations with nongroup members should be carried on, how family life should be preserved, and how group and societal values should be retained.

In recalling his early twentieth-century years as a Russian immigrant, George Papashvily wrote that though he had American friends, there was still a gnawing at his heart. "In fact the more American friends I made, [it] seemed the lonelier I got. I felt like an ax had chopped my life in two and I missed the part that was left in Georgia. I wanted my new friends but I wanted somebody, too, that I could remember home with. Then I could be a whole man again." Said a University of Chicago Filipino student in 1930: "Try as we will, we cannot be Americans. We may go to the farthest extreme in our effort to identify ourselves with the ways of the Americans, straightening our noses, dressing like the American in the latest fashion, pasting our faces with bleaching cream, and our hair with stacomb—but nevertheless we remain sensitive . . . that we are being slighted because we are Filipinos. Always there lurks over us a trace of suspicion that perhaps after all, we do not belong." [8]

Of course, some immigrants were more optimistic. For example, Farzad Ghorbi, a recent Iranian immigrant living in Massachusetts, said, "I love this country. But one day I want to take my son to Iran and show him how we used to make a soccer goal from pieces of wood, not bought from Toys 'R Us." Wendy Law-Yone, who emigrated from Burma in 1972, preferred homelessness to hopelessness, because, "I have seen that here the condition of homelessness is typical rather than special. This land of the exile is the archetype of all exile, a country where everybody is from somewhere else. If I must be rootless, then, I'd rather be rootless here, where at least in my dislocation, I am not alone." [9]

In looking closer at minority and majority groups, it must be remembered that over time most groups change, and that whatever they become, not all members or succeeding generations will necessarily agree.

## MINORITY GROUP GOALS

### Assimilation

The goal is to lose all group characteristics that are different from those of the majority society—language, dress, customs, behavior, even names. When foreign ways are abandoned and when minorities become indistinguishable from the majority of people, it is believed that discrimination against them will then end and their children will be able to achieve socioeconomic success, or at least more of it than their parents have achieved.

If some must hold on to old-country ways, it should be done in the privacy of their homes. Thus, to avoid as far as possible offending others, Orestes Brownson in 1854 urged Irish immigrants not to make "their new home an arena for fighting the battles of the country they have left; let them organize no military companies composed exclusively of foreign-born citizens; let them publish no journals, and organize no associations for political purposes to be effected in foreign countries. These things give offence, and not unreasonably, to the national feeling." Israel Zangwill was no less adamant in his turn-of-the-century play, *The Melting Pot,* wherein his Jewish protagonist defines America as "God's crucible," in which immigrants should happily "melt" and "re-form," and not care a fig about old-country "blood hatreds and rivalries." [10]

Many second and third generation offspring do assimilate. Gone today are the old Irish Protestant and Catholic fights in America over William of Nassau's 1690 defeat of the Catholic King James II. For example, in New York City, bloody fights broke out in 1870 and 1871 between the two faith groups, when in the latter year, according to a pro-Protestant pamphlet, "a mob of brutalized foreigners who, transplanting their bigotry and their incapacity for self-government from the Old World, determined to renew their fight in the home of their adoption—proving for the thousandth time that they know nothing, and under their leaders learn nothing, and practice nothing, common to a liberty loving citizen of the United States." [11] Today, such fights are limited to Northern Ireland, with little interest by their counterparts in America.

True, some elderly Americans retire to their ancestral land, where social security payments go further, and some offspring of immigrants travel to the old country to vacation rather than to relive old ways or revenge old wrongs. In recent years, some Eastern European and Asian immigrants, or their children, began returning as business entrepreneurs or agents.

Some examples follow: When several thousand American Scots visited Scotland, it mattered not that some of their hosts were descendants of those who had brutally forced their forebears off the land. In fact, one Scottish American judge said he was grateful to the first Duke of Southerland for doing so, because his ancestors did so well in America. When Boston's Mayor Thomas Menino visited, in 1994, the Italian town that his grandfather had left at the turn of the century, he said, "You don't always appreciate your heritage till you're a bit older. I couldn't help but wonder—if my grandfather hadn't left, where would I have been?" To Lan Vu, who left Vietnam as a youngster and returned twenty years later as a business expert, the more time she spent there, the more she felt at home: "Probably intellectually I'm American, but the emotional part of me is Vietnamese." Still, she said, "I can't wait to go back [to Oregon] and go skiing. I miss mountain biking. I miss the winter."[12]

Of course, for people of color and for Asians, assimilation is the most difficult, unless they are so light skinned that they can pass as whites or, as in the case of some Asians, have plastic surgery on their epicanthic folds. English professor Shelby Steele wrote that, psychologically and socially, being black meant the likelihood of enduring "more wounds to one's self-esteem than others" and having the capacity for self-doubt born of these wounds intensified "by the black race's reputation of inferiority."[13]

For immigrant offspring, the loss of fluency, and then any knowledge of, their ancestral language are among the first signs of assimilation. For example, Swedish residents in mid–eighteenth-century New Jersey increasingly spoke English, wrote Peter Kalm at the time, and were "ashamed to talk in their own tongue because they fear that they may not in such a case be real English. . . . The Swedish language is doomed to extinction in America." A few decades later, a German American in Philadelphia lamented that young people were gradually becoming ashamed of the German language. Though early Welsh immigrants in Pennsylvania spoke and published in their homeland language, by the time the Welsh Society of Pennsylvania was founded in 1798, its members had little command of the language.[14]

And so it is with most immigrant groups. By 1810, a European Jesuit visitor wrote of Americans, "About nine-tenths speak precisely the same language, which is a national unity probably not to be found, without source variation of dialect, among the same number . . . in any other quarter of the world . . . it is probable that in one century, there will be 100 millions of people in America, to whom English speech, in its purity, will be vernacular." The prediction proved true, for in 1920 a Foreign Language Information Service publication reported that not only did children of immigrants prefer American papers, but so did the foreign born, who "as soon as they have acquired sufficient English, turn to the American papers for American and general news, depending on the press of their language for little more than news of the home country." [15]

A later study by Joshua Fishman found that while in 1960 slightly more than 2,300,000 second-generation Italians spoke Italian, only 147,000 did so among the third generation; the number of American Jews speaking Yiddish dropped from 422,000 to 39,000 in the second to the third generation; and for Poles, the number of those speaking Polish dropped from 1,516,000 to 87,000. Similar developments are now taking place among Asians. For example, studies by the Christian Korean American Alliance in California found that more than 60 percent of English-speaking Koreans in their twenties and thirties quit attending Korean churches because they were unable to adequately understand Korean. [16]

Clearly, the longer foreign-language groups reside in America and the more they live or work alongside members of other groups, the more they and succeeding generations learn English and lose familiarity with their ancestral tongue. Thus, a recent study found that although most United States residents born in Mexico speak Spanish in their homes, almost two-thirds of those born in America of Mexican ancestry speak English at home. Another study showed that even in Miami, which proportionately has more foreign-born residents than any other American city, English is the preferred language of immigrant offspring, including those raised in the heart of the Spanish-speaking community. A third study revealed decade-by-decade increases in the English-speaking ability of immigrants who had arrived in Southern California in the 1970s: for Europeans and Middle Easterners, the percentage of English speakers rose from 62 percent in 1980 to 80 percent in 1990; for Asians, from 39 percent to 53 percent; and for Latinos, from 13 percent to 21 percent. Last, a study of Cuban, Haitian, Filipino, Mexican, and Vietnamese children of immigrants found them becoming so fluent in English that they were "on the way to monolingualism. It is the parents' language, not English, that is endangered." [17]

For slightly different and more grievous reasons, the number of Native American languages declined from some 500 when Columbus arrived to some 205 today. One recent anthropologist estimates that one-third of the latter are doomed to further extinction. Here, too, the causes vary: the large number of adult aboriginals killed by European and American military might and by disease, the destruction of native ways of life, the overwhelming number of Anglophones and their culture, and, until recent decades, the banning or discouragement of traditional languages by governmental and educational public officials.

In Alaska, for example, where some twenty native languages once flourished, only two of five Eskimo languages remain viable and none of the fifteen native Indian ones survive. According to Professor Michael Krauss, the number of fluent Native American language speakers, as of 1992, progressively declined—leaving Mandan with six, Osage five, Abenaki-Penobscot twenty, Iowa five, Tuscarora less than thirty, and Menomini fewer than fifty. Though Congress passed legislation in 1990 to encourage and support the use of Native American languages in classroom instruction, successful results are scant, while fears mount that once the present tribal elders die, so will their languages and ancient traditions, especially among smaller tribes. The Pequots in Connecticut, whose numbers had declined from a few thousand in the seventeenth century to some 260 in 1993, recently sponsored a national Indian powwow (with earnings from its highly successful gambling casino) in order to revitalize the learning of their language, customs, and ceremonial dances.[18]

The fear of losing ancestral languages exists as well among some new immigrants, who seek help in preserving them from sources outside their own groups, especially public schools and universities. Took Took Thongthiraj, a Thai American student, in 1991, felt that the establishing of Hindi, Tagalog, Thai, and Vietnamese language and culture classes would help college students reconnect with their communities and break their invisibility: "And to do that, we need to speak with our communities in the language they know best."[19]

In the desire to assimilate, minority group members sometimes change their names, which many did until the recent explosion of ethnic pride. Apollon Rivoire, Paul Revere's father, changed his "merely on account that the bumpkins pronounce it easier." Other French names like Bon Coeur and de l'Hotel became Bunker and Doolittle. German Hubers and Pfoerschings became Hoovers and Pershings, Dutch Kuiper and Van Kouwenhoven became Cooper and Conover, and Lebanese Maronite names like Aoun and Howayek were transformed to Owen and Howard. The Greek names of Triantaflyllos, meaning rose, became Rose and Mylonas became Miller, Slavic Kovar somehow became Smith and Zeleny became Green. Norwegian Praestegaard became Prescott, and Syrian Al-Khuri became Khoury, Courey or Corey. Swedish Cock was changed to Cox, Kyn to Keen, and Joccom to Yocum.[20]

For offspring of Japanese immigrants, Mokoto became Mac and Isamu became Sam; others adopted the English meaning of their Japanese names, such as Lily for Yuriko or Violet for Sumire. K. W. Lee, an editor at the *Sacramento Union,* recalled in 1993 how, when he began his career in journalism some forty years earlier, he not only changed his first name from Kyung Won to K. W., but also, "became Chinese because no one knew what Korean was." Some recent Vietnamese refugees adopted the names of the relocation camps in which they were held, such as Camp

Chafee or Camp Pendleton, with one refugee calling himself Nguyen Pendleton Chin.[21]

Many English-speaking immigrants or their offspring, like the Irish, Scotch and British (whom many non–English-speaking immigrants thought were Americans), changed their names, particularly those with pejorative or funny-sounding ones, such as Butter, Gutters, Milkhouse, Lavender, Dunce, Gout, Bones, and Snake. Others did so to avoid job discrimination. John Cole, editor of the *Maine Times,* recalled how his immigrant great-grandfather changed his name from Darragh to Darrow, because "signs in every window in the city read 'No Irish Need Apply.' Instead of shaking his bricklayer's fist, my great-grandfather tried to write the Irish from his name and masquerade as whatever a Darrow might be."[22]

More reflective of assimilation today is the skyrocketing rate of intergroup marriages, which in the pre–World War II period were generally limited and disapproved of. Nevertheless, in early American history, some groups engaged in intermarriage more readily than others, as in the case of the French. From a clearly discriminated-against identity in the seventeenth century, Huguenots moved to a highly assimilated one by the early nineteenth century, as their children married Puritans in New England, Anglicans in New York and South Carolina, and Scotch-Irish Presbyterians in the South and West. Their industriousness and success prompted their being viewed as "honorary Anglo-Saxons." As historian Jon Butler noted, the net result was: "Everywhere they fled, everywhere they vanished."[23]

It was after World War II that attitudes toward ethnic, religious, and to a much lesser extent, racial intermarriages began dramatically changing, especially among the American-born young. For example, Gallup polls between 1968 and 1978 reveal that the proportion of Americans approving of marriages between Catholics and Protestants rose from 59 percent to 73 percent and of those between Jews and non-Jews from 59 percent to 69 percent. The same trend can be seen in the approval of interracial relations: A survey by the Times Mirror Center for the People and the Press showed a rising percentage of people feeling that it was all right for blacks and whites to date, going from 43 percent in 1987 to 65 percent in 1994.[24]

Not surprisingly, attitudes soon became facts. What Edward S. Shapiro said of Jews is no less true of other groups. They "did not intermarry because they wished to assimilate; they intermarried because they were already largely assimilated." Thus, Jewish interfaith marriages rose from some 5 percent before 1965 to over 50 percent in the early 1990s. Similar percentages of young Christians began marrying spouses of different denominations or faiths: about 50 percent of Catholics, 69 percent of Methodists, 70 percent of Lutherans, and 75 percent of Presbyterians. Though no intermarriage statistics exist as of 1993 for Muslims in America, one expert assumed that intermarriages are taking place at no lower a percentage than in Canada, where 2 out of 3 Muslim women marry a non-Muslim. As for interethnic marriages, a 1976 study of first and fourth generations of Irish, German, French, Polish, Italian, and Eastern Europeans revealed that by the third generation, a substantial majority in all groups had married members of other groups, with more than three-quarters of the Irish having done so. Among Greek Americans, a recent study revealed that while 51.6 percent of the first generation preferred marrying other Greeks, only 25 percent of the third generation did so. The number of Hispanics marrying non-Hispanics went from 584,000 in 1970 to 1,155,000 in 1992, representing 26 percent of the total number of Hispanic married couples.[25]

Though the number of interracial marriages almost quadrupled from 1970 to 1992, going from 310,000 to 1,161,000, their proportion of total marriages remains small, rising only from 0.6 percent to 2.2 percent. Among black householders in 1990 only 6 percent were married to nonblacks. Much greater is the percentage of American Indian-white and the percentage of white-Asian marriages. Some 70 percent of American Indians marry outside their group. In Hawaii, "the melting pot of the Pacific," interracial marriages zoomed from 13 percent in 1912–13 to 46 percent in 1991, and in California, where the Asian population is also quite mixed, the rate of marriages in 1980 to whites for Chinese was 14 percent, for Vietnamese 15 percent, for Koreans 19 percent, for Asian Indians 23 percent, for Filipinos 24 percent, and for Japanese 32 percent. By 1993, the rate of the latter's intermarriage with whites was 65 percent. Though opposed by some minorities, transracial adoptions have also been increasing. In 1992, an estimated 12 percent of all adoptions were transracial, mostly by whites of black children. Two years later, Congress passed the Multiethnic Placement Act, which bans child welfare agencies from discriminating against would-be parents solely because of their race, color, or national origin.[26]

Socially, economically, politically, and of course linguistically, the British have been the most successful foreign group in America, though among them are many poor, such as those called "swamp Yankees" or "Appalachians." Their general success far exceeds their percentage of the total American population. For example, in the 1930s, two-thirds of all New Haven, Connecticut, professionals and managers were British Americans, though the latter constituted only 12 percent of the total city's population; in the 1950s, 65 percent of the top executives of America's largest companies were of British descent, as was a disproportionately high percentage of those in the legislative and judicial branches of federal government.[27]

Among the more militant or ethnocentric group members, anyone who assimilates with the larger society or overly identifies with it is vulnerable to being ridiculed as a defector or self-hater. For example, in 1994, when Idaho's attorney general Larry EchoHawk, who is proud of his Pawnee roots, opposed establishing gambling casinos on reservations, he was criticized by some tribal leaders. "He looks like an Indian, but I don't believe his heart is totally Indian," said one leader. A more common put-down is the labeling of such a person as an uncle, such as Uncle Tom for an African American, Uncle Jake for a Jew, Uncle Giovanni for an Italian, Uncle Tom Tom for an American Indian, and Uncle Ahmad for an Arab. In 1993, the term was extended to the world of sexual identification when a gay rights militant called Congressman Barney Frank a "homosexual Uncle Tom" because he had fired an unpaid gay intern for becoming involved in gay rights activities not approved of by Frank.[28] In response, many of those who are criticized accuse their attackers of being too black, Jewish, Italian, Indian, or Arab, wanting everyone to live in a ghetto, and, in their view, stunting individual creativity and producing further hostility toward the entire group.

While historian John Higham was basically correct in 1975 when he wrote that no established immigrant group in America ever entirely disappeared, some groups did move a great deal toward disappearance and most are a far cry in beliefs, appearances, and behaviors from their predecessors.[29]

### Acculturation

Less demanding than assimilation is acculturation, which Milton Gordon defined as "behavioral assimilation," wherein immigrants absorb the cultural behavior patterns of the host society without necessarily entering its social cliques, organizations, institutional activities, and general civic life.[30] To varying degrees, they also adopt the biases of born-and-bred Americans.

In the process of acculturation immigrants don't necessarily become official citizens, with citizenship depending largely on age, date of arrival, country of origin, and on whether they intend to remain in America. For example, in the early twentieth century, immigrants from northern and western Europe had much higher percentages of naturalized citizens than newer immigrants from southern, central, and eastern Europe. In 1920, 63 percent of English-born immigrants, 69 percent of Swedish-born immigrants, and 72 percent of German-born immigrants were naturalized, compared to 7 percent of Albanians, 12 percent of Bulgarians, and 17 percent of Greeks. From a broader geographic perspective, a radical change in percentages of naturalized foreign-born residents started occurring in recent decades. For example, in the decade 1961–70, 62.4 percent of Europeans, 12.9 of Asians, and 2.2 percent of South Americans were naturalized; but for 1991–93, the naturalization rate was 51.4 percent of Asians, 11.3 percent of Europeans, and 7.8 percent of South Americans.[31]

Research shows that recent immigrants fleeing political persecution and those coming from the farthest lands more readily become citizens than those coming for solely economic reasons or from nearby countries. For example, Vietnamese immigrants were found to be eight times more likely than Canadians to become citizens; and while more than 50 percent of Russian, Chinese, and Filipino immigrants between 1977 and 1989 became citizens, only 28 percent of Jamaicans, 18 percent of Dominicans, and 17 percent of Trinidadians did so. By the mid-1990s, however, record numbers of legal immigrants from nearby lands, particularly Mexico, began applying for citizenship because of growing American domestic political pressure to exclude all noncitizens from state and federal aid programs.[32]

Research also shows that with second-generation Americans, interest in homeland politics usually shifts to local or mainstream party politics, though still with a group flavor, wherein the group's well-being in America becomes more important than that of their kinsmen back home. For example, American-born children of Vietnamese, Cuban, and Chinese immigrants who fled communist governments are not as hostile as their parents to those governments or to America establishing full diplomatic and business relations with them.[33]

Instinctively and socially, if not intellectually, immigrants and particularly their offspring favor acculturation, which allows them to maintain their group traditions, languages, and institutions, except when they violate the law. By modifying some but not abandoning all group values and behaviors, they hope to blend their old- and new-country ways without alienating their families and yet gaining the respect of society at large. Thus, an early twentieth-century Korean newspaper proudly said that the reason why many Americans love and help Koreans but not Japanese "is that we Koreans gave up old baseness, thought and behavior, and became more westernized."[34]

Whatever the group, however, acculturation does necessitate abandonment of some traditional values and behaviors. For example, most early twentieth-century Hindu immigrants to the West Coast totally abstained from liquor, tea, or coffee, but after "getting something of a greater degree of freedom from the customs of their own country, some have been changed . . . to rather free users. . . . " Intergenerational tensions and conflicts are frequent. When, in the early 1920s, young Syrian immigrant Salom Rizk hesitated to contribute to buying a bottle of liquor, his friends taunted him for being a "sissy," which he sensed from the scorn in their voices was something terrible. "So I chipped in. . . . Then I was no longer a sissy. . . . I was an American, a real American. . . . I wasn't one of them darn furriners." More recently, a study of Jewish philanthropy found that as each of four generations of Jews became "more integrated into the general society," it contributed less to Jewish charities, intermarried more, and had fewer Jewish friendship, neighborhood, and communal ties.[35]

Depending on the immigrant group and where it settles, some members adopt the antiblack, anti-Indian, anti-Mexican, anti-Asian, or anti-Semitic prejudices of their American-born neighbors, fellow workers, or classmates. Being of the same religion, ethnicity, or race as native-born Americans does not preclude such biases developing. For example, after immigrating to America, many black Jamaican and Haitian immigrants took to viewing African Americans with disdain. In some poor inner cities, however, black immigrant offspring began to imitate the talk, the walk, and the values of their African-American classmates, much to the unhappiness of their parents. For some immigrant offspring, the process of acculturation can lead to a decline in educational achievement. For example, while first- and second-generation children of Asian, Latino, and black immigrants did better in school than their American-born counterparts, those of the third generation did less well because they were emulating their American-born age peers rather than their parents.[36]

Criminality, too, is subject to acculturation, and in America a plethora of crime is available to replicate. As an early twentieth-century immigration commission noted, immigrant offspring criminality is "much more frequently in the direction of the criminality of the American-born or non-immigrant parentage than it is in the opposite direction." In recent years, young Salvadoran criminals who have been deported form gangs along American lines back in El Salvador. "They left to escape the war here," explained one El Salvadoran woman, "but in the United States they learned to be criminals. Now the young people who stayed here think joining these gangs is good." For some groups, the less they acculturate, the less their crime rate. For example, a 1935 study of Detroit's Hungarian Americans revealed that those who remained together in special colonies tended to experience lower crime rates than those more widely dispersed.[37]

To many nativists, however, criminality simply reflects the genetic makeup of immigrants or minority groups, an interpretation they never seem to apply to their own criminals however, whose rates of crime in past decades were often, but not always, higher. For example, the crime rates among German, Dutch, Scandinavian, Japanese, and Chinese immigrants are generally lower than those for native-born Americans.[38] Nevertheless, when immigrants commit crimes, the media and Hollywood often sensationalize them, portraying the immigrants' inability to speak English as a sign of stupidity, their poverty a sign of their refusal to accept honest work, and their old-country ways a sign of their inability to adopt American ways.

A few early twentieth-century observers did blame the criminal behavior of some immigrant children on such environmental factors as miserable tenement housing conditions, child labor, and the decline of parental influence, particularly in large cities. In 1906, Howard Grose wrote: "The fathers and mothers who cannot speak English, but whose children have learned it at school or on the street, soon lose control over them. The children come to feel superior to their parents and look down on them as 'foreigners.' " Such factors are no less absent today, as inner city children often reject the work, family, and sexual behavior patterns and values of their immigrant parents and adopt a scepticism, if not hostility, to education as a way of socioeconomic advancement. Nu Yeng Yang, a Hmong immigrant whose son and two other Hmong teenagers robbed and fatally shot two German tourists in 1994, lamented: "Back in our country, you never saw things like this happen. . . . We have lost all control. Our children do not respect us. One of the hardest things for me is when I tell my children things and they say, 'I already know that.' When my wife and I try to tell my son about Hmong culture, he tells me people here are different, and he will not listen to me." [39]

## Separation and Secession

Differing only in degree, both goals seek to preserve group identity by defining as good and necessary that which differentiates one's own group from another and by doing everything possible to avoid contact with non-group members. Members are enjoined to live among group members, marry each other, oppose transgroup adoptions, develop businesses, own land, manage economic resources, and control educational institutions—as happens among Chassidim, Mormons, Amish, Mennonites, and Black Muslims.

Religionists long advocated the need for a separate existence, labeling all dissenters as schismatics, heretics, or blasphemers. Until relatively recent centuries, Jewish, Protestant, and Catholic religious and political leaders believed the security of the faith and of the community sometimes required the imprisonment, mutilation, expulsion, or killing of obstinate dissenters. In colonial America, particularly in New England, Quakers, both male and female, and religious dissenters were flogged and hanged, and at Harvard College, a student was whipped publicly and expelled for aspersing the Holy Ghost.[40]

Though no longer subjecting dissenters to harsh physical punishments, some contemporary religionists believe the very concept of diversity or equality to be anathema. As one Christian fundamentalist said, "At no point in the Scripture do we read that God teaches, supports or condones pluralism. To support pluralism is to recognize all religions as equal." Within a group also, such is believed. "We cannot accept pluralism if it means legitimating different definitions of Jewishness and of marital status," said Orthodox Rabbi Marc D. Angel. "Pluralism ultimately must lead to the total splinterization of the Jewish people." In writing about her Mennonite upbringing, Laura H. Weaver told how her community objected not only to its children "joining a 'worldly' church or marrying outsiders with names like McDonald or Woodward but even to their joining or marrying into a more liberal, 'worldly' Mennonite group."[41]

Ethnically, one researcher noted that any Lithuanian immigrant "who attempted to integrate even minor local customs was immediately faced with community sanctions in the form of gossip, ridicule and open hostility, though the customs be as insignificant as a woman shaving her legs or wearing nail polish, or a man drinking mixed drinks." Early twentieth-century Japanese immigrants in one California farming town built a Japantown, which barred fellow group members who were gamblers, vagrants, or business owners in the area's Chinatown. Today, in many large public school lunchrooms and hallways, students segregate themselves by socioeconomic class, ethnicity, and race, and pressure others not to befriend or try to "act white" or "act black." In one South Philadelphia school, Asians tend to meet on the second floor, whites on a section of the third floor, and blacks on a section of the fourth floor.[42]

Racially, too, there are some whites and blacks who advocate separation, if not for racist reasons than for group biological survival or socioeconomic success. Many blacks, especially women, resent black males marrying white women, which, they feel, serves "to either reinforce the historically exploitative relationships between white men and black women" or "to rob the black community of the needed resources found in the black men who marry white women." Also, a white woman dating a black man is criticized by some whites as being sexually promiscuous and can be subjected to a white boycott should her relationship with the black man end. The statistics on the black family are especially ominous. For example, from 1947 to 1980, the percentage of never-married black women ages 25 to 44 doubled from 10.5 to 21.3 percent, while the number of 18- to 19-year-old marriageable males able to support a family declined from 55 for every 100 black females of the same age in 1954 to 29 in 1982, and for males 25 to 34 years old, the number dropped to 60 from 68.[43]

If not total, then partial or selective separation is often sought by some groups. Many minority groups believe in having their own school systems or supplementary programs for their children. Within the public schools, too, some groups want separation, particularly those lacking the resources to establish their own private institutions. For example, though not giving up entirely on the public schools, Cherokee chief Wilma Mankiller said in 1994 that "we're never going to have school systems that truly respond to Native needs until we run them ourselves. . . . The fact is Native students do better when they have the support and sustenance of other Native students, faculty, and staff."[44]

Separation, if not isolation, is also believed essential to building member self-esteem, cooperation, and even social peace with other groups. Writing on the increasingly strained relations between Hispanics and blacks in 1991, two Hispanic experts saw relatively little difference in behavior by African Americans or whites toward their community. "In both cases, raw political and economic power is brought to bear to deny equality for Hispanics," thereby creating the belief that "an Hispanic-specific, 'quasi-separationist' approach is the only viable way of achieving full equality." [45]

In more extreme cases, some groups seek legal secession, as did a few black groups and the early Mormons. U.S. military opposition ended such Mormon aspirations in the late nineteenth century, and governmental rejection ended them for black separatist groups in the early twentieth century. For example, in vain, the African Blood Brotherhood, in 1917, asked for 10 percent of the country, particularly in California and Nevada. Seven decades later, the Black Muslims urged that they "be allowed to establish a separate state or territory of their own—either on this continent or elsewhere." As late as 1985, some Boston black leaders formed the Greater Roxbury Incorporation Project (GRIP), which demanded a city referendum on giving the black community the right to secede. "We want to govern ourselves," explained GRIP's leaders. Nationally, a 1994 poll showed that while black support for a separate nation was minimal, support for a national black political party increased to 50 percent, double that of five years earlier. With the rise of "Chicano" identity in the 1960s and 1970s, some advocates projected the goal of Atzlán—a Mexican-American homeland in the southwest, with cultural and possibly political ties to Mexico. [46]

## Dominance

A minority seeks to gain control over a majority by force of arms, economics, religion, politics, expanding settlements, and/or sheer increase in number. That is how the early minority European invaders conquered and subjugated Indian majorities. A short while later, the Spanish, French, and British colonial powers received similar treatment from minority Americans, who utilized every tactic from intimidation to warfare to gain control. In Spanish Florida, for example, American settlers revolted in 1810 with the help of U.S. troops in the hope of being annexed by America, which did happen nine years later when the Spanish government reluctantly accepted an offer of $5 million for the land, knowing that otherwise it would be taken without any compensation.

Less obvious was the conflict after the Louisiana Purchase in New Orleans between the French and Spanish majority on one hand and the incoming rough-and-tumble American minority. Both sides spoke different languages, had different social philosophies and systems, and "the fact that the Creoles were Catholic whereas most of the Americans were Protestant did little to foster mutual affection. . . . The Americans were . . . in no psychological mood to be a minority group." [47]

It was also a minority of American intruders and settlers on Mexican land who provoked the 1836 Texas Revolution, which led to the formation of the Lone Star Republic and then to America's annexation of Texas in 1845. As Stephen F. Austin said, "Texas should be effectually, and fully, Americanized—that is—settled by a population that will harmonize with their neighbors on the *East,* in language, political principles, common origin, sympathy, and even interest." With equal deviousness, but with less bloodshed, a minority of American settlers, missionaries, and entrepreneurs took over Hawaii against the wishes of its native residents, whose numbers and land ownership then decreased with each passing decade. By 1980, only nine-tenths of 1 percent of the population of some 1 million people were pure Hawaiian and 19.9 percent were pure or mixed. Similar to the plight of many Native Americans on the continent, aboriginally descended Hawaiians today experience a high school drop-out rate, low-paying jobs, welfare dependency, a high incarceration rate, and short life expectancy.[48]

Takeovers of areas and neighborhoods in which minorities live continue in present-day America, largely by natural resource explorers, real estate developers, young professionals, and new immigrants, who eagerly buy up the property of local natives, whether in Alaska, Hawaii, or the Southwest. For example, in Santa Fe, New Mexico, Mexican Americans and American Indians have increasingly resented the coming of "Anglos," who in 1990 became the majority in the city and in some of the nearby Indian pueblos. "These are conquerors who did not need arms to take over the town," complained a member of the city council. "They have come instead with their big money and their higher education." Likewise, in South Dakota, Sioux Indians have protested white New Age practitioners who meet on land they consider holy and, they feel, desecrate it with distortions of Indian traditions.[49]

Globally, white minority expansion and domination over indigenous majorities has a long history. What was manifest destiny to some white minorities was, of course, ruthless oppression and exploitation to those they vanquished. European settlements in America, Africa, and Australia, wrote Herman Merivale in 1861, "presents everywhere the same general features—a wide and sweeping destruction of native races by the uncontrolled violence of individuals, if not of colonial authorities, followed by tardy attempts on the part of governments to repair the acknowledged crime." In his 1936 study, Grover Clark pointed out that Europeans ruled 9 percent of the earth in 1492, a third by 1801, yet another third by 1880, nearly another fifth by 1913, and 85 percent by 1935. On the eve of World War II, they ruled almost 70 percent of the world's population.[50]

Since the end of World War II, however, colonialism and imperialism crumbled rapidly under the force of national liberation and self-determination movements in Africa, Asia, and, most recently, Eastern Europe. Minority and majority tension and conflict still exist in those areas, except that today they are between different indigenous ethnic groups and tribes in a given country.

### Fight

Minority groups sometimes adopt a policy of fighting, either to defend themselves against attacks and encroachments by majority or other minority groups, to take the property and possessions of others, or to gain public attention to their plight. The fighting can range from armed force to nonviolent resistance. Indian, Mexican, and Mormon use of armed force proved futile in stopping American expansionism. As one Kiowa Indian chief said, reluctantly agreeing in 1867 to move to a reservation:

We have warred against the white man, but never because it gave us pleasure. Before the day of oppression came, no white man came to our villages and went away hungry. . . . In the far distant past . . . (h)e once came to trade; he now comes to fight. . . . He now covers his face with a cloud of jealousy and anger and tells us to be gone, as the offended master speaks to his dog. . . . We once gave you our hearts; you have them now.[51]

Similarly, rebellions, riots, or violent strikes by black African slaves and European immigrants were quickly repressed. On the other hand, post–World War II demonstrations, rallies, lobbies, sit-ins, pray-ins, and so forth, to obtain racial justice, civil rights, civil liberties, and religious freedom were increasingly successful, so much so that other ethnic and racial minorities, as well as women, the handicapped, and senior citizens replicated some of those actions.

### Flight

Because of prejudice, discrimination, or denial of the right to live the way they wish, some minority groups believe it better to flee than to remain, and so they go into hiding, move to another area, or leave America entirely. For millennia before Columbus' arrival in the western hemisphere, native bands and tribes fled from one another across Asia to Alaska, down to the tip of South America.

After the Revolutionary War thousands of Loyalists fled to England, the West Indies, and Canada. Following the enactment of the Alien and Sedition Acts, hundreds of French nationals in America returned to France or to Santo Domingo. During and after the Revolutionary War, the War of

1812, and the Civil War, blacks fled from American to Spanish and English territories, and from slave to free states. Some runaway slaves, called "maroons," formed small communities deep in forests, swamps, or other inaccessible terrain. Some Indian tribes fled to Canada and Mexico to escape white American attacks or to avoid being confined to reservations. While most twentieth-century immigrants settled in areas where they would be with their own people, some did so to avoid living near people they considered to be undesirable, as in the cases of nineteenth and early twentieth centuries, south, central, or Eastern Europeans, Afro-Americans, Chinese, Japanese, Filipinos, and Spanish-speaking groups.

## Millennialism

Some people and groups turn to God for immediate redress and eternal salvation, which they believe will occur on a predetermined day when God begins to reign for a thousand years. To Christians, generally, the millennium will come either immediately before God returns for the second time (premillennialism) or immediately after (postmillennialism).

Christian, Jewish, or Native American millennialists always differ among themselves over the exact day or year when that great event will begin. Sixteenth-century Anabaptists believed it would occur in 1533. Columbus thought it would be in the 1650s. Others pinpointed the year 1666. One seventeenth-century German mystic set sail for America, hoping to greet the millennium's beginning in 1694. In eighteenth-century colonial America, many educated people studied biblical prophecy to detect God's plan for the world. Mid–nineteenth-century Millerites were convinced that the Second Coming would take place in 1843.[52]

Millennialist groups still exist. Periodically, some believers give up their possessions and climb to their rooftops to await a miraculous ascension to heaven, only to be disappointed, but not dissuaded. Some small groups of ultra-Orthodox Jews, particularly in America and Canada, refuse to settle in Israel, "the promised land," because, "until G-D chooses to end history as we know it, with redeeming us by miraculous acts, we are commanded by Him to live as cooperative, law abiding and patriotic citizens in our countries of residence."[53]

Other forms of millennialism include: The Plains Indians, whose ghost dance ritual posits the eventual disappearance of whites, the resurrection of the dead, the restoration of the buffalo to the plains, and a return to former days of peace and happiness; the Ras Tafari, whose numbers are small in America but large in Jamaica, believe that Emperor Haile Selassie of Ethiopia, though dead, is a living God, that white people are inferior to blacks, that the latter represent the reincarnation of ancient Israel, that their return to Ethiopia is imminent, and that they are destined to rule the world. In Chicago, a black group, the House of Israel Cultural Center, believes that their members will leave America in the year 2019 for the "promised land," Israel, because, as their leader said, "You just can't fight prophecy."[54]

### Sojourn and Asylum

Other than as students, many immigrants come to America for a short time to earn a certain amount of money and then return home to help family, buy property, start a small business, or, in the case of some pregnant women, to give birth here so their children will be American citizens. In most cases, however, these immigrants are young men. "It was to be for just a little while," recalled one Basque immigrant, "just enough time to make some money and go back to help Papa and Mama with the care of the property. . . . I wanted stock and the land to move in, and we didn't even own the property where we lived." In contrast, among refugees from disasters, the male-female ratio is more evenly balanced.[55]

On an even more temporary basis come foreign nationalists, radicals, revolutionaries, and royalists, who seek sanctuary until conditions back home stablize, or until they can muster political or financial support from their ethnic kinsmen in the United States or from the federal government.

During the French Revolution, some 10,000 to 25,000 Frenchmen—royalty as well as disenchanted revolutionaries—took refuge in America, including the Duke d'Orleans, who later returned home and became King Louis Phillipe. In the 1850s, Giuseppe Garibaldi settled here, first as a candlemaker on Staten Island and then as a ship's captain, after which he returned home to once again fight for a united Italy. Syngman Rhee, the first Korean to obtain a doctorate from an American university, returned to his homeland in 1948 to become the first president of the Republic of Korea. In recent decades, deposed and overthrown presidents, generals, officials, and royalty have sought refuge in America, such as General Battista of Cuba, President Somoza of Nicaragua, the Shah Reza Pahlavi of Iran, and President Jean-Bertrand Aristide of Haiti. By the late 1980s, the number of people seeking political asylum climbed to 60,000 and then to more than 103,000 in 1992, representing 154 countries.[56]

Also numerous are the foreign statesmen who regularly visit America and their expatriate communities in search of political and financial support. In the early decades of the twentieth century, men like Ignace Paderewski of Poland, Thomas G. Masaryk and Eduard Benes of Czechoslovakia, Chaim Weizmann of Israel, Eamon de Valera of Ireland, Karlis Ulmanis of Latvia, came to the United States. Dr. Sun Yat-sen, who raised much money here, credited the Chinese diaspora for being "the mother of the revolution" in China in 1910.[57] In recent decades, Miami, Florida, has become known as the Latin Capital in Exile, where large numbers of Cubans, Nicaraguans, Salvadorans, Haitians, Jamaicans, Panamanians, Hondurans, and Colombians reside.

At times, prominent emigres, immigrants, and naturalized citizens return to their homeland. Simeon Vratzian left his pre–World War I American editorship of the Armenian weekly *Hairenik* to become prime minister of the then short-lived Armenian Republic. After becoming an American citizen and serving in the U.S. Navy, Andreas Papandreau returned to Greece to become its prime minister. Another naturalized American, Peter Zwak, became Hungary's ambassador to America. With the breakup of the Soviet Union, American-born Raffi K. Hovannisian was appointed Armenia's foreign minister; Milan Panic, a naturalized American citizen and millionaire, became prime minister in 1992 of the reconstituted Yugoslavia; Alexander Einseln, who had immigrated to America in 1949 and joined and then retired from the U.S. Army as a colonel, returned to Estonia in 1993 to become its military commander-in-chief.[58]

## Proportional Representation

In proportional representation, a group seeks to be included or represented numerically or by a percentage in various societal arenas. The formulations and rationales for representation differ, depending largely on the group, its organizational strength, and/or its leaders. The goal can be representation equal to a group's percentage of the local, statewide, or national population; representation equal to its percentage of the national or local workforce, whichever is higher; representation as a reflection of the nation's diversity; representation as proof of nondiscrimination against its members; representation as compensation for past discrimination; or representation until its members no longer lag behind other groups in earnings.

Such goals are particularly true of people of color, who were long ignored, discouraged, or excluded from the processes of acculturation and economic advancement. Ironically, as they began obtaining proportional representation, other groups less historically oppressed than they began emulating and at times competing with them, such as other ethnics, women, the elderly, the handicapped, and gays and lesbians. For example, the Italian-American Defense and Higher Education Fund won a suit against City University of New York, in which Italian Americans claimed they were discriminated against because their percentage of staff and faculty was not proportionate to their numbers in the qualified labor pool or student body. Some Hispanic leaders have claimed that their members, 9 percent of the total U.S. population, were greatly underrepresented in elected offices and government positions. In Los Angeles, Chinese Americans wanted the police department to increase their representation on the force from 4.1 percent to 10 percent, which was their share of the city's population. Since women comprise 53 percent of the American population, wrote a *Boston Globe* editor, it would be fair and just that they have a quota "of slightly more than half of all the jobs and the payroll, the promotions, elected offices and political appointments." [59]

However, not all minority groups (except for a few dissenting members) seek proportional representation, such as Armenians, Greeks, Japanese, Jews, Koreans, black West Indians, and Asian Indians, all of whom have high achievers in some arenas that exceed their respective population percentages, locally or nationally.

## MAJORITY GROUP GOALS

Just as minority groups have a variety of goals, so it is within the larger society, which at the very least expects all citizens to be law-abiding and patriotic, and believes that the faster immigrants and their offspring become so, the better it is for them and for society. The U.S. government, however, was not that even-minded or even-handed when it came to specific racial, religious, or ethnic groups, some of whom it welcomed, tolerated, ignored, oppressed, rejected—or even changed its attitudes about from negative to positive and vice versa.

Some examples: Early nineteenth-century Chinese were welcomed on the West Coast, then attacked, segregated, urged to leave, and by the latter part of the century totally banned from immigrating to America. Only in the post–World War II decades did anti-Chinese immigration laws begin to be eliminated. Native Americans were first viewed by the government as tribes or nations to be conquered, converted, or enlisted as allies, with relations formalized by treaty. However, as the government grew stronger and white settlers and land speculators grew greedier, Indians were deemed wards, to be relocated and restricted to specific areas, without rights of citizenship, and urged to surrender their tribal identities. Not until 1924 were all Indians born in America granted citizenship.

Generally, the government's goals can be characterized as assimilation, cultural pluralism, legal protection, separation and segregation, population transfer or deportation, invidious immigration policies, violence and mass murder, obviation, and proportional representation.

### Assimilation

Minority group members are expected to accept, absorb, and conform to the values and behaviors of the dominant society, wherein immigrants renounce all old-country values and ways that differ with those of the established English-speaking population. Such an outlook of what has been termed "Anglo-conformity" underlay George Washington's questioning of whether people should be allowed to come to America as a group, because "by so doing, they retain the language, habits and principles (good or bad) which they bring with them." [60]

Totally excluded from any expectations of assimilation were black African slaves, who were deemed biologically and theologically destined to remain slaves and forgo whatever languages they brought with them—whether African or the French, Spanish, Portuguese, or Dutch they had learned from various colonial enslavers. Under English and then American colonial rule, Indians were viewed slightly less severely, though encouraged to adopt white Christian ways and beliefs, except for marriage with white Protestants. To the Reverend John Eliot, the seventeenth-century missionary who has been called the "Apostle to the Indians," Indians lacked repentence, prayer, and industry: "Would they but doe as wee doe in these things, they would be all one with English men." As Americans moved westward, various Protestant denominational missionaries competed with one another and with Catholics and Mormons to convert the Indians, who at times were accused by Protestants of conspiring with Catholics and Mormons to wipe out their settlers.[61]

In the late nineteenth and early twentieth century, as wave after wave of European immigrants arrived, the melting pot goal took form. The wise thing for an immigrant to do, said Theodore Roosevelt, was "to become thoroughly Americanized . . . [and] revere only our flag: not only must it come first, but no other flag should even come second. He must learn to celebrate Washington's birthday rather than that of Queen or Kaiser, and the Fourth of July instead of St. Patrick's day." Their children, too, were expected to assimilate, at least if they were to gain acceptance in the larger and higher society. In the 1930s, some college professors wrote recommendations for talented Jewish graduate students, noting that one of them "measures up to the whitest Gentile I know" and that another has "none of the offensive traits which some people associate with his race." Having a foreign accent or using a foreign language in school was criticized. " 'Speak White,' we were told, to take away our heritage," recently wrote one Franco-American songwriter. As late as the 1950s, Catholics were still seen by many a nativist as a threat to democracy: "When the individual Roman Catholic gets courage enough to tell his hierarchy what he wants done—and makes them do it—instead of groveling under fear and threats of the Church, then the individual Catholic will find himself welcomed by his fellow citizens as a part of true American society and democracy." [62]

Neither the Anglo-conformity nor the melting pot goal totally succeeded or failed, especially with second and succeeding generations of white immigrant offspring, who though progressively knowing less about their ancestral language, country, and history still held on to some degree of group identity. In contrast, little hope for assimilation was given blacks, Indians, Asians, and Mexican Americans, though some of them, particularly blacks and Indians, had been born in America and had family roots far older than those of many white Europeans.

## Cultural Pluralism

After World War I, the concept of cultural pluralism gained popularity, wherein philosophers like Horace Kallen and John Dewey encouraged native-born and naturalized Americans to respect and take pride in the diversity of group life about them, which they said enriched America. Dewey argued that the typical or genuine American is truly "hyphenated," which did not mean "he is part American and that some foreign ingredient is then added. It means that . . . he is international and interracial in his makeup. He is not American plus Pole or German. But the American is himself Pole-German-English-French-Spanish-Italian-Greek-Irish-Scandinavian-Bohemian-Jew—and so on."[63] Also, anthropologists like Franz Boas and Margaret Mead stressed the essential equality of all people and the relativity of all cultures. Lectures and courses on comparative religion grew in popularity. New metaphors like symphony, tossed salad, stew, and minestrone began replacing melting pot in describing the multivaried population. Still in those years, positive discussion of assimilation of people of color was scant.

Only as a result of World War II idealism, black protests, and the entire civil rights movement did newer, broader and tougher laws and legislation begin decisively outlawing racial, religious, ethnic, and sexual discrimination, ending invidious and racist immigration policies, and mandating bilingual education and foreign languages in public institutions, elections, and government agencies. No longer were the problems of race to be avoided or treated as afterthoughts to religious or ethnic bigotry. Whether in the name of blind justice, equal opportunity, fair employment practices, desegregation, or integration, all people of color were believed equally assimilable or, at the very least, not to be prevented from assimilating or being represented in all arenas of life. Thus, the Supreme Court in 1967 declared unconstitutional state laws banning interracial marriages. Rainbow became the newest metaphor for the ideal America.

## Legal Protection

By specific treaty, law, legislation, or conquest, the government often promises to protect a minority group, as happened with Indians and Eskimos. Congress passed legislation to help perpetuate Native American languages, as well as, in the 1978 Indian Child Welfare Act, to protect Native American reservation families and tribes against a state abusively taking away children from allegedly unfit parents and turning them over to non-Indian couples or foster homes for adoption.[64] The Thirteenth, Fourteenth, and Fifteenth Amendments, as well as twentieth-century civil rights legislation, were basically designed to ensure equal rights for African Americans, though they inspired other groups qua groups to seek similar treatment.

On the Atlantic and Pacific islands that America conquered, occupied, and/or annexed, the natives were at first protected by U.S. military forces to prevent lawlessness or rebellion, to better control the native group, and to preclude other foreign countries from entering. After the intrusion of the military came missionaries and merchants to save native souls and to reap profits, respectively. Even then, for many decades the natives were denied U.S. citizenship, equal protection of the law, representation in Congress, or self-determination. Not until 1952 did Puerto Rico become a self-governing commonwealth of America, whose residents do not pay any federal taxes to America though they are deemed American citizens, and who can travel freely to and from the mainland.

Whether at home or abroad, governmental promises of protection required the protectee's submission to American rule, with sometimes disastrous results for those who declined or opposed it. As one late nineteenth-century Sioux Indian said, the government "made us many promises, more than I can remember, but they never kept but one: they promised to take our land and they took it."[65]

### Separation and Segregation

In the name of maintaining domestic tranquility, intergroup peace, control over an area or group, or even protecting a victimized group, a national or local government sometimes passes laws or adopts policies to keep groups separate. In the past, this separation was achieved by dividing land for use only by Indians or white settlers, establishing free and slave states, creating separate schools and public facilities for racial and gender groups, organizing segregated work and military forces, legalizing racial and religious restrictive housing covenants, banning interracial marriages and transracial adoptions, or by generally validating social practices that excluded people from joining, recreating, or living in another group's clubs, resorts, or housing, including signs proclaiming "No Irish Need Apply" and "No Dogs or Mexicans Allowed."

However well intentioned, those who engaged in such actions were rarely free of believing themselves superior to those they avoided or restricted. At their worst, they allowed others to harass, intimidate, or aggress other groups, sometimes participating themselves.

### Population Transfer or Deportation

More aggressive than separation and segregation is the governmental policy of population transfer or deportation. As noted earlier, black Africans and, to a much lesser degree, European criminals and convicts were transported against their will to colonial America. In the immediate post–War of 1812 decades, free Negroes were encouraged to immigrate to Africa, while Indian tribes on the East Coast were forced to relocate west of the Mississippi, ever subject to further relocation when they were in the path of white expansion or when valuable minerals were discovered beneath their newly settled lands.

During World War II, almost 120,000 Japanese on the West Coast (but not in Hawaii), as well as some 1,000 Aleuts in Alaska, were relocated and interned in militarily restricted camps, though most were American citizens and none had been tried for any crime. Ironically, in some cases, they were confined on Indian land, or that was once owned by Indians, but without the violence that had been used against the Indians. After the war, in order to conduct a series of nuclear weapons tests, America compelled the natives on the Enewetak atoll in the Marshall Islands to relocate to other Pacific islands, where they were forced to remain for some thirty years before being allowed to return home.[66]

At times, a local or national government may expel certain people because of their religious or political views, or because such action is somehow believed essential to national or communal well-being. English military forces in Canada in 1755 compelled thousands of French Canadians (the Acadians) to move to English colonies in America, where most finally found refuge among French and Spanish residents in Louisiana. The Alien and Sedition Acts of 1798 empowered the president to deport all aliens considered dangerous to America, prompting many French residents to voluntarily leave. During the anti-communist Red Scare of 1919–20, some 250 aliens considered radical and revolutionary were deported to Russia. In the early 1950s, almost 2 million Mexican aliens were willingly or unwillingly deported back to Mexico, including many naturalized and American-born spouses and children.

## Invidious Immigration Policies

Depending on the economics and politics of the time, the U.S. government either prefers, restricts, or excludes some immigrants because of race, religion, ethnicity, health, economic status, or political beliefs. Before the American Revolution, the European colonial powers sought to replicate themselves in the New World, and so New England, New France, New Spain, New Netherland, New Sweden came into being, with the hope that they would be populated by people of their own homelands, but when relatively few immigrants came, the colonizers, particularly the English and Dutch, took to recruiting and admitting others.

After the Revolution, America's immigration doors were widened, except to blacks. By passing the Naturalization Act of 1790, Congress specifically restricted citizenship to free white persons. Broad ethnic, racial, and social exclusionary policies began being instituted in the late nineteenth century, chiefly against Chinese, Japanese, Mexicans, and Asians.

Some states, too, expressed similar preferences, particularly in the South. For example, a 1907 Alabama statute sought prospective residents from "white citizens of the United States first, and then citizens of English-speaking and Germanic countries, France and the Scandinavian countries, and Belgium. . . ."[67]

Increasingly wanted were people of Anglo-Saxon descent, and unwanted were south, central, and eastern Europeans. In the 1920s, the government instituted national origins quotas, with the support of racist groups like the Ku Klux Klan, some Ivy League and self-styled geneticists and eugenicists, and urban reformers, all of whom deemed immigrants from south, central, and eastern Europe a menace to democracy and the cause of urban blight and crime. Writing in *Good Housekeeping Magazine,* in 1921, Calvin Coolidge (then vice president-elect) stressed the allegedly scientific reasons for being selective: "Biological laws tell us that certain divergent people will not mix or blend. The Nordics propagate themselves successfully. With other races, the outcome shows deterioration on both sides. Quality of mind and body suggests that observance of ethnic law is as great a necessity to a nation as immigration law."[68]

Today, too, calls are made for limiting or stopping immigration—but not so much because of a group's race, religion, or ethnicity, but rather the fear that more immigrants cannot be absorbed economically.

### Violence, Disease, and Mass Murder

Some of the oldest practices used to control minorities involve the use of force, terrorism, and mass murder, with the cooperation at times of other minority groups. In North, Central, and South America, the sword, the gun, alcohol, and especially disease decimated large numbers of natives, if not entire tribes. In fact, it was against Native Americans and not countries abroad that America fought its longest and most frequent wars.

From the fifteenth through the nineteenth centuries, the Spanish, French, Dutch, British, or American powers waged limited to broad military actions against tribes in the Caribbean and the Americas to advance Christian civilization, convert natives, obtain food, extract mineral wealth, confiscate lands, force natives to work the fields or mines, prevent native or slave rebellions, punish marauders and thieves—or simply to protect themselves and what they had conquered. To the Europeans, the natives were filthy heathens. "They are not wild because we believe them to be mad and insane, but on account of their idolatry and error in religion," noted Peter Lindestrom in seventeenth-century New Sweden.[69]

The same psychology and brutality that the Elizabethan English had used against the Irish were used against the Indians, who were demonized as barbarians and terrorized by the burning of their crops, food storages, and villages. Certainly, some Indian tribes hated each other more than they did the Europeans and allied themselves with one or another foreign power to attack an enemy tribe or European power. In one case, white settlers and the Micmac Indian invaders from Nova Scotia succeeded by 1830 in what has been termed the genocidal destruction of the Beotucks of Newfoundland. Ironically, when not fighting each other, the early European powers all the more aggressed the natives.[70]

Also, in war or peace, thousands of Indians died from transplanted European and African diseases, which according to some experts caused more deaths than European military might. Nor were the early settlers above engaging in murderous treachery. In 1623, during peace talks with the Pamunkey tribe, Virginia colonists killed some 200 of them with poisoned wine. During the 1763 so-called Pontiac's War, a British commander surreptitiously gave smallpox infected blankets to the Indians. At other times, colonists refrained from inoculating Indians, whose subsequent deaths they happily credited to God's will. Likewise, in Hawaii, European and American diseases resulted in increased deaths and decreased birthrates among the natives, whose numbers fell from some 400,000 in 1778 to 40,000 in 1883, rendering them a minority in their homeland.[71]

Into the early twentieth century, massive violence, shootings, and lynchings took place against American blacks, Mexicans, Asians, and Pacific Islanders, often with the approval or indifference of public opinion and local, state, or federal governments, which considered the victims little better than animals. "I thought I could shoot Mexicans as well as I could shoot Indians, or deer, or turkey," recalled an early nineteenth-century Texan. Senator J. J. Ingalls, in 1890, well characterized America's racial attitudes and behaviors: The "race to which we belong is the most arrogant and rapacious, the most exclusive and indomitable in history. It is the conquering and the unconquerable race, through which alone man has taken possession of the physical and moral world. All other races have been its enemies or its victims."[72]

### Obviation

Local or national governments and communities often adopt a formal or informal policy of not seeing, hearing, admitting, or stopping injuries inflicted upon minorities, and when challenged, either deny any wrongdoing, blame the victim, defend their behavior in the name of a higher calling, acknowledge wrongdoing but say it is best forgotten, or delay rectification as long as possible:

—Centuries passed before American Indians received any fair hearing in the courts, and when they did, it was after long and costly suits. Not until Congress passed laws in 1989 and 1990 did museums receiving federal funds begin returning Indian bones and funeral relics to their tribal descendants, and not until 1993 were Indians granted the legal right to use the stimulant drug peyote derived from the mescal cactus in religious ceremonies, for which hitherto they could have been arrested in twenty-two states. Post–Civil War proposals for a "mule and forty acres" to each former slave, as well as contemporary demands for reparations for past injustices, remain totally ignored by the U.S. government, which in 1994 rejected such claims on the income tax returns of some 20,000 African Americans. In 1995, Mississippi finally ratified the Thirteenth Amendment abolishing slavery. Almost four decades passed before Congress voted compensation to American Japanese and Aleuts unjustly interned, detained, or forcibly relocated during World War II. Not until 1990 did the federal government stop using a small Hawaiian island, which natives held sacred, for naval gun and bomber practice. In addition, the government has yet to explain why it subjected more than 100 Alaskan natives in the 1950s to radioactive drugs without telling them they were part of a dangerous medical experiment to find better ways for soldiers to survive the arctic climate. On a community level, records on the brutal killing of thirty-one innocent Chinese goldminers in Oregon in 1887 were recently made public because they had been deliberately hidden at the time.[73]

—When Congress declared Puerto Rico an unincorporated territory in 1900, it not only appointed the island's governor and members of the legislative upper house, but also denied the residents citizenship and misnamed the area "Porto Rico," much to the consternation of the natives and Representative William Jones, who at the time pointed out, "There does not even exist the pretext of changing the name to Americanize it, since porto is not an English but a Portuguese word," which "some Republican politician, ignorant of its derivation and meaning, and insensible to the wishes and the feelings of those who are attached to it, had arbitrarily and wickedly determined."[74]

—Only in recent decades have major American and world Protestant and Catholic leaders apologized for the wrongs of the past inflicted in the name of religion, such as their churches' historic role in the destruction of American Indian spiritual practices and lives, the maintenance and spread of slavery, and the propagation of anti-Semitism. For example, on a global level, Pope John Paul II deplored the excesses of the Crusades and the Inquisition, and in 1995, while on a trip to the Czech Republic, apologized in the name of all Catholics for the wrongs done to non-Catholics. Domestically, in that same year, on the 150th anniversary of its founding, the Southern Baptist Convention overwhelmingly voted to apologize and ask forgiveness of all African Americans for their forebears' behavior in defending the right of people to own slaves and failing to support civil rights for black Americans.[75]

In other cases, as long as minorities do not cause public or governmental problems; do not become uppity, pushy, or aggressive; do not live on land containing valuable natural resources; do not move into areas where they are not wanted; and are not perceived as causing the spread of disease, blight, or crime, they are usually allowed to do as they please. While today's inner-city blacks and Hispanics are largely the victims of such attitudes, in the past the victims were various European ethnic groups and American Indians. For example, when Italian immigrants murdered each other, editorialized one newspaper in 1891, "Americans are not likely to pay much attention to their performances, although nothing can be more demoralizing to society than the immunity of criminals." When the government does pay attention to the wrongdoing of minorities, it often does so in a self-serving manner. As Major General John Pope wrote in 1865, "It is only what the Indian does to the white man (nine times out of ten in the way of retaliation) which reaches the public."[76]

### Proportional Representation

As with minorities, majorities can adopt the goal of proportional representation for a variety of reasons. In the name of justice, morality, or compensation for past exclusion, it is believed that different groups should be represented in government and societal institutions in proportion to their percentage of the electorate, workforce, or total population. More pragmatically, the government, politicians, educators, and businessmen see proportional representation as a way of winning votes, obtaining federal, state or city contracts, gaining local community and media support, and/or preventing demonstrations, strikes, or even violence.

Governmental proportional representation is not new. In the early twentieth century, municipal reformers advocated it as a way of insuring minority views in government and combating election corruption and machine politics. With the civil rights movement of the 1960s and the introduction of affirmative action legislation and practices primarily for blacks, both local and federal government and private industry began adopting and extending proportional representation to other groups as well.

As a result, some people are hired, awarded contracts, or given loans because of their group affiliation—specifically African Americans, Hispanics, Asians, Pacific Islanders, American Indians, Alaskan Natives, women, and the handicapped. To encourage small minority owners of wireless telephone businesses, the Federal Communications Commission allows them a 25 percent discount and ten-year period to pay off successful bids. The secretary of the navy ordered that contract preferences be given to the maximum extent possible to businesses owned by native Hawaiians for environmental work on and about the island of Kaho'olawe. The Department of Housing and Urban Development added Hasidic Jewish Americans to its Minority Business Enterprise procurement list of preferred groups. The Defense Department requires that 5 percent of the total value of its various contracts be awarded to socially and economically disadvantaged individuals. Under that rubric, the Small Business Administration includes Subcontinental Asian Americans as being eligible for its assistance programs, namely, those from India, Pakistan, Bangladesh, Sri Lanka, Bhutan, Maldive Islands, or Nepal. In addition to the above categories, the minority business outreach program of Fairfax County, Virginia, includes "all persons with a physical or mental impairment that substantially limits one or more of the major life activities of such individuals, a record of such impairments, or who are regarded as having such impairments." [77]

Not only have the courts upheld many of these practices, particularly when there is a history of past discrimination against a group, but increasing numbers of political leaders, educators, social reformers, and business executives are redefining equality and fairness in terms of a particular group's statistical representation in a given geographic area or labor force rather than in terms of equal opportunity for each individual regardless of group origin. The difference between the minority and majority goal of proportional representation is that in the latter case the government has the power to determine who the recipients of affirmative action and proportional representation are, without necessarily including all groups seeking such recognition. Excluded thus far are religious and European nationality groups, as well as white Americans in general and white males in particular.

In summary, both majority and minority groups often have similar, competing, or overlapping goals, which are not always formally proclaimed or free of ambiguity. While the very plurality of minority groups inhibits any one group from dominating all others, it also creates or intensifies intergroup differences, particularly when government favors some groups and not others, thereby thwarting coalitional efforts to resolve commonly held problems and straining, if not threatening, national unity.

Before exploring those developments, a closer look at the benefits and disadvantages of group identity is in order.

## NOTES

1. Betty-Bright Low, *French in North America* (Philadelphia: Balch Institute Reading Lists, no. 4, 1974), 1.

2. Alan Conway, "Welsh Emigration to the United States," in *Perspectives in American History*, Vol. 7, ed. Donald Fleming and Bernard Bailyn (Cambridge: Harvard University Press, 1974), 221.

3. Merle Curti, *The Roots of American Loyalty* (New York: Atheneum, 1968), 84.

4. Marc Pachter, *Abroad in America: Visitors to the New Nation* (Reading, Pa.: Addison-Wesley Publishing Company, 1976), 43.

5. Leo Schelbert, "On Becoming an Emigrant: A Structural View of Eighteenth- and Nineteenth-Century Swiss Data," in *Perspectives in American History*, Vol. 7, ed. Donald Fleming and Bernard Bailyn (Cambridge: Harvard University Press, 1974), 493.

6. William J. Baker, *America Perceived: A View from Abroad in the 19th Century* (West Haven, Conn.: Pendulum Press, 1974), 139; Susan M. Papp, *Hungarian Americans and Their Communities of Cleveland* (Cleveland: Cleveland State University Press, 1981), 164; John J. Bukowczyk, *And My Children Did Not Know Me: A History of Polish-Americans* (Bloomington: Indiana University Press, 1987), 16; Nancy Faires Conklin and Nora Faires, " 'Colored' and Catholic—The Lebanese in Birmingham, Alabama," in *Crossing the Waters,* ed. Eric J. Hooglund (Washington, D.C.: Smithsonian Institution Press, 1987), 78.

7. Fred Alvarez, "Coming Home," *Los Angeles Times,* 1 January 1995, A35; David Cressy, *Coming Over: Migration and Communication between England and New England in the Seventeenth Century* (Cambridge: Cambridge University Press, 1989), 194.

8. George Papashvily and Helen Waite Papashvily, *Anything Can Happen* (New York: Harper & Brothers Publishers, 1945), 55; Ronald Takaki, *Strangers From a Different Shore* (New York: Penguin Books, 1989), 331.

9. *Boston Globe,* 27 March 1993, 5; Wendy Law-Yone, "Becoming American," *The Washington Post Magazine,* 10 April 1983, 20.

10. Charles F. Donovan, *Nineteenth Century Boston College: Irish or American?* (Boston: Boston College, undated pamphlet), 13; Israel Zangwill, *The Melting Pot* (New York: Macmillan, 1913), 37.

11. Richard Hofstadter and Michael Wallace, *American Violence* (New York: Vintage Books, 1971), 322.

12. Roy Reed, "Gathering Clans Find the Scots Aflame Over a Bitter Past," *New York Times,* 16 May 1977, 2; Paula Butturini, "Menino's Roots: A Town in Italy Finds a Grandson," *Boston Globe,* 30 September 1994, 1; Seth Mydans, "Former Refugees See Opportunity in Vietnam," *New York Times,* 5 December 1994, A8.

13. Shelby Steele, *The Content of Our Character* (New York: St. Martin's Press, 1990).

14. E. Clifford Nelson, *The Lutherans in North America* (Philadelphia: Fortress Press, 1975), 19, 42; Conway, "Welsh Emigration to the United States," 188.

15. Peter C. Marzio, ed., *A Nation of Nations* (New York: Harper & Row, 1976), 245; Humbert S. Nelli, *Italians in Chicago, 1880–1930* (New York: Oxford University Press, 1970), 169.

16. Stephen Steinberg, *The Ethnic Myth* (New York: Atheneum, 1981), 45; Doreen Carvajal, "Trying to Halt 'Silent Exodus,' " *Los Angeles Times,* 9 May 1994, A1.

17. Philip Martin and Elizabeth Midgley, "Immigration to the United States: Journey to an Uncertain Destination," *Population Bulletin* 7, no. 2 (Washington, D.C.: Population Reference Bureau, September 1994): 38; Alejandro Portes and Richard Schauffler, "Language and the Second Generation: Bilingualism Yesterday and Today," *International Migration Review* (Winter 1994): 658–59; Patrick J. McDonnell, "Study Disputes Immigrant Stereotypes, Cites Gains," *Los Angeles Times,* 3 November 1995, A1, A28; Deborah Sontag, "A Fervent 'No' To Assimilation in New America," *New York Times,* 29 June 1993, A10.

18. Shannon Henry, "Native Americans Attempt to Save Tribal Languages for the Next Generation," *Christian Science Monitor,* 29 June 1993, 1; Michael Krauss, "The World's Languages in Crisis," *Language* 68, no. 1 (1992): 4; Felicity Barringer, "Tongues that Dance with Wolves," *New York Times,* 8 January 1991,

A14; Lee Dye, "Alaskans Speak Out to Save Dying Languages," *Los Angeles Times,* 7 July 1994, A8; Kirk Johnson, "Seeking Lost Culture at a Powwow," *New York Times,* 19 September 1993, 45.

19. Took Took Thongthiraj, "The Demand for Hindi, Tagalog, Thai, and Vietnamese Language and Culture Classes at UCLA," *Crosscurrents, Newsmagazine of the UCLA Asian American Studies Center* (Fall/Winter 1991): 2.

20. Ted Morgan, *On Becoming American* (Boston: Houghton Mifflin Company, 1978), 76; Mary Helen Dohan, *Our Own Words* (Baltimore: Penguin Books, 1974), 147–48; George T. Labaki, "Struggle of the Maronite," *Migration World* 67, no. 1 (1989): 25; H. L. Mencken, *The American Language* (New York: Alfred A. Knopf, 1963), 580–90; Nelson, *The Lutherans in North America,* 42; Samuel P. Orth, *Our Foreigners* (New Haven: Yale University Press, 1921), 24–30.

21. Takaki, *Strangers From a Different Shore,* 215; *New York Times,* 21 December 1975, 2; K. Connie Kang, "Images of Asian Americans Change Slowly—If at All," *Crosscurrents, Newsmagazine of the UCLA Asian American Studies Center* (Fall/Winter 1993): 4.

22. Orth, *Our Foreigners,* 24; *Boston Globe,* 23 December 1977, 17.

23. Charles H. Anderson, *White Protestant Americans* (Englewood Cliffs, N.J.: Prentice Hall, 1970), 70–71; Stephan Thernstrom, *Harvard Encyclopedia of American Ethnic Groups* (Cambridge: Harvard University Press, 1980), 385, 387; James Stuart Olson, *The Ethnic Dimension in American History* (New York: St. Martin's Press, 1979), 126–27; Roger Daniels, *Coming to America: A History of Immigration and Ethnicity in American Life* (New York: Harper Perennial, 1990), 95.

24. *Boston Globe,* 6 August 1979; Richard L. Berke, "U.S. Voters Focus on Selves, Poll Says," *New York Times,* 21 September 1994, A21.

25. Edward S. Shapiro, "The Ordeal of Success: American Jewry Since World War II," *American Jewish History* (Autumn 1993): 99; Jonathon D. Sarna, "The Secret of Jewish Continuity," *Commentary* (October 1994): 57; Steinberg, *The Ethnic Myth,* 68; Alice Scourby, "Three Generations of Greek Americans: A Study in Ethnicity," *International Migration Review* 14 (Spring 1980): 48; *JTA Community News Reporter,* 18 January 1991, 1; 10 June 1991, 1; Peter Steinfels, "Despite Role on World Stage, Muslims Turn to the Personal," A20; Arlene F. Saluter, *Marital Status and Living Arrangements: March 1992, Series P20–468* (Washington, D.C.: U.S. Department of Commerce, 1992), x.

26. Takaki, *Strangers From a Different Shore,* 473; Charisse Jones, "Debate on Race and Adoptions Is Being Reborn," *New York Times,* 24 October 1993, 35; Glen Grant and Dennis M. Ogawa, "Living Proof: Is Hawaii the Answer?" *Annals of the American Academy of Political and Social Science* (November 1993): 151; *Jet,* 8 March 1993, 32; Lawrence Wright, "One Drop of Blood," *The New Yorker,* 25 July 1994, 49; "The Numbers Game," *Time, Special Issue* (Fall 1993): 14; *Boston Globe,* 6 October 1994, 10.

27. Anderson, *White Protestant Americans,* 17–19.

28. David Foster, "Indian Candidate Seeks Top Idaho Post," *Boston Globe,* 6 September 1994, 3; Anastasia Bastea, "Group Blasts Frank Over Firing of Gay Intern," *Boston Globe,* 26 June 1993, 9.

29. John Higham, *Send These To Me: Jews and Other Immigrants in Urban America* (New York: Atheneum, 1975), 234.

30. Milton M. Gordon, *Assimilation in American Life* (New York: Oxford University Press, 1964), 279.

31. Thernstrom, *Harvard Encyclopedia of American Ethnic Groups,* 747; *Statistical Yearbook of the Immigration and Naturalization Service, 1993* (Washington, D.C.: U.S. Government Printing Office, 1994), 125.

32. Deborah Sontag, "Immigrants Forgoing Citizenship While Pursuing American Dream," *New York Times,* 25 July 1993, 1; Sam Howe Verhovek, "Legal Immigrants Seek Citizenship in Record Numbers," *New York Times,* 2 April 1995, 1.

33. Raymond A. Mohl, "The Politics of Ethnicity in Contemporary Miami," *Migration World* 14, no. 3 (1986): 8.

34. Takaki, *Strangers From a Different Shore,* 277.

35. Jeremiah W. Jenks and Jett W. Lauck, *The Immigration Problem* (New York: Funk & Wagnalls Company, 1913), 256; Salom Rizk, *Syrian Yankee* (Garden City, N.Y.: Doubleday & Company, 1954), 147–48; Gary A. Tobin and Adam Z. Tobin, *American Jewish Philanthropy* (Waltham, Mass.: Brandeis University Press, 1995), 27.

36. Mary C. Waters, "Ethnic and Racial Identities of Second-Generation Black Immigrants in New York City," *International Migration Review* (Winter 1994): 797; Elaine Woo, "Immigrants Do Well in School, Study Finds," *Los Angeles Times,* 3 April 1995, A1.

37. Gerald Rosenblum, *Immigrant Workers* (New York: Basic Books, 1973), 32; Mike O'Connor, "A New U.S. Import in El Salvador: Street Gangs," *New York Times,* 3 July 1994, 3; Anthony Bottoms, "Crime and Delinquency in Immigrant and Minority Groups," in *Psychology and Race,* ed. Peter Watson (Chicago: Aldine Publishing Company, 1973), 436.

38. James Q. Wilson and Richard J. Herrnstein, *Crime & Human Nature* (New York: Simon & Schuster, Inc., 1985), 459.

39. Howard B. Grose, *The Incoming Millions* (New York: Fleming H. Revell Company, 1906), 101; Seth Mydans, "Laotians' Arrest in Killing Bares a Generation Gap," *New York Times,* 21 June 1994, A10; George F. Will, "Misreading Immigration," *Boston Globe,* 12 August 1994, 19.

40. Leonard W. Levy, *Blasphemy* (New York: Alfred A. Knopf, 1993), 46–47, 66–67, 261.

41. *The Religious Right: The Assault on Tolerance & Pluralism In America* (New York: Anti-Defamation League, 1994), 121; Albert Vorspan, "Is American Jewry Unraveling," *Reform Judaism* (Summer 1995): 14; Laura H. Weaver, "Forbidden Fancies: A Child's Vision of Mennonite Plainness," *The Journal of Ethnic Studies* 11 (Fall 1983): 56.

42. Liucija Baskauskas, "The Lithuanian Refugee Experience and Grief," *International Migration Review* 15 (Spring-Summer 1981): 282; Eiichiro Azuma, "Interethnic Conflict under Racial Subordination: Japanese Immigrants and Their Asian Neighbors in Walnut Grove, California 1908–1941," *Amerasia Journal* 20, no. 2 (1994): 32–35; David Rohde, "Racial Code in High School: Tolerance, Not Integration," *Christian Science Monitor,* 8 March 1994, 2.

43. Richard Lewis, Jr., and George Yancey, "A Comparison of the Acceptance of Hyperandry and Hypergyny Interracial Relationships: A Test of Sexual Racism," *The Journal of Intergroup Relations* (Winter 1994–1995): 46–47; Tracy Thompson, "The Way Off Welfare: Work or a Wedding Ring," *Washington Post National Weekly Edition,* 22–28 May 1995, 32.

44. "Wilma Mankiller—Destined To Lead," *NEA Today* (October 1994): 7.

45. Charles Kamasaki and Raul Yzaguirre, "Black-Hispanic Tensions: One Perspective," *Journal of Intergroup Relations* (Winter 1994–1995): 34.

46. "The Muslim Program," *Muhammed Speaks,* 29 January 1971, 32; *Christian Science Monitor,* 25 November 1985, 3; Michael Conlon, "Poll Finds a More Radical Black US," *Boston Globe,* 15 April 1994, 17; James Crawford, *Hold Your Tongue—Bilingualism and the Politics of 'English Only'* (Reading, Pa.: Addison-Wesley Publishing Co., 1993), 82.

47. H. W. Gilmore, "The Old New Orleans and the New: A Case for Ecology," in *Neighborhood and Ghetto,* ed. Scott Greer and Ann Lennarson Greer (New York: Basic Books, 1974), 260–61.

48. Aronoldo De Leon, *They Called Them Greasers* (Austin: University of Texas Press, 1994), 3; *New York Times,* 24 December 1980, A11; Carey McWilliams, *Brothers Under the Skin* (Boston: Little, Brown and Company, 1951), 182; Eileen H. Tamura, "Review of *A Call for Hawaiian Sovereignty (A Hawaiian Nation II),* by Michael Kioni Dudley and Keoni Kealoha Agard," *Journal of American Ethnic History* (Winter 1995): 116.

49. Dirk Johnson, "Lure to Affluent, Hispanic Santa Fe Loses Itself," *New York Times,* 21 June 1993, A12; *New York Times,* 27 June 1994, A14.

50. John H. Bodley, *Victims of Progress* (Menlo Park: Benjamin/Cummings, 1975), 23; Harold R. Isaacs, *Idols of the Tribe* (New York: Harper & Row, 1975), 6.

51. Stan Hoig, *Tribal Wars of the Southern Plains* (Norman: University of Oklahoma Press, 1993), 285.

52. Richard Hofstadter, *America at 1750* (New York: Vintage Books, 1973), 19; Nathan O. Hatch, *The Democratization of American Christianity* (New Haven: Yale University Press, 1989), 184; Robert Royal, *Columbus on Trial: 1492 v. 1992* (Herndon, Va.: Young America's Foundation, 1992), 11.

53. "A Clarification of Torah Doctrine," [a paid advertisement] *New York Times,* 6 February 1994, E17.

54. Hans Toch, *The Social Psychology of Social Movements* (New York: Bobbs-Merrill Company, 1965), 31; Leonard Barrett, *The Rastafarians* (Boston: Beacon Press, 1977), 103–45; Israel J. Gerber, *The Heritage Seekers* (Middle Village, N.Y.: Jonathan David Publishers, 1977), 100.

55. Robert Laxalt, *Sweet Promised Land* (New York: Harper & Brothers, 1957), 50; Thomas Sowell, *Race and Culture* (New York: Basic Books, 1994), 46.

56. Durand Echeverria, *Mirage in the West* (Princeton: Princeton University Press, 1968), 176; John P. Diggins, *Mussolini and Fascism* (Princeton: Princeton University Press, 1972), 111; Tim Weiner, "Pleas for Asylum Inundate System for Immigration," *New York Times,* 25 April 1993, 1, 50.

57. Louis L. Gerson, *The Hyphenate in Recent American Politics and Diplomacy* (Lawrence: University of Kansas Press, 1964), 14; Joel Kotkin, *Tribes* (New York: Random House, 1992), 193.

58. *The Armenians in Massachusetts* (Boston: The Armenian Historical Society, 1937), 50; *New York Times,* 15 July 1992, A6 and 24 October 1991, A7; *Boston Globe,* 5 May 1993, 14; *Unum,* a Newsletter on American Diversity and Unity (Summer 1993): 5.

59. Eric Dixon, " 'Systemic Discrimination' Against Italian-Americans," *Kingsman* (Brooklyn College's Weekly Newspaper), 10 September 1990, 1; Kama-

saki and Yzaguirre, "Black-Hispanic Tensions: One Perspective," 26–27; K. Connie Kang, "Building Bridges to Equality," *Los Angeles Times,* 7 January 1995, A1; Loretta McLaughlin, "Gender Wars in the Boardroom," *Boston Globe,* 27 February 1995, 15.

60. Gordon, *Assimilation in American Life,* 90.

61. Irving H. Bartlett, "The Puritans as Missionaries," *The Boston Public Library Quarterly* (April 1950): 101; Philip Perlmutter, *Divided We Fall: A History of Ethnic, Religious, and Racial Prejudice in America* (Ames: Iowa State University Press, 1992), 129; Kenneth H. Winn, *Exiles in a Land of Liberty* (Chapel Hill: University of North Carolina Press, 1989), 86–89.

62. Theodore Roosevelt, "True Americanism," *History of the American Nation,* Vol. 9, ed. William J. Jackman (Chicago: Western Press Association, 1923), 2,625; Shapiro, "The Ordeal of Success: American Jewry Since World War II," 93; Royal Ford, "Franco Americans Struggle to Preserve Their Heritage," *Boston Globe,* 28 October 1994, 16; Mark J. Hurley, *The Unholy Ghost: Anti-Catholicism in the American Experience* (Huntington, Ind.: Our Sunday Visitor Publishing Division, 1992), 174.

63. Horace M. Kallen, *Culture and Democracy in the United States* (New York: Boni and Liveright, 1924), 131–32.

64. Timothy Eagan, "A Cultural Gap May Swallow a Child," *New York Times,* 12 October 1993, A16; Mitchell Zuckoff, "More and More Claiming American Indian Heritage," *Boston Globe,* 18 April 1995, 9; Alvin M. Joseph, Jr., *The Indian Heritage of America* (Boston: Houghton Mifflin Co., 1991), 363.

65. Hofstadter and Wallace, *American Violence,* 278.

66. Richard Drinnon, *Keeper of Concentration Camps* (Berkeley: University of California Press, 1989), xxiii; *New York Times,* 17 October 1982, 7.

67. Thomas Muller, *Immigrants and the American City* (New York: New York University Press, 1993), 19, 27; Conklin and Faires, " 'Colored' and Catholic— The Lebanese in Birmingham, Alabama," 74.

68. Allan Chase, *The Legacy of Malthus* (Urbana: University of Illinois Press, 1980), 175.

69. Francis Jennings, *The Invasion of America* (New York: W. W. Norton & Co., 1975), 48.

70. Ibid., 46; *The World Book Encyclopedia,* s.v. "Newfoundland"; Frank Chalk and Kurt Jonassohn, *The History and Sociology of Genocide* (New Haven: Yale University Press, 1990), 36; Richard White, Review of *Warpaths: Invasions of North America* in *The New Republic* (23 January 1995): 42.

71. Ian K. Steele, *Warpaths: Invasions of North America* (New York: Oxford University Press, 1994), 22, 47; Grant and Ogawa, "Living Proof: Is Hawaii the Answer?," 141.

72. Frank H. Tucker, *The White Conscience* (New York: Frederick Ungar Publishing, 1968), 3; De Leon, *They Called Them Greasers,* 11.

73. *New York Times,* 10 October 1993, 32 and 20 March 1995, A10; *Boston Globe,* 9 May 1994, 3, 4 May 1993, 10, 20 October 1994, 15, 17 March 1995, 3; "Files Found in Oregon Detail Massacre of Chinese," *New York Times,* 20 August 1995, 30.

74. Jose A. Cabranes, *Citizenship and the American Empire* (New Haven: Yale University Press, 1979), 1.

75. Celestine Bohlen, "Pope Asks Czechs to Forgive Sectarian Wrongs," *New York Times,* 22 May 1995, A3; Desmond O'Grady, "The Perils of Penance," *Commonweal,* 21 October 1995, 7; Gustav Niebuhr, "Baptist Group Votes to Repent Stand on Slaves," *New York Times,* 21 June 1995, B7.

76. Thomas Monroe Pitkin and Francesco Cordasco, *The Black Hand* (Totowa, N.J.: Rowman and Littlefield, 1977), 28; Hoig, *Tribal Wars of the Southern Plains,* 6.

77. Steven A. Holmes, "Clinton to Review Federal Affirmative Action Programs," *New York Times,* 25 February 1995, 9; Edmund L. Andrews, "Court Stalls F.C.C. Program for Women and Minorities," *New York Times,* 16 March 1995, A22; Charles V. Dale to Sen. Robert Dole, letter, 17 February 1995, "Compilation and Overview of Federal Laws and Regulations Establishing Affirmative Action Goals or Other Preference Based on Race, Gender, or Ethnicity" (Washington, D.C.: Congressional Research Service, Library of Congress), CRS-11, CRS-12; *Code of Federal Regulations,* No. 13 (Washington, D.C.: Office of Federal Register, National Archives and Records Administration, 1993), 457; Jeffrey Rosen, "Affirmative Action: A Solution," *New Republic,* 8 May 1995, 25.

# 7

# The Benefits of Group Identity

Men have learned what wonders can be accomplished in certain cases by union, and seem to think that union is competent to every thing. You can scarcely name an object for which some institution has not been formed. Would men spread one set of opinions, or crush another? They make a society. Would they improve the penal code, or relieve poor debtors? They make societies. Would they encourage agriculture, or manufactures, or science? They make societies. Would one class encourage horseracing, and another discourage travelling on Sunday? They make societies.

—William Ellery Channing,
*The Works of William E. Channing*, Vol. 1

Regardless of the problems minority groups confront relating to the dominant society, there are many benefits in belonging to a group. The attention, respect, status, and friendliness that minorities would like to receive from the larger society are more easily obtainable in their own community. Likewise, the attention, respect, and status they may not receive from their family or friends may also be more easily obtainable by becoming active in their own group's voluntary organizations, in which a person can become a president, vice president, treasurer, and so forth, be listed on a letterhead, be cited in the group's bulletin or newspaper, or be thanked or acknowledged at a group function or celebration.

Society, too, benefits from having many voluntary groups, as noted by some early nineteenth-century observers. The prominent American church leader Lyman Beecher, in 1812, argued that "wise and good" local voluntary groups were needed "to enlist and preserve the public opinion on the side of law and order," and that they served as "a sort of disciplined moral militia, prepared to . . . repel every encroachment upon the liberties and morals of the State." Some eighteen years later Alexis de Tocqueville made his memorable observation about Americans constantly forming all kinds of associations: "They have not only commercial and manufacturing companies, in which all take part, but associations of a thousand other kinds— religious, moral, serious, futile, extensive or restricted, enormous or diminutive. The Americans make associations to give entertainments, to found establishments for education, to build inns, to construct churches, to diffuse books, to send missionaries to the antipodes; and in this manner they founded hospitals, prisons, and schools. If it be proposed to advance some truth, or to foster some feeling by the encouragement of a great example, they form a society."[1]

And indeed, with each passing decade, more and more voluntary organizations came into being in the United States, so that by 1980, some 6 to 7 million voluntary groups existed, with 84 percent of the adult population contributing funds to one or more group. The United Way agencies alone had gross annual receipts, which if included in the Fortune 500 listing, would have put them in the top 200. By 1988, some 80 million Americans—45 percent of all adults—did some kind of voluntary work, with uncounted numbers of youths doing the same by visiting people in nursing homes, manning hot lines, helping in soup kitchens, cleaning up parks, and so forth. By 1994, 62 cents out of every charitable dollar in the United States went to a religious institution. Also, social activism led to the creation of tens of thousands of public-interest groups and committees, which in the 1990s raised more than $4 billion a year from 40 million citizens.[2]

With the examples cited above as a background, a closer look will now be taken at the benefits of creating, joining, and maintaining a minority group, remembering that the benefits are often multidimensional, overlapping, and reciprocally reinforcing. In brief, they may be described as offering ease of organizing, opportunity for economic improvement, effectiveness in combating bigotry, a basis for gaining societal respect and power, help in acculturation, and multiple ways of achieving personal self-fulfillment.

## EASE OF ORGANIZING

Group identification is a convenient way for people to organize, whether around a church, fraternal organization, neighborhood, or even a gang. It fosters communal trust, friendship, and solidarity, whether among new minority members or longtime American-born residents. At its simplest, little more is required for membership than having been born of a particular religion, race, nationality, or neighborhood. As Kipling wrote in his defense of Englishmen:

> The men of my own stock
>   They may do ill or well,
> But they tell the lies I am wonted to,
>   They are used to the lies I tell.
> And we do not need interpreters
>   When we go to buy and sell . . .
> This was my father's belief
>   And this is also mine:
> Let the corn be all one sheaf—
>   And the grapes be all one vine,
> Ere our children's teeth are set on edge
>   By bitter bread and wine.[3]

Such beliefs and behaviors are commonplace, particularly among immigrants. An early Swedish pioneer in Wisconsin noted that when his compatriots first arrived and found the best land already taken, they refused to settle a few miles away where there was much better land and greater economic opportunity, but preferred, "for the sake of being close to their countrymen, to dig in among the hills, hollows and rocks." Norwegian immigrants settled among people from the same "bygd" (valley community). "If you travel from Black River Falls to Mondrove," wrote an early observer in western Wisconsin, "you will pass through 'Little Norway' where every soul hails from Ringebu. West of there lies a series of long valleys . . . where only the sons of Solor thrive." City neighborhoods, streets, and even saloons likewise attracted immigrants from the same country, region, or village. For example, sameness of language rather than land of origin attracted many recent Brazilian immigrants to some New Jersey communities where immigrants from Portugal had previously settled.[4]

Transplanted intergroup associational patterns also occur. Just as some upland Hungarian villages were composed of Magyars, Slovaks, Ruthenes, Jews, and Germans, so were some urban ethnic enclaves in America. Old-country antagonisms notwithstanding, Bohemian immigrants generally settled close to Germans, particularly in St. Louis, Milwaukee, Cincinnati, and Detroit, where they were "drawn to the Germans by a similarity, if not identity, in customs and mode of life; besides, educated as many of them had been in German-language schools, the pioneers felt pretty much at home among the Germans." Similarly, the first Poles in American urban areas settled near other Slavs, Russians, or Germans. In Milwaukee, many Polish social, cultural, and fraternal organizations patterned themselves after earlier German ones, as with the Polish Falcons and the German Turners.[5]

Central to such patterns are religious institutions, which not only attract those of the same religion, but also those of a different ethnicity, at least until the latter build their own churches. Jay Dolan credits the immigrant Catholic parish for helping establish a sense of community: "As an educational organization, it taught both young and old the meaning of America, its language as well as its culture; as a religious organization, it brought the presence of God to the neighborhood, nurturing and sustaining the presence of the holy through worship, devotional services, and neighborhood processions." In more contemporary times, Korean churches in southern California were described as offering "not only spiritual comfort, but worldly advice on every topic from paying traffic tickets to finding a job or the best school. People could pray to God, find a mate, make business connections, and read about a young member's acceptance to Harvard in the Sunday bulletin." In Boston, churches, which number more than 500 and represent 110 denominations and 32 languages, aid new immigrants with housing, job-training, legal help, and English language instruction. Many immigrants have a sense of loss, said one religious leader, "and the church gives them an affirmation of culture and who they are and also provides love in the sense of helping with jobs and schools."[6]

Just as there has always been a plethora of local and national social and fraternal organizations among native-born Americans, so there has also been with minority groups. In Boston, in 1756, the first St. Andrew's Society was formed "to assist Scots and those of Scottish descent in distress and to provide for social intercourse among members." Likewise, in Philadelphia, in 1772, the Society of Sons of St. George was formed "for the Advance and Assistance of Englishmen in Distress." The first Chinese "tong" was formed in 1852 in California, because as one later member explained, "We are strangers in a strange country" and "must have an organization to control our country fellows and develop our friendship." The Bohemian-Slavonian Benevolent Organization was formed in 1854, the Uniao Portugueza do Estado da California in 1880, the Danish Brotherhood of America in 1881, the Hungarian Verhovay Fraternal Insurance Association in 1886, the Allianza Hispano Americana in 1894, and the Croatian Fraternal Union of America in 1894. The B'nai B'rith, organized in 1843, became so successful that Jews in other countries replicated it. To one degree or another, all such organizations provided, among other things, health benefits, burial sites, pensions, college scholarships—and, at times, served as centers for union organizing and the planning of labor strikes.[7]

In writing what the County Armagh Men's Association meant to him, one anonymous Irishman wrote:

A place where I can spend an evening for less than 50 cents

A little time that takes me back to fond memories of my birthplace

An organization with a human heart

A right to the free expression of my thoughts

A friendly debate and a view of the other fellows side

Warm friends who will give me a hand when I'm down

A tradition carried on by the Nugent's, McCooey's, Byrnes, Callaghan's, Kane's and McCoy's

A pride in the things that are best in men.[8]

In recalling his first days in New York City in 1891, Syrian immigrant Abraham Rihbany credited the Syrian colony there with providing him with a temporary home. "To me the colony was a habitat so much like the one I had left behind me in Syria that its home atmosphere enabled me to maintain a firm hold on life in the face of the many difficulties which confronted me in those days, and just different enough to awaken my curiosity to know more about the surrounding American influences."[9]

Chinatowns grew out of a variety of happy and unhappy circumstances. At first, in nineteenth-century California, Chinatown was the only area where Chinese could obtain inexpensive housing, as well as find sanctuary from attacks by white nativists. In subsequent decades, Chinatowns throughout the United States served as marketplaces, social gathering places, residences, places of employment, recreational, educational, and religious centers, industrial areas, and—unlike most other minority group neighborhoods—tourist attractions for non-Chinese. A similar evolution is occurring with Little Saigon in Westminster, California, which grew from having a handful of stores in the late 1970s to more than 1,600 businesses in 1994. Though relatively few Vietnamese actually live there, its shops, bakeries, and markets attract residents from throughout the state. "I don't come to buy things," said one elderly Vietnamese woman. "I come to see people, strangers mostly, who come . . . to do ordinary, everyday things, but in an environment where, because of the familiarity of faces and language, we never feel out of place."[10]

Wherever immigrants settle they create or subscribe to foreign-language publications that provide them with news about the old and new worlds. In Chicago, at least twenty Italian newspapers appeared between 1886 and 1921. Massachusetts had fifty-four ethnic newspapers in 1914, published in such languages as Albanian, Arabic, Armenian, French, German, Greek, Italian, Lettish, Lithuanian, Polish, Portuguese, Swedish, Syrian, and Yiddish. Between 1898 and 1929, Arab Americans had slightly more than 100 Arab language newspapers and periodicals. Like many other publications, Boston's Irish Catholic weekly *The Pilot* informed nineteenth-century readers of old-country births, deaths, and marriages, and its classified section was "a primitive missing persons bureau as newcomers fresh off the boat sought the whereabouts of fathers, sons, and brothers who had preceded them." The ethnic press also carried articles on American politics and history, especially when they involved successful group members. However, with the decline of foreign-language literacy by second- and third-generation immigrant offspring, many newspapers began publishing columns and pages in English, and then switching entirely to English. By the 1930s, 20 percent of the Eastern European immigrant press published an English page.[11]

However, the recent influx of large numbers of immigrants not only inspired the creation of new publications, it prompted older ones to resume publishing foreign-language sections and supplements, as with American Jewish papers adding Russian-language features. A few started reaching out to wider ethnic audiences, such as *East/West* no longer calling itself "A Chinese American Newspaper" and the Japanese-American *Pacific Citizen* reporting on other Asian countries.

Inadvertently helping the development of the ethnic press was the American press, which in prior decades did not report minority group events, unless they involved crime. Gino Speranzo, an Italian-American attorney, in 1904, actually credited the unfriendliness of the American press as the reason why Italians created their publications, which told "them what Italy is bravely doing at home and abroad." Similar views are sometimes still heard. At a 1993 meeting of the Minnesota Advisory Committee to the U.S. Commission on Civil Rights, several African, Asian, Indian, and Spanish-speaking Americans complained of adversarial and patronizing major media coverage, which "don't tell (minority) stories and when they do tell them, they get it wrong." [12]

Also, just as old-line white Protestants established patriotic historical societies to trace and celebrate their Anglo-Saxon roots in America (especially before, during, or right after the American Revolution), so it was with late nineteenth-century offspring of immigrants from other parts of Europe, Africa, and Asia, whom the former excluded from their histories, or, if included, were treated with disdain.[13] They formed hundreds of local and national groups, such as the Irish Ancestral Research Association, the Norwegian-American Historical Association, the Swedish Historical Society of Rockford, Illinois, the African American Museum in Cleveland, the Amana Heritage Society, the Cherokee National Historical Society, the Polish American Historical Association, and the Germans from Russia Heritage Society.

The role of immigrant women, other than as wives and housekeepers, was long neglected by historians, though they played major roles in the formation and maintenance of voluntary clubs and organizations, which were either affiliates of male groups or entirely independent of them. "When I was growing up, it seemed to me that, in my house at least, the

Syrian Ladies' Aid Society of Boston [formed in 1917] ranked in importance somewhere ahead of the church and only slightly behind the family itself" and served as "an island of familiarity in an alien world," wrote Evelyn Shakir. And so it was with other groups. The Finnish Woman's Cooperative Home was established in 1910 to help servant girls between jobs or immigrant girls adjust to their new country. The Slovenian Women's Alliance, organized in 1926, helped immigrant women obtain a "social, moral, and intellectual education." Some groups provided special services for women, such as the National Desertion Bureau, which aided Jewish women locate missing husbands, and the Central Japanese Association, which sent members to meet Japanese brides at San Francisco's docks when their grooms were sick or lived too far away to greet them.[14]

Although some organizations began as branches of those in the old country, they invariably assumed new functions and developed new kinds of leaders. Unlike in Italy or Ireland, wrote Dennis Clark, a Catholic church structure emerged in America without government aid: "The American Irish launched innovations on a large scale in building their independent parish schools, medical facilities, colleges, libraries, and financial systems . . . in a most American pattern of efficiency with committees of all kinds, reports, diocesan land banks, seminary recruiting drives, and missionary funds."[15]

New immigrants are also creating their own local and national organizations. Though relatively small in number (85,000 to 100,000), Copts from Egypt settling largely in New York and Los Angeles formed the Egyptian National Committee in 1972 and the American Coptic Association in the following year. Between 1975 and 1980, Indochinese refugees formed more than 260 associations, some primarily cultural, religious, professional, educational, political, fraternal, social, or recreational; many of these also had a specific ethnic base—195 being Vietnamese, 29 Cambodian, 19 Laotian, 5 H'Mong, 4 Chinese, and a few "Indochinese," whose members included Vietnamese, Cambodians and Laotians. In Los Angeles, the Korean Capital of America, Koreans in 1980 had over fifty high school and college alumni associations, some eighty churches, and more than fifty non-profit organizations. In 1993, there were some thirty Muslim women's social, philanthropic, and professional organizations (in contrast to about five groups ten years earlier).[16]

Past and present teenagers often form gangs based not only on ethnicity, race, sex, or geographical location, but also on motivation, ranging from the peaceful to the criminal. The number of street gangs and their members, particularly 12 to 25 year olds, has been increasing rapidly, so that by 1993 there were more than a 1,000 gangs whose total membership in 1993 exceeded half a million. As a Los Angeles gang leader said, "human nature wants to be accepted" and "all kids want to belong." A former gang member told an American Asian youth conference that gangs aren't necessarily all bad, because they enable young people to "feel they belonged and find the love and respect they craved." To others, being a gang member insures protection against attack. Among today's Navajo, Apache, and Sioux youngsters in Arizona, gangs exist similar to those in the large urban areas, replete with the wearing of baggy clothes and tattoos totally unrelated to Indian traditions. "It's about respect—respect and power," explained a 19-year-old Navajo. "People fear you." [17]

## ECONOMIC IMPROVEMENT

Group identification provides opportunities for economic stability and advancement, particularly for immigrants unfamiliar with the English language and American customs. Friends, relatives, and neighbors frequently help immigrants locate jobs and housing, act as translators, vouchsafe their honesty, and help those in need of temporary living quarters or small loans. "The only way you got a job," said one early twentieth-century immigrant, "was through somebody at work who got you in." Over 75 percent of Italian working girls in the 1920s credited getting their first jobs to help from friends or family. Such was also true of large numbers of Poles and Hungarians entering the coal mines of Pennsylvania, the Portuguese to Massachusetts fishing industries, French Canadians to New England textile mills, and Jews to New York City garment shops. Intragroup help is no less apparent today. In describing Asian Indian employees, a New York City official admired how they alert kinsmen of job openings, "network like crazy" and "look out for each other." The large number of Brazilian immigrants working in the resort hotels of Ellenville, New York, resulted from post–World War II immigrants telling family and friends back home of available jobs. [18]

Among small businessmen and professionals, start-up money or goods are more easily and inexpensively borrowed from family or friends than from regular banks or suppliers, which until recent decades usually ignored them. As with prior immigrant generations, entire families sometimes work and live in crowded quarters today. Long working hours are common, as exemplified by Korean grocers in New York City who, in 1988, were found to work sixteen to eighteen hours per day. In areas where group and nongroup businesses compete, such as furniture stores, groceries, and haberdasheries, community leaders and ethnic publications usually urge consumers to patronize the establishments of their own kinfolk, who are also more culturally equipped to meet a group's special needs, especially in burial services, restaurants, grocery stores, and the sale of religious objects. For example, some recent Salvadoran immigrants in Hempstead, Long Island, took to selling goods and services at much lower prices than were available elsewhere—or used their residences as unlicensed restaurants, pharmacies, lodgings, or medical offices. "For me, what was important was price," said one Salvadoran patient about going to an unlicensed dentist. "He's a good, honest man who would help any time. When I had a toothache late at night, he told me to come over right away and he gave me medicine for my pain. He also speaks my language." [19]

Similar developments prevailed in earlier Irish and Eastern European saloons at the turn of the century, where simple drinks, soup, and cold cuts were served by the proprietor or a member of his family. For many Greek, Italian, Armenian, Jewish, and Syrian immigrants, peddling was a relatively fast way of earning a living, since it required little or no language skills, funds, or technical training, but rather friends or relatives willing to provide merchandise on credit and directions on where to start selling it.[20]

Not all such entrepreneurialism was "made in America." Historian John Bodnar believes that nearly all turn-of-the-century immigrant business operators arrived with some prior experience, and the greater it was, the more likely it was utilized. The same was seen with other skills, as in the case of early twentieth-century Jews, two-thirds of whom were skilled workers, especially in tailoring. Other scholars credit some groups with possessing certain social and work characteristics that they display no matter where they live, such as a readiness to work long hours, save money, and be reliable and clannish. Conversely, the lack, or comparative lack, of entrepreneuralism and skills in some groups is due either to historic conditions in their ancestral homeland, the American economy at the time of their arrival, or the institutionalized bigotry they confronted. Ronald Takaki notes that the Spanish administrators in the Philippines did not develop a native capitalist economy, but rather allowed Chinese merchants to service the local populace; consequently, when Filipinos first came to America they found "the Chinese and Japanese already established, with footholds in the retail trade that accommodated the needs of the Filipino newcomers and that preempted the entry of Filipino retailers." Until recent decades, African American small businesses confronted a host of discriminatory societal problems, as well as internal group difficulties, in borrowing money from banks, family, or the community.[21]

Similar patterns are evident among recent immigrant groups, some of which are highly entrepreneurial—or are more so than other immigrant groups or native-born Americans. In Miami, about 20,000 Spanish-speaking enterprises existed in 1980, ranging from small stores and restaurants to construction companies and auto dealers. Immigrants from India, Pakistan, and Bangladesh succeeded Jews and Italians in New York City as newsstand workers, managers, and owners; and in 1985 controlled more than 1,000 newsstands and greeting card shops in Manhattan and Queens. In Detroit and San Francisco, many Palestinians opened small convenience stores. According to 1990 census figures, while 6.8 percent of immigrant workers are self-employed compared to 7 percent of native workers, the percentages varied greatly for specific groups: 18 percent for Koreans, 15 percent for Greeks, 6 percent for Vietnamese, and 5 percent for Mexicans. Professor Julian Simon, of the University of Maryland, claims that contemporary immigrants participate at a higher rate in the labor force than resident Americans, tend to save more money, apply more effort at work, have a higher propensity to start new businesses, and to be self-employed.[22]

Unfortunately, being a member of a minority group also facilitates illegal economic success, particularly by criminal gangs and syndicates, which usually exclude outsiders, exploit same-group members, and compete with other gangs for territory and influence. To Police Commissioner Theodore Bingham, in 1907, New York City attracted the "predatory criminals of all nations, as well as the feuds of the Armenian Hunchakists, the Neapolitan Camorra, the Sicilian Mafia, the Chinese Tongs, and other quarrels of the scum of the earth." During the Prohibition years (and for some years afterward), Irish, Italian, and Jewish criminal gangs grew in sophistication and ruthlessness. Less extreme, but no less greedy, were immigrant labor contractors and businessmen who exploited newly arrived kinfolk, as happened, for example, among Jews, Italians, Austrians, Bulgarians, and Mexicans in clothing factories, construction sites, lumber camps, and farms. Greek recruiters brought over youngsters to become bootblacks who were then compelled to live together, work long hours, and not learn English in school, lest they discover how shabbily they were being treated.[23]

Recent ethnic and racial criminal gangs are just as competitive, brutal, or exploitative of innocent group members as those in the past. For example, in New York City, American-born and Hong Kong–born Chinese feud with and prey on Chinese merchants. Bloody gang warfare has also erupted between Chinese and Vietnamese, and between Chinese and Koreans. In Los Angeles, Mexican and African-American gangs in and out of prison periodically fight over control of street narcotic sales.[24]

Some immigrants simply transplant their criminal activities here or come as temporary representatives of international syndicates. With the help of Russian nationals and emigres in America, criminal gangs in Russia laundered their earnings through American financial institutions, prompting the FBI in 1994 to open an office in Moscow to work with Russian law enforcement officials. A few years ago, some two dozen Armenians, many of whom were Lebanese and Syrian nationals, were charged with being part of an international drug network.[25]

Various groups specialize in different crimes, though not exclusively so. Drug smuggling in Miami is mostly controlled by rival gangs of Cuban and Colombian "cocaine cowboys." In Los Angeles, extortion, insurance fraud, and the narcotics trade are carried on by a gang of Israeli ex-convicts and former army commandos. On the East Coast, Albanian criminal gangs, with some Croat and Serb members, specialize in sophisticated burglaries of jewelry stores, supermarkets, bank automatic teller machines, and other retail outlets. A *New York Times* investigation in 1993 of immigrant life in New York City found that prostitution attracted poor South American and Korean women; cocaine street dealing, Dominicans; smuggling, Nigerians; smuggling illegal immigrants and running gambling houses, Chinese; fraudulent oil distribution schemes and tax avoidance, Russians.[26]

Also at work are minority businessmen who hire immigrants, including illegal ones, and either underpay them, don't pay them, or delay their payment. Many of the estimated 2,000 sweatshops throughout New York City in the 1990s were owned by Chinese and Korean immigrants, who like their early twentieth-century European predecessors have no qualms about exploiting fellow immigrants. These exploited workers, reported the *New York Times,* "do not speak English, possess little education and few skills, and do not understand their considerable rights as underground workers." Similar abuses occur in California, where in 1995 nine Thai nationals were indicted for holding seventy-two immigrants, mostly fellow Thais, in virtual slavery as workers in a garment factory surrounded by razor wire. On both coasts Asian men have smuggled women from their respective countries to become—or to continue being—prostitutes, especially from Hong Kong, Taiwan, Korea, and most recently Thailand.[27]

As in regular commerce, some criminal groups cooperate with each other, like Japanese "yakuza" criminals and Italian-American "Cosa Nostra" members in gambling clubs in New York, drug traffic in Hawaii, and California real estate deals. In 1994, the president of the League of United Latin American Citizens and three Taiwanese men were indicted for operating a multimillion dollar immigration fraud business, in which large fees were charged for helping wealthy Asians file false citizenship eligibility claims. Criminal connections are also said to exist between Russians, Colombians, and Sicilians; Chinese and Taiwanese; Chinese, Burmese, and Thais; Burmese, Chinese, and Nigerians; and Puerto Ricans and African Americans.[28]

In short, like birds, people flock together, though often for more reasons than similarity of feathers. Doing so helps advance their socioeconomic status, especially the more entrepreneurially oriented, whether the businesses be legal or illegal.

## COMBATING BIGOTRY

Group identification serves as a refuge from bigotry and/or a basis from which to combat it, particularly for those living in areas where they are in the minority. By forming or joining a social, fraternal, or business organization—or even a gang—individuals develop a sense of security, power, and retaliation not otherwise available. In their own organizations, they are spared the pain or possibility of rejection by outsiders, and are insulated from being confused with other minority groups, which may be more stigmatized than theirs.

For example, by creating their own burial society, early twentieth-century Lebanese immigrants in Birmingham, Alabama, avoided the "possible exclusion of their dead from 'white only' city cemeteries." By sending their children to parochial schools, they shielded them from the pervasive racial segregation of the time. "Only unity can save the Serbs" is a historic slogan of Serbian Orthodox church members. In response to Christian missionizing and criticism, the editor of the first American Jewish newspaper, *The Jew,* in 1823, declared, "not to defend Judaism, would be considered a tacit acknowledgment that it was indefensible, or at least that we thought so. Not to defend our character as a people, as Jews, by repelling detraction, would be a dereliction of duty, and might be considered as a proof either that we had not a character worth defending, or that we despised the good opinion of our fellow citizens, and of the world. . . ." In planning the first Armenian Orthodox church in Worcester, Massachusetts, in the late nineteenth century, its trustees resolved: "Whereas the Armenian people, by reason of persecution and abject poverty, are immigrating to America, in order to preserve these immigrants from being alienated, we hereby decide to build a church."[29]

Being alone or few in number in a majority setting means feeling, if not being, vulnerable to ridicule and oppression. This is particularly true of racial minorities, non-English speaking ethnic immigrants, and generally those from lands where they were in the majority. For example, in recent years, some African Americans began abandoning social, educational, and residential goals for alternative goals of separation. Such people seek "comfortable places to breathe and be themselves," said David Dent, a New York University professor of history. "They're saying to themselves: 'I'm not going to set myself up in a hostile world for the sake of integration. . . .'" In the case of Peter John-Baptiste, a 1993 freshman at the University of Massachusetts, he felt disturbed at being the only black in many classes, "especially coming from St. Croix, where I never was a minority."[30]

To one degree or another most minority groups establish self-defense committees and organizations. In the early twentieth century, Jews created the American Jewish Committee and the Anti-Defamation League of B'nai B'rith, Italians the Sons of Italy, blacks the Urban League and the National Association for the Advancement of Colored People, and Greeks the American Hellenic Educational Progressive Association. The Catholic League for Religious and Civil Rights was formed in 1973, whose goals include combating defamation of Catholics and Catholicism, ending employment and university discrimination, and stopping abortion and pornography. In 1990, the Reverend Pat Robertson founded the Christian

Anti-Discrimination Committee to combat defamation and discrimination against Christians, whether in television, print, or public meetings.

Self-protective group measures have also taken place in many labor unions, professions, political parties, and schools. On a city level, street gangs protect members and their turf, as well as revenge wrongs done to members. In explaining the clashes in 1994 with African Americans in Palm Springs, California, a Mexican-American former gang member noted that when his group's population was small, "the black guys were hitting South of the Border kids, punching them and stuff for no reason. Now the numbers of Mexicans have gotten big and the paybacks are coming in." At a middle school, Asian and Latino youngsters joined separate gangs to insure protection from one other. As one school counselor explained: "The Asian kids are after the Latino kids and vice versa and they get fed up with getting bullied so they have their older friends come over to retaliate." [31]

In prisons, too, group-specific defense associations exist. Some years ago, the Islamic chaplain for the Washington, D.C. Department of Corrections stated that inmates often joined the Islamic Brotherhood for "protection from assaults and sexual abuse. . . . If you fight one Muslim, you have to fight them all." In Massachusetts, Hispanic prisoners formed Latino Unity because they felt they were being treated like second-class citizens by other inmates and prison personnel: "Nobody fights for the Latinos. We want to be heard by somebody." Police personnel have long had ethnic, racial, and religious subgroups, including the Association of White Male Peace Officers, in Los Angeles, which opposes prejudice or preferential treatment based on "race, creed, color, gender, ethnicity, sexual orientation or national origin." [32] Trite, but true. In unity there is always strength—or, at the very least, less weakness than in division.

## GAINING RESPECT AND POWER

Being a member of a minority group provides a psychological, moral, and, especially since the civil rights movement, a legal and even opportunistic basis for gaining recognition, entrance, and power on many levels of society. When prior generations of immigrants first arrived, they were at best tolerated, and when they became citizens, wooed for their votes by the dominant political machines of the day, which often served as a quasi-welfare system in helping them obtain jobs, get emergency funds for rent or heat, and become naturalized. African Americans, who had preceded most other minorities in coming to America, were long denied similar opportunities, protections, and resources.

Numbers, particularly at the ballot box, are crucial to a group's socio-economic and political well-being. Simply put, the more votes a group can cast, the more attention and patronage it receives; and the more members it elects, the more political power and role models it has. As one early twentieth-century politician told an audience of fellow Catholics, "Our preparation is education, our strength lies in our unity; our battleground the ballot box."[33] Like the Irish on the East Coast, Scandinavians in the Midwest began electing their own kinsmen, with Knute Nelson, in 1882, becoming the first Norwegian Senator in Minnesota. Except for the Reconstruction period, African Americans were overwhelmingly denied the right to vote until the 1960s when they began electing black mayors, as in Newark, Atlanta, Chicago, and Detroit. To a lesser extent, Chinese and Japanese began achieving political victories and appointments where they were numerically dominant or significant, as in Hawaii and California.

In areas where no one group had sufficient numbers to win an election, but enough to influence who would, political coalitions and "balanced tickets" were organized, in which the top offices were earmarked for representatives of the major groups. At the same time, throughout most of the first half of the twentieth century, reforms in civil service employment sought to eliminate political corruption and patronage, particularly in entry-level positions. Applicants were required to pass objective tests and possess a set number of years of schooling, with the understanding that the highest scorers and most qualified would be the first hired.

With the rise of group pride and rights, the politicization of ethnicity as well as the ethnicization of politics intensified. Group identity in and of itself became a legally validated political asset, if not requirement, for position and benefits, especially for minorities that had experienced or were still experiencing discrimination. The goal was no longer equal opportunity, but specific group entitlement, proportionate to their population numbers. A first step required gaining—or maintaining—governmental recognition as a minority group. Thus, in congressional hearings on how the Census of 2000 should classify people, the National Coalition for an Accurate Count of Asian Pacific Americans wanted Cambodian and Laotian added to the list of choices, the National Council of La Raza wanted Hispanics listed a race, the Arab American Institute wanted Arabs to be counted as a separate category and not as whites. In contrast, many black organizations have taken to opposing any modification in census terminology to include biracial or multiracial, which they fear would lower the national African-American population percentage and therefore their number of affirmative action preferences.[34]

Politicians who in the pre-civil rights movement decades avoided discussing their personal racial or ethnic roots now freely affirm them, not merely to win votes, but also to attract campaign contributions from likeminded or like-descended people throughout the country. Some, however, brazenly exploit existing prejudice against or within their own group. For example, in the 1994 mayoral election in New Orleans, a white Jewish candidate, Donald Mintz, admitted sending potential Jewish contributors across the country copies of anti-Semitic fliers attacking him, which his critics claimed he or his staff deliberately manufactured in order to muster sympathy. In areas with heavy concentrations of a specific minority, many candidates claim that no outsider could represent them as effectively as they could.[35]

Also, like other groups of Americans, minority groups form their own political, professional, or community action associations, networks, and coalitions. For example, the National Association of Latino Elected Officials (NALEO) was founded in 1975; a year later, five of the six Hispanic-American Congressmen formed the Congressional Hispanic Caucus, which by 1993 had grown to nineteen members. At times, differing Hispanic groups work together for common goals. In 1995, the first Latino Community Leadership Conference in Massachusetts took place, calling for "Unidad, Camino al Poder—Unity, the Road to Power." New immigrants are also organizing, as in Brooklyn, New York, where Muslim residents— primarily from Yemen, Iran, Turkey, and Bangladesh—succeeded in petitioning the city to block off traffic in front of their mosques during major festivals, as well as to inform school officials about the origin and customs of Ramadan.[36]

Psychologically, politically, and socially, what was once a stigma or burden is now a source of pride and comfort. As Phoebe Eng, the Chinese-American editor of A. *Magazine,* said, with the rise of multiculturalism, "if you don't have something to separate you as a distinguishing characteristic, like your racial background, then you're almost left out in the cold in the '90's." [37]

## FOSTERING ACCULTURATION

Group identification facilitates acculturation. By settling among or intermarrying with people who speak the same language and practice the same customs, people gain a pragmatic knowledge of how to adjust to the new society about them. Among kindred folk, they learn without embarrassment what being an American is all about. Their group institutions function as educational devices, enabling them to feel secure about the compatibility of their ancestral heritage and the principles of their adopted country. For example, to some recent Jamaican immigrants in New York City, joining a cricket club that has other West Indian members allows them to continue a sporting tradition they grew up with, and as one player said: "Coming to the park and playing cricket with other West Indians helped me adjust to life in this country. It made me feel more at home." [38]

Even the retention of a foreign language does not necessarily impede acculturation, but can actually help, particularly for adults unable to master English but who want to learn more about their new home. If they are literate in their ancestral tongue, they can read about and discuss what is happening in the larger society and back home. In much the same manner that bilingual education is defended today, so many nineteenth- and early twentieth-century ethnic leaders argued that by using native languages, English was learned all the faster. To Charles Reemelin, a prominent German-American journalist and politician in the early nineteenth century, linguistic pluralism aided the commitment of immigrants to democratic ideals and therefore merited state support of German instruction in the public schools and the printing of important state documents in German.[39]

Acculturation also results from what Yusuf Dadabhay terms "circuitous assimilation," wherein, for example, Punjabi men in northern California in the 1950s entered the dominant society by working with, living alongside, and marrying Mexican Americans, who were less prejudiced against them than the Anglos.[40] Such, of course, is true of many immigrant group members who settle among different groups or convert to their faith, and then adopt their Americanized ways and values.

## SELF-FULFILLMENT

Lastly, group identification represents a way of fulfilling and validating one's historical, social, and psychological identity. Since the dawn of history, wrote Carlton Hayes, a mark of nature has been for human beings to possess some consciousness of nationality and "some feeling that linguistic, historical and cultural peculiarities of a group make its member akin among themselves and alien from all other groups." Thus exist memories, loyalties, contributions, political support, trips to the homeland, language retention, and endogamy.[41]

As noted earlier, when among their own kind, whether racially, religiously or ethnically, people feel emotionally secure and socially acceptable. It is the common "ground" upon which they stand, wrote social psychologist Kurt Lewin, providing or denying them social status and security. The firmness of their actions and the clarity of their decisions depend "largely upon the stability of this 'ground.' . . . Whatever a person does or wishes to do, he must have some 'ground' to stand upon."[42]

Researchers also point out that instead of handicapping people, the maintenance of group identity strengthens their mental health by providing a sense of historical continuity and self-pride. Just as good fences can make good neighbors, so group separation and social distancing can create secure egos. Even the once ridiculed ethnic family is today applauded, if not envied, as a transmitter of benign values and customs, as well as a possible deterrent to asocial behavior. Also, some second and third generation European immigrant offspring are reaffirming their ancestral roots and no longer changing their names in order to appear American or to succeed socioeconomically, with a few even readopting the names their parents abandoned.

As never before, African Americans are also studying their past in America and Africa, and instead of feeling shame about their historic enslavement, they are confronting it, with some terming it "the black Holocaust" or the "maafa," the Swahili word for "unspeakable horror." Velma Maia Thomas, a black curator, called it a healing process: "Every group of people is allowed to remember the past and pay homage to those who have come before them. Why shouldn't we? It's that whole ritual of memory and honor. That's part of being human." Other blacks—both nationalists and intellectuals—assert pride in being part of a group that challenges, if not rejects, the belief that all-black schools are necessarily inferior, and that blacks cannot succeed without the benefit of white presence.[43]

Whatever the group, more and more young minority people are demanding and enrolling in courses in order to better understand themselves and their history. As Sarah Chee, a 1993 college undergraduate wrote, because of her contact with Asian American Studies at the University of California, Los Angeles, "I realized that all Asian Americans are not rich or great at math. I realized that I needed to stop hating myself because I did not have blond hair and blue eyes. I realized that the prejudices I have toward others were neither justified nor inherent, but taught to me by society. . . . Most importantly, I began for the first time to feel proud about my family and the struggles we had to overcome."[44]

In spite of all the above advantages in belonging to a group, there are also disadvantages, which will now be explored.

## NOTES

1. Robert T. Handy, *A Christian America* (New York: Oxford University Press, 1984), 39; Michael McGiffert, *The Character of Americans* (Homewood, Ill.: Dorsey Press, 1968), 45–46.

2. Stuart Langston, "The New Voluntarism," *Journal of Voluntary Action Research* 10 (January 1981): 7; *Christian Science Monitor,* 5 December 1988, 7; Gustav Niebuhr, "Pious in Public and Proud of It," *New York Times,* 4 December 1994, 6E; Jonathan Rauch, "The Hyperpluralism Trap," *The New Republic,* 6 June 1994, 22.

3. *Rudyard Kipling's Verse* (Garden City, N.Y.: Doubleday, Page & Company, 1920), 616.

4. Charles H. Anderson, *White Protestant Americans* (Englewood Cliffs, N.J.: Prentice Hall, 1970), 52; Frank C. Nelson, "Norwegian-American Attitudes Toward Assimilation During Four Periods of Their History in America," *Journal of Ethnic Studies* 9 (Spring 1981): 61; Ron Rothbart, "The Ethnic Saloon as a Form of Immigrant Enterprise," *International Migration Review* (Summer 1993): 341; Ashley Dunn, "Starting Over Without Fear," *New York Times,* 16 January 1995, B1, 4.

5. Howard F. Stein and Robert F. Hill, *The Ethnic Imperative* (University Park: Pennsylvania State University Press, 1977), 27; Thomas Capek, *The Cechs (Bohe-*

*mians) in America* (Westport, Connecticut: Greenwood Press, 1970), 112; Theresita Polzin, *The Polish Americans* (Pulaski, Wis.: Franciscan Publishers, 1972), 97; Dorota Praszalowicz, "The Cultural Changes of Polish-American Parochial Schools in Milwaukee, 1866–1988," *Journal of American Ethnic History* (Summer 1994): 25.

6. Jay P. Dolan, *The American Catholic Experience* (Garden City, N.Y.: Doubleday & Company, 1985), 204; Doreen Carvajal, "Trying to Halt 'Silent Exodus,'" *Los Angeles Times*, 9 May 1994, A16; Diego Ribadeneira, "Immigrants Find Ally in City's Churches," *Boston Globe*, 6 August 1995, 1, 31.

7. Kathleen Teltsch, "Women and St. Andrews: Old Society's New Issue," *New York Times*, 27 May 1993, B3; Stephan Thernstrom, *Harvard Encyclopedia of American Ethnic Groups* (Cambridge: Harvard University Press, 1980), 323, 915; Ronald Takaki, *Strangers From a Different Shore* (New York: Penguin Books, 1989), 118; Stanley Aronowitz, *False Promises* (New York: McGraw-Hill Book Company, 1973), 152.

8. Edward Wakin, *Enter the Irish-American* (New York: Thomas Y. Crowell, 1976), 149.

9. Abraham M. Rihbany, "A Far Journey, 1913," in *Sources of the American Social Tradition*, ed. David J. Rothman and Sheila Rothman (New York: Basic Books, 1975), 359.

10. Stan Steiner, *Fusang: The Chinese Who Built America* (New York: Harper Colophon Books, 1979), 195–96; Betty Lee Sung, *Transplanted Chinese Children* (New York: City College of New York, 1979), 30; Lily Dizon, "Little Saigon Is Big in Hearts of Vietnamese," *Los Angeles Times*, 14 June 1994, A3.

11. Humbert S. Nelli, *Italians in Chicago, 1880–1930* (New York: Oxford University Press, 1970), 158; Stanley Feldstein and Lawrence Costello, *The Ordeal of Assimilation* (Garden City, N.Y.: Anchor Press, 1974), 103; Raouf J. Halaby, "Dr. Shadid and the Debate over Identity in the *Syrian World*," in *Crossing the Waters: Arabic-Speaking Immigrants to the United States before 1940*, ed. Eric J. Hooglund (Washington, D.C.: Smithsonian Institution Press, 1987), 56; *New York Times*, 24 April 1994, 21; Francis R. Walsh "From 'The Jesuit' to 'The Pilot,'" *The Pilot*, 1829–1979 150, no. 38 (1979): 35; Kathleen Neils Conzen et al., "The Invention of Ethnicity: A Perspective from the U.S.A.," *Journal of American Ethnic History* (Fall 1992): 25; Yen Le Espiritu, *Asian American Panethnicity* (Philadelphia: Temple University Press, 1992), 41.

12. Thomas Monroe Pitkin and Francesco Cordasco, *The Black Hand* (Totowa, N.J.: Rowman and Littlefield, 1977), 43; *Civil Rights Update*, U.S. Commission on Civil Rights, September/October 1992, 4.

13. Wesley Frank Craven, *The Legend of the Founding Fathers* (Westport, Conn.: Greenwood Press, 1983), 158.

14. Evelyn Shakir, "Good Works, Good Times," in *Crossing the Waters: Arabic-Speaking Immigrants to the United States before 1940*, ed. Eric J. Hooglund (Washington, D.C.: Smithsonian Institution Press, 1987), 133; Maxine Schwartz Seller, *Immigrant Women* (Philadelphia: Temple University Press, 1981), 158–60.

15. Dennis J. Clark, "The Irish Catholics," in *Immigrants and Religion in Urban America*, ed. Randall M. Miller and Thomas D. Marzik (Philadelphia: Temple University Press, 1977), 56.

16. Thernstrom, *Harvard Encyclopedia of American Ethnic Groups*, 242–43,

604; Diana Bui, "The Indochinese Mutual Assistance Associations," in *Bridging Cultures: Southeast Asian Refugees in America* (Los Angeles: Asian American Community Mental Health Training Center, 1981), 167–92; *New York Times,* 8 November 1993, B9.

17. Ann Scott Tyson, "Combatting the Allure of Gangs," *Christian Science Monitor,* 13 November 1995, 1, 14; Hugh B. Price, "Making Our Multicultural Society Work," *Journal of Intergroup Relations* (Winter 1994–95): 61; Gloria Negri, "Conference Targets Asian Stereotypes," *Boston Globe,* 17 March 1995, 24; Seth Mydans, "Gangs Reach a New Frontier: Reservations," *New York Times,* 18 March 1995, 1.

18. John Bodnar, *The Transplanted* (Bloomington: Indiana University Press, 1987), 61–62; William M. Leiserson, *Adjusting Immigrant and Industry* (New York: Harper & Brothers, 1924), 31; Roger Waldinger, "The Making of an Immigrant Niche," *International Migration Review* (Spring 1994): 22; "Beans and Rice in the Borscht Belt," *New York Times,* 21 October 1995, 23.

19. Ivan H. Light, *Ethnic Enterprise in America* (Berkeley: University of California Press, 1972), 12; *Washington Post,* 7 September 1988, A22; Doreen Carvajal, "Making Ends Meet in a Nether World," *New York Times,* 13 December 1994, B1.

20. Rothbart, "The Ethnic Saloon as a Form of Immigrant Enterprise," 341.

21. Bodnar, *The Transplanted,* 131; Thomas Sowell, *Race and Culture* (New York: Basic Books, 1994), 46–47; Takaki, *Strangers From a Different Shore,* 336.

22. George J. Borjas, "Nine Immigration Myths—Know The Flow," *National Review,* 17 April 1995, 49; Raymond A. Mohl, "An Ethnic 'Boiling Pot': Cubans and Haitians in Miami," *Journal of Ethnic Studies* (Summer 1985): 57; *New York Times,* 3 January 1986, B2; Joel Kotkin, *Tribes* (New York: Random House, 1992), 236; "The Impact of Immigrants on the U.S.: Shattering the Myths" (Washington, D.C.: National Immigration, Refugee and Citizenship Forum, undated report), 2.

23. Pitkin and Cordasco, *The Black Hand,* 90; Feldstein and Costello, *The Ordeal of Assimilation,* 300–305; Leonard Dinnerstein and David M. Reimers, *Ethnic Americans: A History of Immigration and Assimilation* (New York: Dodd, Mead & Company, 1975), 45; Theodore Saloutos, *The Greeks in the United States* (Cambridge: Harvard University Press, 1964), 48; Henry Pratt Fairchild, *Greek Immigration to the United States* (New Haven: Yale University Press, 1911), 172–73.

24. *New York Times,* 1 December 1976, B14; Donatella Lorch, "3 Are Found Slain Execution Style Near City Hall," *New York Times,* 16 October 1994, B1; George James, "33 Suspected Chinatown Gang Members Are Indicted," *New York Times,* 22 November 1994, B1; Jesse Katz, "Clashes Between Latino, Black Gangs Increase," *Los Angeles Times,* 26 December 1993, A38; Seth Mydans, "Racial Tensions in Los Angeles Jails Ignite Inmate Violence," *New York Times,* 6 February 1995, A13.

25. "Russia's Notorious Mafia Spreads Tentacles of Crime Around the Globe," *Christian Science Monitor,* 11 January 1995, 1, 6; *Armenian Weekly,* 4 March 1989, 3.

26. Mohl, "An Ethnic 'Boiling Pot': Cubans and Haitians in Miami," 57; *Newsweek,* 5 January 1981, 40; *Time,* 11 November 1984, 30; *Washington Post,* 25

October 1984, A19; Matthew Purdy, "Police Say Albanian Gangs Are Making Burglary an Art," *New York Times,* 17 December 1994, 1; Ian Fisher, "A Window on Immigrant Crime," *New York Times,* 17 June 1993, B1.

27. Alan Finder, "Despite Tough Laws, Sweatshops Flourish," *New York Times,* 6 February 1995, B4; Deborah Sontag, "Emigres Battling Abuse Flex Rights as Workers," *New York Times,* 15 June 1993, A1, B8; Kenneth B. Noble, "Thai Workers Held Captive, Officials Say," *New York Times,* 4 August 1995, A1; "9 Charged in LA Sweatshop Case," *Boston Globe,* 18 August 1995, 6; Carey Goldberg, "Sex Slavery, Thailand to New York," *New York Times,* 11 September 1995, B1.

28. *Boston Globe,* "Japanese Gangs Invade US," 6 February 1994; *New York Times,* 7 April 1994, A17; "Russia's Notorious Mafia Spreads Tentacles of Crime Around the Globe," *Christian Science Monitor,* 6; Charles A. Radin, "Burma Heroin Finds Chinese Path to West," *Boston Globe,* 12 January 1995, 1, 4; Peter Kerr, "Chinese Now Dominate New York Heroin Trade," *New York Times,* 9 August 1987, 1, 30; Steven Greenhouse, "Burmese Lead in Heroin Supply and U.S. Tries to Respond," *New York Times,* 12 February 1995, 5.

29. Conklin and Faires, " 'Colored' and Catholic—The Lebanese in Birmingham, Alabama," in *Crossing the Waters,* 80; John Kifner, "Through the Serbian Mind's Eye," *New York Times,* 10 April 1994, 4; Morris U. Schappes, *A Documentary History of the Jews in the United States* (New York: Schocken Books, 1971), 164–66; Robert Mirak, "The Armenian Orthodox and Armenian Protestant Churches in the New World to 1915," in *Immigrants and Religion in Urban America,* ed. Randall Miller and Thomas D. Marzik (Philadelphia: Temple University Press, 1977), 141–42.

30. Sam Fulwood III, "Black Attitudes Shift Away From Goal of Inclusion," *Los Angeles Times,* 30 October 1995, A1, A16; Alice Dembner and Cate Chant, "Progress on UMass Race Relations is Fragile," *Boston Globe,* 2 October 1993, 8.

31. Seth Mydans, "Desert Playground for Rich Is Turf for Racial Gang War," *New York Times,* 18 March 1994, A16; Denise Hamilton, "Principal Calls Meeting to Fight Racial Tension," *Los Angeles Times,* 8 December 1994, 3.

32. *Washington Post,* 27 February 1978; Jennifer McKim, "Hispanic Inmates Form Rights Group," *Boston Globe,* 26 March 1995, 33; *New York Times,* 19 November 1995, 36.

33. Richard Krickus, *Pursuing the American Dream* (Garden City, N.Y.: Anchor Books, 1976), 167; Lynn Dumenil, "The Tribal Twenties: 'Assimilated' Catholics' Response to Anti-Catholicism in the 1920s," *Journal of American Ethnic History* (Fall 1991): 37.

34. Lawrence Wright, "One Drop of Blood," *The New Yorker,* 25 July 1994, 47; Michael K. Frisby, "Multiracial Debate," *Emerge* (December/January 1996): 48–54.

35. Ronald Smothers, "Ex-Mayor's Son Wins Election in New Orleans," *New York Times,* 7 March 1994, A10.

36. Manny Lopez, "Seeking Political Strength, Hispanics Gather for Unity," *Boston Globe,* 18 June 1995, 28; Randy Kennedy, "Jews and Muslims are Sharing Borough Park," *New York Times,* 17 August 1995, A1.

37. Felicia R. Lee, "Conversations/Phoebe Eng," *New York Times,* 10 October 1993, E7.

38. Victor R. Greene, *American Immigrant Leaders, 1800–1910* (Baltimore: Johns Hopkins University Press, 1987), 16; *New York Times,* 11 July 1983, B1.

39. Greene, *American Immigrant Leaders, 1800–1910,* 50.

40. Karen Leonard, "Historical Constructions of Ethnicity: Research on Punjabi Immigrants in California," *Journal of American Ethnic History* (Summer 1993): 10.

41. Harold R. Isaacs, *Idols of the Tribe* (New York: Harper & Row, 1975), 172.

42. Kurt Lewin, *Resolving Social Conflict* (New York: Harper & Row, 1948), 145.

43. Charisse Jones, "Bringing Slavery's Long Shadow to the Light," *New York Times,* 2 April 1995, 1, 43.

44. Sarah Chee, "Why I Got Arrested for Chicana/o Studies," *Crosscurrents, Newsmagazine of the UCLA Asian American Studies Center* (Fall/Winter 1993): 2.

# 8

# Disadvantages of Group Identity

Those whose narcissism refers to their group . . . react with rage to any wound, real or imaginary, inflicted upon their group. . . . One's own group becomes a defender of human dignity, decency, morality, and right. Devilish qualities are ascribed to the other group; it is treacherous, ruthless, cruel, and basically inhuman. The violation of one of the symbols of group narcissism—such as the flag, or the person of the emperor, the president, or an ambassador—is reacted to with such intense fury and aggression by the people that they are even willing to support their leaders in a policy of war.

—Erich Fromm,
*Anatomy of Human Destructiveness*

In spite of the many benefits of group identification, there are disadvantages to individuals, groups, and society at large, depending on who is being identified and who is doing the identifying, as well as when and where it is taking place. In life, rather than logic, contradictions are many, so that while being a member of a minority group provides a sense of strength, it also makes one vulnerable to bigotry. And almost always, it means not having the political power of a majority in determining the group's present and future situation.

At one time or another all American minority groups were victimized, though to differing degrees, forms, and durations. For example, if being dispossessed of one's home and then subsequently murdered are the worst things that can befall human beings, then certainly the native American Indians were the most victimized of all groups, followed by blacks, who, as noted previously, were the only group brought here against their will and enslaved for the rest of their lives. Mexicans throughout the Southwest became strangers in their own land, as did native Hawaiians, both of whose lands were taken by deceit and conquest. Alaskan natives were not asked by their Russian rulers if they wanted their land sold to Americans, who, in turn, had no concern for their wishes either. Asians, particularly Chinese and Japanese, were the most unwanted ethnoracial group, opposed by both native-born Americans and by European immigrants, and when not completely barred from immigrating to the United States were victimized by state and local laws and officials.

Catholics were the most and longest hated religious group in America until they began outnumbering and outvoting their neighboring Protestant oppressors. Mormons were the next most persecuted religious group, forced to flee from state to state until they settled in Utah. Anti-Semitism, the oldest form of religious intolerance, was transplanted from Europe, and readily practiced by Catholics and Protestants alike. At their worst, however, Protestant-Catholic-Jewish relations were never as bad or as bloody as they were in Europe, where, when Protestants and Catholics weren't killing one other, they fell upon the Jews, and, with the dawning of the age of exploration and expansion, they began to oppress or convert all non-Christian believers in various parts of the world.

Just as all minority groups did not suffer equally, so it was with all members within a particular group. Much depended on where they lived, their socioeconomic standing, and their aspirations for their offspring. African Americans in the South and Asians in the West suffered from a broader and longer range of bigoted actions than their counterparts in the North and East. Also, within each minority group, those who were somewhat successful socioeconomically were better able to shield themselves from the harsh realities of bigotry by creating their own social and fraternal organizations, and/or by becoming more involved in the larger society and its problems.

It is against the above background that the disadvantages of group identity will now be examined. Here, too, as in the case of the benefits of group identity, the disadvantages are often multidimensional, overlapping, and reciprocally reinforcing. They may be characterized as creating an invitation to societal criticism, causing intergroup envy and conflict, encouraging discrimination against other groups, becoming vulnerable to exploitation, generating insecurity and foreboding, contributing to self-hatred, and prompting the reestablishment of invidious social preferences.

## INVITATION TO CRITICISM

To the extent that group members retain ancestral languages, practice endogamy, avoid contact with outsiders, do not become citizens, and/or establish separate schools, enterprises, social clubs, and newspapers, they are vulnerable to criticisms of being clannish, intolerant of others, fearful of competition with nongroup members, derelict in civic responsibility, and of being unpatriotic. Throughout American history various religious, racial, and ethnic groups—such as the French, the Irish, Germans, Jews, Catholics, Russians, Asians—were criticized for such ethnocentrism.

Just as majority groups have always justified limiting, avoiding, or excluding minorities, so have minorities justified separation from majorities, either partially or fully. For example, Catholic parochial schools "are not established and maintained with any idea of holding our children apart from the general body and spirit of American citizenship," noted a group of bishops in 1919, but "are an example of the use of freedom for the advancement of morality and religion." In recent years, some Native American leaders urged the establishment of separate public schools for their children, which would "affirm tribal membership and use group approaches and culturally relevant curriculum to help any student survive the gauntlet of the majority educational system," said John E. Beaulieu, chair of the Indian Education Advisory Committee of the Minneapolis public school system. Deaf students at Gallaudet University in Washington, D.C., in 1988, and at the Lexington School for the Deaf in New York City, in 1994, held successful demonstrations demanding their institutions be headed respectively by a deaf president and a deaf executive officer. "We don't have to depend on hearing people" to make decisions, said one of the latter school's demonstrators. "We can do it ourselves." [1]

Sex and gender separation are likewise defended by some groups. Some Hispanic and black minority leaders have called for separate public schools for troubled male students in the belief that their learning and social problems could be more effectively addressed separately. Judith Shapiro, president of Barnard College, endorsed all-female colleges and schools because they "are places where girls and women get more attention, more respect and more room to be individuals." There are also gay, lesbian, and transsexual militants who insist upon having separate social clubs. "Males are the oppressors of females," said one lesbian recently, "and all oppressed groups have the right to be with each other away from their oppressors." [2]

More prevalent and surprising is the growing self-segregation of minority groups in colleges, which aid the process by providing them with funds, facilities, and support staff. Institutions do so in the belief that they are helping minorities develop self-esteem, and that their assistance prevents minority protests and demonstrations. And, in fact, many minority students do feel uncomfortable in a largely white setting and resent the widespread ignorance of minority life. These students believe that college is where they should learn more about their own group than about others, and so the call on campuses across the country for separate dorms, yearbooks, graduation exercises, and parties.[3]

At Cornell University, separate dormitories, called residential colleges, were established first for black students in 1971 and then in the early 1990s for Native Americans and Hispanics (though they were denied to gays). At Brandeis University, in 1994, during Black History Month, a student organizer of an "All Black Affair," party to which no white students were invited, said that people should have "a safe place to retreat to and build among themselves before they run out and try to be one with everyone." Support has also grown to maintain historic black colleges and all-black private boarding schools. "Blacks have realized that integration didn't work," said Frank McDuffie, Jr., president of the private college preparatory Laurinburg Institute in North Carolina. "Blacks gave up their institutions in the '50's and early '60's, thinking they would be welcomed into the nation's fold. It didn't happen, and blacks are beginning to look around and create their own villages again."[4]

Institutionalized self-segregation is further encouraged by an earlier noted peer group pressure on group members to stick together, whether it be in the form of cliques, gangs, social clubs, or living patterns. At one California high school, Korean students socialize in one section of the school grounds, whites in another, and Latinos in a third. "The Asians don't like the whites because they're all sports," claimed one student, "and the whites don't like the Asians because they're all academics and money." To cross-socialize is to open oneself up to criticism from within the home group. As an Asian American college student described her experience: "Students of color are looked down upon and sometimes openly criticized by their peers for having too many white friends, not doing enough for their respective multicultural groups, or just being too 'Americanized' or trying too hard to blend in. . . . [T]erms like 'banana' (yellow on the outside, white on the inside) are sometimes used and questions like 'How come you don't have an Asian first name?' come up in everyday conversation." Such experiences are not unusual. A 1987 national study and follow-up four years later reported that college students feel pressured not to socialize with members of other groups: among blacks, 37 percent had such feelings; Asians, 19 percent; Chicanos, 15 percent; and whites, 13 percent.[5]

Similar separation has been urged for minority doctors, police, social workers, reporters, and so forth, who are believed by some to be best able to relate only to other members of their group. For example, upon assuming the presidency in 1993 of the country's largest black physicians group, the National Medical Association, Dr. Leonard Lawrence declared that minority patients are often better served by physicians of the same group background. Also, at a 1994 convention of Native American, Asian American, Hispanic, and black journalists, the Native American organizational president asked: "How long will we allow somebody else to shape the picture we see in the mirror each day?" [6]

Even at its mildest, the minority press is permeated with ethnocentrism. It has become commonplace that if a tornado strikes a town, the Hispanic press will tell of the damage to an iglesia, the Jewish press of the damage to a synagogue, the Afro-American press of damage to the black church, and so on, with each group telling only of the damage suffered by its members. Should a group's newspaper not report on the tornado, it is safe to assume that none of its members were affected.

## INTERGROUP ENVY AND CONFLICT

Group identification can generate intergroup envy, competition, and conflict, particularly when accompanied by varying degrees of racial or ethnic superiority.

From a historical viewpoint, there was always a simultaneity, succession, and proliferation of victims, who, prior to being physically attacked, were invariably verbally stereotyped and defamed. Mid–nineteenth-century Missouri residents disdained and feared newly arriving Mormon settlers from Ohio and New York not only because of their religious beliefs, but also "from their appearance, from their manners, and from their conduct," they generally seemed to be from "the very dregs of that society from which they came, lazy, idle, and vicious." A century later, Emily Greene Balch described another group as follows: "A Slovak comes over with a group of his fellows, goes to a Slovak boarding house, a Slovak church, a Slovak saloon, and a Slovak bank; knows his 'boss,' himself very likely a foreigner, only by his orders and oaths, and deals with Americans only as the street car conductor shouts to him, 'What do you want, John?' or the boys stone his children and call them 'Hunkies.' " More recently, Ramon Bosque-Perez of the Center for Puerto Rican Studies in New York noted a chain of victimization: "Haitians are discriminated against in the Dominican Republic. And that happens to Dominicans in Puerto Rico. And that happens to Puerto Ricans and Dominicans here." [7]

The continuing existence of xenophobic attitudes toward a variety of groups is reflected in a 1982 Gallup poll, which asked whether some immigrant groups are "a good thing or a bad thing for this country." The older the group in America, the better it was regarded, and, conversely, the newer the group to America, the less well it was regarded. The percentages for those who had a clear opinion (other than "mixed feelings" or "don't know") were: [8]

|              | Good | Bad |
|--------------|------|-----|
| English      | 66   | 6   |
| Irish        | 62   | 7   |
| Jews         | 59   | 9   |
| Germans      | 57   | 11  |
| Italians     | 56   | 10  |
| Poles        | 53   | 12  |
| Japanese     | 47   | 18  |
| Blacks       | 46   | 16  |
| Chinese      | 44   | 19  |
| Mexicans     | 25   | 34  |
| Koreans      | 24   | 30  |
| Vietnamese   | 20   | 38  |
| Puerto Ricans| 17   | 43  |
| Haitians     | 10   | 39  |
| Cubans       | 9    | 59  |

In addition to the plurality of victims, there is always a simultaneity of them. In colonial times, Quakers, Baptists, Catholics, Presbyterians, and, of course, Indians and blacks were victimized. In the nineteenth century, Chinese and Japanese on the West Coast were targeted, as were Mormons in the Midwest, and south, central, and Eastern European immigrants on the East Coast—all at a time when African Americans were held in slavery or in segregated peonage and when Indians were warred upon and forcibly relocated to federal internment areas.

As noted earlier, today's victims are frequently new immigrants from Asia, the Middle East, and South and Central America. As they increasingly move into an area, established residents feel threatened, and intercultural incidents multiply, such as between American shoppers (black and white) and immigrant Korean, Chinese, and Arab merchants, who are often accused of being disrespectful and arrogant for not making eye contact or engaging in small talk with customers, although this behavior is uncommon in the merchants' countries of origin. For example, in Korea saying "hello" and shaking hands is usually done only among friends and family. Koreans, especially men, are "brought up not to be expressive," said the Reverend Hee-Min Park, a Presbyterian minister in Los Angeles. Scapegoating and the harassment of newcomers are also common. While growing up in a Bronx Italian neighborhood, Dion DiMucci and his friends liked to chase kids of other groups: "If I could just put somebody under me because he's poorer, Puerto Rican, black, Chinese or whatever." [9]

A 1993 Ford Foundation study of "newcomers and established residents" in six major communities found a major source of conflict was over language usage in governmental offices, street and store signs, and church services, whether it was between Caucasians and Asians in Monterey Park, California, or between Latinos and Anglos (white and black) in Miami and Houston, or between Spanish, Asian, and Polish groups in Philadelphia. Other conflicts also took place, such as the spray-painting of a Chinese immigrant girl's face by teenagers of another group; the taunting, kicking, and eventual murder of a 21-year-old Cambodian by a dozen white men; the vandalism by three teenagers of an Asian Indian's home and messages left such as, "Indians go home" and "Leave or die"; the regular spitting on of a Mexican selling flowers at a street intersection; the repeated calling of Egyptian immigrants "camel jockeys" by a supervisor and the threat of being sent back to Egypt; the fatal attack on an Ethiopian with a baseball bat; the beating to death of a Vietnamese premedical student when he objected to racial slurs directed at him; and the fatal attack on an Ecuadorean adult by a group of youths carrying lead pipes and two-by-fours.[10]

Contemporary American Indians have not been spared from attack, particularly in regions where they compete or differ with white residents over water, hunting, fishing, or gambling casino rights. For example, in Montana, Idaho, and Washington, bumper stickers and T-shirts with the message "SAVE A FISH—SPEAR AN INDIAN" were sold, and an organizer of an anti-Indian group declared that "blacks, Indians, and others have no right to be U.S. citizens even if they are born in this country. Those people . . . should be asked to leave so the United States can provide a peaceful place for whites to live by themselves." In 1995, conservationists threatened to use a large ship and submarine to stop Makah Indians in the state of Washington from reenacting their ancient tradition of killing five whales each spring, which was assured them in an 1855 treaty with the U.S. government. However, an official of the Sea Shepherd Conservation Society stated that, "They used to keep slaves, as well. I don't see the point in making a distinction between natives having more of a right to kill whales than nonnative people."[11]

According to the Southern Poverty Law Center, hate crimes in 1992 involving mainly race, religion, ethnicity, and sexual orientation resulted in at least 31 killings and 322 acts of vandalism. In the previous year Arab Americans alone suffered 119 attacks, and then 222 attacks within just three days after the 1995 bombing of the federal building in Oklahoma City, although no members of their community were actually involved. Incidents of violence against Asian Americans rose from 335 in 1993 to 452 in 1994, motivated largely by anti-immigration sentiments. Violence against gays and lesbians between 1992 and 1994 resulted in 151 deaths, nearly half of which were motivated by antigay bias or the suspicion of such. In Massachusetts alone, hate crimes jumped from 304 in 1991 to 480 in 1992, of which 30.6 percent were motivated by bias against blacks, 17.4 percent by bias against whites, 14.4 percent against Jews, 11.4 against Asians, 10.8 percent against gays, 7.5 percent against Hispanics, and 5.1 percent against lesbians. Whether on a local or a national level, the actual number of hate crimes—such as name-calling, threats, personal assaults, and property damage—exceeds those reported because of inadequate recording procedures or the refusal of victims to report them. In most cases, the perpetrators were males in their teens or twenties, operating in groups of four or more, whose targets were often people walking, driving through, or working in a neighborhood, or families moving into areas where they were not wanted.[12]

Contrary to the conventional belief, being young or educated offers no immunity or antidote to bigotry or violence. On 79 college campuses, hate incidents against Jews increased in 1994 to 143 compared to 54 in 1988. Other studies show that anti-Catholic views are more likely held by educated people, including college faculty members, than by the poor and less educated. Teenage crime, in particular, has also been rising, and alarmingly so. According to a national survey of tenth, eleventh, and twelfth grade students in 1990, racially motivated crime skyrocketed 149 percent in two years, wherein about 57 percent of students reported seeing such an attack; 47 percent indicated they would join in if they came across such a fight because they felt that the victims probably deserved what was happening; and only 25 percent said they would report the incident to a school official. In fact, while overall crime rates have been declining, those for young males have been climbing, particularly for violence by 14 to 17 year olds, whose rate of committing murder between 1985 and 1992 rose almost 50 percent for whites and more than 300 percent for blacks.[13]

## DISCRIMINATION AGAINST OTHERS

As seen earlier, being a member of a minority group, even one that experiences discrimination does not prevent some members from discriminating against members of other groups, or denying them rights they want for themselves. For example, the early church theologian St. Augustine distinguished between "unjust persecution which the wicked inflict on the Church of Christ" and "just persecution which the Church of Christ inflicts on the wicked." Though Puritans settled in New England to exercise "the liberty of their consciences," wrote a Quaker minister in 1742, they soon forgot "the golden rule of doing to others as they would be done unto [and] became, to their lasting ignominy, persecutors of the Quakers."[14] In the decades that followed, so some American Indians behaved toward blacks, Mormons toward Gentiles, Irish toward Jews, and Japanese toward Chinese. Nor did being a persecuted minority prevent some members from owning slaves, as did some early American Catholics, Jews, Huguenots, Quakers—and even blacks.

More recently, the Southern Poverty Law Center reported that racially motivated crimes by blacks had soared and that in the three years prior to 1993 they had committed 46 percent of all murders of whites, Asians, or Hispanics. What was said of some whites began being said of some blacks. For example, in Compton, California, where blacks held most elected offices, though the population was about evenly divided between blacks and Hispanics, the head of the Latino Chamber of Commerce, Arnold Alatorre, claimed in 1994 that Latinos "are treated worse by the blacks in the government than the blacks are treated by the white government in South Africa."[15]

The rationale behind such interminority animosities is frequently similar to that of minority-majority animosities, wherein one group justifies its behavior by claiming the other group is bad. For example, early twentieth-century immigrant Japanese farmworkers in California not only resented Asian Indian, Chinese, and Filipino workers for accepting lower wages, but opposed their children (the Nisei) socializing with them, particularly with Filipinos, lest the latter's "lazy blood" become part of "the Japanese race through interethnic marriage" and gradually "offset the racial superiority of the Japanese," warned a Japanese-American newspaper editorial. More recently, in Brooklyn, a group of blacks and Hispanics physically assaulted a black man and his white girlfriend, demanding to know why they were together.[16]

Also, like majorities, minorities may deny being bigoted, claiming that as a past or present discriminated-against group they would never discriminate against other people or that they do not have the power to do so. "After 500 years of having to endure slavery, oppression, exploitation in our community, our people are in no way, shape or form able to discriminate," said one Mexican-American leader in defense of a fellow Mexican American's public disparaging of homosexuals.[17]

## VULNERABILITY TO EXPLOITATION

Wherever differences or animosities exist between groups, groups are vulnerable to exploitation by other, more powerful groups. Thus, there were European colonists who exacerbated tensions among Indians so that they fought each other rather than the colonists; slave owners who purchased Africans from different tribes and industrial and agricultural employers who hired ethnic and racial workers from different groups to prevent their conspiring or organizing against them; and employers who replaced one group of workers with another to keep wages low or prevent unionization.

More specifically, on the West Coast and in Hawaii, white employers exploited cultural differences and animosities between Chinese, Japanese, Korean, and Filipino workers, while in mainland America, employers did the same with European immigrant groups, and with the latter and American blacks. To avoid interethnic fighting and work stoppages, some early twentieth-century employers hired separate Irish and Italian work crews, just as later agricultural employers did with Mexican and West Indian migratory laborers. In describing the replacement process, an early twentieth-century scholar noted, "As rapidly as a race rises in the scale of living and . . . begin[s] to demand higher wages and resist the pressure of long hours and over-exertion, the employers substitute another race and [the] process is repeated."[18]

Though such gross labor exploitation has largely disappeared, many politicians, demagogues, and minority group militants readily exploit intergroup animosities for personal gain or for that of their group. In the process, political ambitions may replace ethical principles, and more energy is then expended on maintaining or obtaining separate group power than in resolving problems that affect their group and other groups.

In recent years, as some minority groups started gaining political power (such as African Americans) and others began striving for it (such as Hispanics), tensions and rivalries have grown between blacks and Koreans in Los Angeles, Jews and Hispanics in New York City, Cubans and Haitians in Florida, Mexicans and Indochinese in Denver, and Asians and native Hawaiians in Hawaii. In Florida, African Americans opposed an affirmative action plan for the state's corrections department, while Hispanics endorsed it, claiming they were underrepresented and blacks were overly so; similar charges were made in Los Angeles about the U.S. Postal Service, 15 percent of whose employees in 1993 were Hispanic though Hispanics comprised 35 percent of the regional labor force, while blacks constituted 62 percent of postal employees though only 10 percent of the regional labor force. In Boston, in 1993, Chinese and Hispanic leaders complained that the state-funded program that bused inner-city children to 32 suburban schools favored African Americans, who constituted 48 percent of the Boston school population, but 94 percent of the busing program.[19]

Nor, as noted in chapter 3, does minority membership preclude some members from discriminating against other members of the same group. In fact, this intragroup discrimination can facilitate oppression, exploitation, swindling, or even murder, whether through robbery, extortion, the sale of fictitious land or stock, payment of substandard wages, or being overcharged for merchandise or services. On a subtler level, when a group's leaders or major organizations insist that all members conform with the group's norms, values, and political interests, creativity is stifled and learning the ways of more successful groups is inhibited. One of the great sources of cultural achievement for groups, nations, and even civilizations, wrote Thomas Sowell, "has been a borrowing of cultural features from others who happened to be more advanced in given fields at a given time."

Likewise, in his study of how race, religion, and identity determine a group's success in today's global economy, Joel Kotkin emphasizes the value of "passion for technical and other knowledge from all possible sources, combined with an essential open-mindedness."[20]

## INSECURITY AND FOREBODING

While associating with "one's own kind" generates a sense of security, pride, and power, it can also create feelings of insecurity, shame, and foreboding. In its extreme form, this association leads to paranoia, wherein members feel that all nonmembers are alike and are enemies, latent if not active. And so there are Jews who believe that most or all Christians hate them, blacks who believe that most or all whites hate them, Catholics who think most or all Protestants hate them, Asians who think most or all Occidentals hate them, and so forth.

Those who are paranoid usually refuse to acknowledge that any progress has been made in improving the group's existence. Rather, they see a plan, conspiracy, or pattern perpetrated by nonmembers to destroy them. Otherwise, they reason, so many fellow members would not have been or are currently being demeaned, discriminated against, or physically attacked. Paranoid group members are also highly suspicious of forming alliances with members of other groups, who they believe will sooner or later betray them.

Nongroup members can share or defend minority group paranoia, though their motives are sometimes suspect. For example, as Native American Vine Deloria, Jr., noted, "The white liberal establishment has not yet reached the point of sophisticated thought where it can conceive of demagoguery within projects and programs which it is funding. It is caught in a logical circle of paranoia in which everything is interpreted according to the mythology of oppression. . . . When a white is involved in a task which involves racial minorities, it is paternalism per se."[21]

At the same time, there are minority members who fear that any wrongdoing committed by a fellow member will provoke society to blame all members of their group. "When I hear a news report that implicates an African American, intellectually I know I have nothing to do with that," said Patricia Turner, a professor at the University of California. "I follow all the rules. I'm law-abiding. I stop at stop signs. But I can't stop an emotional response of 'Please, don't let this person be black.' " A Jamaican American, after a fellow immigrant in 1993 had viciously shot twenty-three white train passengers, killing six of them, said that, "You constantly hear statements about Jamaican gangs and how violent they are. I'm concerned that people will look at this and feel this is what you can expect from 'those kind of people.' "[22]

Some extremist fringe groups believe that the U.S. government is conspiring to arrest them or that the Russians, Chinese, or Japanese are about to attack America, after which, "Communists will kill white Christians and mutilate them; witches and satanic Jews will offer people up as sacrifices to their gods, openly and proudly; blacks will rape and kill white women, and will torture and kill white men; homosexuals will sodomize whoever they can. Prisoners from Federal and State prisons will be set free to terrorize, while Cuban refugees will do the same." As of 1994, citizen militia groups existed in thirteen states, all defending their right to purchase and bear arms, including assault weapons. In the same year, the head of the United States Militia Association stated that he believed that President Clinton was planning to bring 100,000 policemen from China to disarm all Americans.[23]

At times, the desire to increase group identity causes some minority members to deliberately exaggerate the amount of bigotry directed at their group, sometimes even manufacturing evidence. For example, after racist letters were clandestinely posted on the door of the Black Student Union at Williams College, in early 1993, a black student confessed he had done it to promote discussion of racial issues on campus. Some years earlier, to awaken the Philadelphia Jewish community to the dangers of anti-Semitism, a member of the militant Jewish Defense League perpetrated a hoax, wherein for a number of days people were convinced that the American Nazi Party, abetted by Ku Klux Klan members, were going to hold a white power rally. At other times, some members exploit the present or past bigotry against their group in order to muster support for their views or to deflect attention from a wrong some members have committed. For example, in 1988, a young black teenager, Tawana Brawley, claimed that she had been raped and abused by six white men, though there was no evidence of such an occurrence. It was later revealed that she had run away from home for several days and wanted to escape punishment from her family.[24]

Whites sometimes engage in similar practices. In 1989, Charles Stewart, a white man, called the police from his car phone, saying that a black man had shot him and his pregnant wife; some days later, it was discovered that Stewart himself had committed the acts. In 1994, Susan Smith, a young white mother in Union, South Carolina, claimed a black man had forced her out of her car and had driven off with her two children, who were later found drowned in a car that she had deliberately allowed to roll into a lake. In the same year, a white coed in Albany, New York, reported that a black man had beaten her in her dormitory room, though in fact it had been her father. As one militant black leader, Khalid Abdul Muhammad, said, "It's a good thing we weren't on the *Titanic,* or they'd blame a nigger."[25]

The paranoia, foreboding, and emotional distress resulting from group affiliation have many forms and roots. For some people, severe psychic stress results from the process of resettlement, as among early nineteenth-century Norwegian immigrants in which a heightened incidence of insanity was found, even though their group affiliation psychologically should have helped shelter them while they were adjusting to American society. Similarly, a New York almshouse physician at the time said young Irish women who came to America alone were often more given to emotional illness than other immigrants because of the "moral and physical influences of their leaving the homes of their childhood, their coming almost destitute to a strange land, and often after great suffering."[26]

Recent research notes that when a minority group constitutes a small proportion of the total population in a given area, "diagnosed rates of mental illness increase both in comparison to the rates for other ethnic groups in that area and to members of the same ethnic group in neighborhoods where they constitute a significant proportion or majority." Among African Americans, too, psychiatrists William H. Grier and Price M. Cobbs found a clash between the psyche and the environment, wherein to survive, "Black people . . . must be ever alert to danger from their white fellow citizens. . . . And it is a posture so close to paranoid thinking that the mental disorder into which black people most frequently fall is paranoid psychosis."[27]

To be sure, being a minority and being paranoid does not preclude having real enemies, who can likewise be paranoid—and at times more so. From America's earliest history, phobias abounded about: foreign countries, domestic ethnic groups, immigrants, and aliens undermining democracy or plotting to take over the country, such as the French, Spanish, Germans, Russians; religious groups seeking to abolish or dominate others, such as Catholics, Mormons, Jews; blacks and Indians conspiring separately or together to rebel and murder all whites; and assorted groups seeking to destroy the country's religious and/or political way of life, such as Masons, Mormons, unions, socialists, communists, and atheists.

In contemporary times, too, though anti-Catholicism is far less prevalent than in the nineteenth century, there are Catholics who believe it is a fact in American life and always will be. They hold this belief because Catholic leaders and teachings are periodically maligned by some government officials, homosexual groups, and people ordinarily considered to be well intentioned. For example, a mandatory employee diversity program in Minnesota, designed to improve intergroup understanding, specified Catholicism as being counter to the goals of cultural diversity and as condoning the persecution of homosexuals. More extreme are anti-Catholic groups, which still claim that a Catholic conspiracy exists, wherein the Vatican controls the government, the postal service, and the telephone companies, as well as owning publications like *People, Time, Newsweek,* the *New York Times,* and the NBC, CBS, and ABC television networks.[28]

## SELF-HATRED

To some degree, self-hatred is a frequent concomitant of minority group affiliation, wherein members ridicule or reject the characteristics of their group, such as speech, dress, values, and even physical appearance. This is particularly true of the decades prior to the rise of ethnic pride and multiculturalism.

As psychoanalyst Erik Erikson noted, "in any system based on suppression, exclusion and exploitation, the suppressed, excluded and exploited accept the evil image they are made to represent by those who are dominant." Likewise, social psychologist Kurt Lewin noted a tendency in every underprivileged group "to accept the values of society's more privileged group and become excessively sensitive, critical, and ambivalent to everything in their own group differing from the larger society." According to Minister Louis Farrakhan, blacks so hate their color, hair, features, and origins that "black young men are the No. 1 destroyers of self." Among many Native Americans living off the reservation, self-hatred took the form of not disclosing their roots. "I remember my father telling us we had Native American blood, but he wouldn't even talk about it," recalled one Native American, while another said that until her teens she thought she was "part Mexican," because her mother "felt Mexicans were treated better than Indians." [29]

Studies have shown a widespread pattern of self-hatred among some groups. A 1969 survey of Boston ethnic groups revealed that 36 percent of Puerto Ricans and 16 percent of the Irish found nothing good about their respective groups; when asked what was embarrassing about their own group members, 43 percent of the Irish pointed to personality, as did 22 percent of the Puerto Ricans, and 18 percent of the blacks and Italians. Also, in the 1960s, a study found that native-born Mexican Americans had internalized many negative stereotypes about themselves and agreed with most of them, such as being authoritarian, emotional, lazy, and unconcerned with education. Among Poles in California it was found that because of their lack of appreciation for their ethnic heritage and because of living in a society that belittled them, many felt inferior and wanted to disappear into the larger society. In a survey of Franco-Americans in nine Maine cities (in four of which they were a majority), only 5 percent were very proud of their ethnicity and achievements and only 6 percent believed using French at home was important. In the early 1970s, the term "ethnotherapy" was coined by psychiatrist Price M. Cobbs, who sought to change negative black identity problems through group interaction and self-exploration. Since then, other groups have adopted similar forms of therapy. [30]

Less extreme is the self-hatred of people who want to assimilate, but find—or found—it difficult to do so. In describing his feelings about his own ethnicity, American Asian author David Hwang wrote, "You think it's great but there is necessarily a certain amount of self-hatred or confusion at least, which results from the fact that there's a role model in this society which is basically a Caucasian man, and you don't measure up to that." Though as an adult, Hollywood director Steven Spielberg is proud of his Jewish roots and wants his children to feel likewise, he recalls how as a youngster: "I was embarrassed because we were Orthodox Jews. I was embarrassed by the outward perception of my parents' Jewish practices. I was embarrassed because I wanted to be like everybody else. I didn't feel comfortable with who I was."[31]

## INVIDIOUS PREFERENCES

Another major disadvantage of group identity results from the U.S. government sometimes viewing individuals according to their ethnic, racial, religious, or sexual group affiliations, thereby creating the kind of invidious preferences that civil service reform, blind justice, and the civil rights movement sought to end, as well as weakening a sense of national unity and undermining both group and individual security. As Supreme Court Justice Sandra Day O'Connor noted in the five to four decision challenging North Carolina's congressional redistricting to insure a black representative:

Racial classifications of any sort pose the risk of lasting harm to our society. They reinforce the belief, held by too many for too much of our history, that individuals should be judged by the color of their skin. . . . Racial gerrymandering, even for remedial purposes, may balkanize us into competing racial factions; it threatens to carry us further from the goal of a political system in which race no longer matters.[32]

Already, social policies based on group identity are exacerbating old and generating new forms of intergroup competition and conflict as increasing numbers of groups demand and lobby for rights, benefits, and entitlements. Comparative or relative group deprivation has become the basis for obtaining special treatment, thereby not only provoking the resentment of those denied it, but also the resentment of those actually or allegedly receiving it. For example, to some Afro-Americans, other groups such as women, Hispanics, and most recently, gays are unfairly benefiting from their struggle for racial justice and programs originally designed for them. When Hispanics wanted inclusion in the 1975 Voting Rights Act extension, an NAACP official exclaimed, "Blacks were dying for the right to vote when you people couldn't decide whether you were Caucasians." The feminist movement "has pimped off the black movement," said Lou Palmer, a black Chicago talk show host, in 1993. "Now here comes the gay movement. Blacks resent it very much, because they do not see a parallel, nor do I." Similarly, the following year, when Northeastern University included gays and lesbians in its affirmative action policies, some critics pointed out that such people were already well represented in universities, especially in the arts. "I don't put gays in the same category as blacks," said one English professor. "I have some relatives who are gay. They are not deprived people."[33]

By providing benefits or preferences to people solely because of their group affiliation, some members of the group are unfairly included and many members of other groups are unfairly excluded. Simply put, not every member of a group is equally disadvantaged or advantaged. In fact, except for a few small religious groups, some members of groups benefiting from the government are socioeconomically better off than some members of groups not recognized by the government.

As law professor William Kai-Shen Wang wrote in the *Christian Science Monitor* in 1978, society should "help *all* those who are poor or culturally deprived, not just those with slanted eyes or darker skins. Why should an impoverished refugee from Chile with a 'Spanish surname' be granted more favorable treatment than a penniless Czech refugee? Why should the black child of a Jamaican doctor be shown more concern than the child of a white Appalachian dirt farmer?" Similarly, Dante Ramos, in 1994, wrote in *The New Republic* on the injustice of governmental classifications:

If Argentines, the highest-paid Hispanic group, receive affirmative action benefits, perhaps the list should include every ethnic category less fortunate than they are. In 1990 Argentines earned $15,956 per year on the job. Less successful were the Dutch, Finns, French, Scotch-Irish, Bulgarians, Croats, Slavic Macedonians, Slovenes, Brazilians, Assyrians, Cajuns and . . . Pennsylvania Germans. . . . On the other hand, the Argentine threshold would *disqualify* such frequent listmakers as Pakistanis, Sri Lankans, Burmese, Chinese, Japanese and Asian Indians, whose earnings average $25,198.[34]

Not only do policies of group favoritism invariably generate envy, resentment, and, at times, rage by those who do not benefit toward those who do, but also by both groups against the government, which cannot possibly meet all competing and conflicting racial, ethnic, sexual, and religious demands. Such dynamics surface even in the matter of immigration policy, which is said to favor, for example, whites over blacks, Cubans over Haitians, immigrants over native-born Americans, or even illegal immigrants over legal ones. "[I]f I ever needed some kind of outside assistance, I couldn't get it because they're (illegal immigrants) taking so much of it," complained a black woman postal service worker in 1994. "You can open your doors to just so many people and, after a while, you just have to say no." Moreover, such policies facilitate the emergence of demagogues. "Whether justified by past oppression or notions of racial superiority," wrote Shelby Steele in analyzing black and white extremists, "a group's entitlements always require thugs and goons to patrol its borders and ignorant mythologies to justify its advantages."[35]

In summary, just as there are individual, group, and societal benefits to group identity, so are there disadvantages. In a democratic, pluralistic society, tensions between the advantages and disadvantages of group identity are inevitable, particularly for new immigrants, whose problems are well summarized by a Trinidad-Tobago immigrant, who three months after arriving wrote that America consisted of so many parts and structures that it was "impossible to be exposed to it all, to see all the realities, to feel every throb. Whatever your circumstances you exist in a world within a world."[36]

However, from a historical perspective it is clear that when a higher value is placed on group rights than on individual ones, and when group affiliation is made the basis for societal recognition or entitlement, then individual uniqueness and freedom become hostage to the passions, prejudices, and politics of the groups in power. Group restrictions often quash individual opportunities and conformity can replace creativity, patronage can replace merit, quotas can replace qualifications, and fear of group reprimand can stifle open communication, civil debate, and intergroup cooperation. But before exploring group restrictions any deeper, a look at how groups respond to bigotry is necessary.

## NOTES

1. Mark J. Hurley, *The Unholy Ghost: Anti-Catholicism in the American Experience* (Huntington, Ind.: Our Sunday Visitor Publishing Division, 1992), 165; Mireya Navarro, "Proposed School May Draw Lawsuit," *New York Times,* 13 January 1991, 21; *Civil Rights Update,* U.S. Commission on Civil Rights (July/ August 1992), 4, 7; David Firestone, "Deaf Students Protest New School Head," *New York Times,* 27 April 1994, B3 and 22 June 1994, B3.

2. Sam Dillon, "Hispanic School Is Put Off Amid Bias Inquiry," *New York Times,* 13 October 1993, B3; *New York Times,* 13 July 1994, B8; Judith R. Shapiro, "What Women Can Teach Men," *New York Times,* 23 November 1994, A23; Stephen Miller, "Gay-Bashing by Homosexuals," *Heterodoxy* (November-December 1994): 4–12; Sarah Horowitz, "Separating the Men from the Womyn," *The Heterodoxy Handbook,* ed. David Horowitz and Peter Collier (Washington, D.C.: Regnery Press, 1994), 99–101.

3. Gabriella Stern and Dorothy J. Gaiter, "Frustration, Not Anger, Guides Race Relations On a College Campus," *Wall Street Journal,* 22 April 1994.

4. Kenneth B. Clark and Michael Meyers, "Separate Is Never Equal," *New York Times,* 1 April 1995, 19; Dan Rademacher, "Black History Month Stresses Action," *The Justice* [Brandeis University newspaper], 1 February 1994, 15; Peter Applebome, "Boarding Schools for Blacks: Need Born of Segregation Is on the Rise," *New York Times,* 21 September 1994, B12.

5. Jodi Wilgoren, "High-Pressure High," *Los Angeles Times,* 4 December 1994, A32; Editor's Comment, "Self-Segregation: A Repudiation of the Vision of a Color-Blind Society," *Lincoln Review* (Spring-Summer 1994): 3–4; Alice Dembner, "Campus Racial Lines May Be Blurring," *Boston Globe,* 5 April 1994, 1.

6. *Boston Globe,* 8 August 1993, 16; William Glaberson, "As Minority Journalists Meet an Example of White Power," *New York Times,* 29 July 1994, A12.

7. Kenneth H. Winn, *Exiles in a Land of Liberty* (Chapel Hill: University of North Carolina Press, 1989), 89; Emily Greene Balch, *Our Slavic Fellow Citizens* (New York: Charities Publication Committee, 1910), 115; Lori S. Robinson, "What Goes Around Comes Around," *Emerge* (October 1995): 10.

8. Rita J. Simon, "Old Minorities, New Immigrants: Aspirations, Hopes, and Fears," *Annals of the American Academy of Political and Social Science* (November 1993): 63.

9. William E. Schmidt, "For Immigrants, Tough Customers," *New York Times,* 15 November 1990, E5; David Gonzalez, "Hate Blasts from the Past: Bias Crimes in New York City are Nothing New," *New York Times,* 1 February 1992, 25; K. Connie Kang, " 'Smile, You're in America,' " *Los Angeles Times,* 22 October 1994, A1, A20.

10. Robert Bach, *Changing Relations: Newcomers and Established Residents in U.S. Communities* (New York: Ford Foundation, 1993), 36–37; Deborah Sontag, "Across the U.S., Immigrants Find the Land of Resentment," *New York Times,* 11 December 1992, A1, B4 and 23 August 1992, 35; *Intelligence Report,* Southern Poverty Law Center (August 1994): 2, 3; Jennifer Steinhauer, "Killing of Immigrant Stuns a Brooklyn Area," *New York Times,* 16 October 1994, 39.

11. *Intelligence Report,* Southern Poverty Law Center (October 1994): 2–3; Timothy Egan, "A Tribe Sees Hope In Whale Hunting, But U.S. Is Worried," *New York Times,* 4 June 1995, 1.

12. *Boston Globe,* 2 March 1993, 10 and 21 September 1993, 19; *Klanwatch Intelligence Report* (March 1995): 4; and idem (August 1995): 5; James Brooke, "Amid Islam's Growth in the U.S., Muslims Face a Surge in Attacks," *New York Times,* 28 August 1995, A1; Sara Bullard, ed., *The Ku Klux Klan: A History of Racism and Violence* (Montgomery, Ala.: Southern Poverty Law Center, 1991), 61; Daniel Goleman, "As Bias Crime Seems to Rise, Scientists Study Roots of Racism," *New York Times,* 29 May 1990, C1, C5.

13. *1994 Audit of Anti-Semitic Incidents* (New York: Anti-Defamation League, 1995), 1, 11; Hurley, *The Unholy Ghost: Anti-Catholicism in the American Experience,* 159; Diego Ribadeneira, "Study Says Teen-agers' Racism Rampant," *Boston Globe,* 18 October 1990, 35; John J. Dilulio, "The Coming of the Super-Patriots," *The Weekly Standard,* 27 November 1995, 24.

14. Carla Gardina Pestana, "The Quaker Executions as Myth and History," *Journal of American History* (September 1993): 466; Leonard W. Levy, *Blasphemy* (New York: Alfred A. Knopf, 1993), 48.

15. *New York Times,* 7 August 1994, 25; Peter Applebome, "Rise Is Found in Hate Crimes Committed by Blacks," *New York Times,* 13 December 1993, A12.

16. Eiichiro Azuma, "Interethnic Conflict under Racial Subordination: Japanese Immigrants and Their Asian Neighbors in Walnut Grove, California 1908–1941," *Amerasia Journal* 20, no. 2 (1994): 42; Dennis Hevesi, "5 Youths Accused of Beat-

ing and Shouting Racial Slurs at Brooklyn Couple," *New York Times,* 15 December 1994, B3.

17. Denise Hamilton, "Seeking Justice for Latinos," *Los Angeles Times,* 3 November 1994, 13.

18. Roger Daniels, *Coming to America: A History of Immigration and Ethnicity in American Life* (New York: Harper Perennial, 1990), 59; Thomas Sowell, *Race and Culture* (New York: Basic Books, 1994), 84–85; Philip Perlmutter, *Divided We Fall: A History of Ethnic, Religious, and Racial Prejudice in America* (Ames: Iowa State University Press, 1992), 176.

19. Clemence Fiagome, "Pendulum of Affirmative Action Swings Both Ways," *Christian Science Monitor,* 10 March 1994, 1; Kelle Walsh, "Critics Say Metco Favors Blacks," *The Tab* (Newton, Mass.), 15 March 1994, 30; Peter Skerry, "The Black Alienation," *The New Republic,* 30 January 1995, 20; Jenifer McKim, "Activists Endorse Metco Outreach Plan to Hispanics, Asians," *Boston Globe,* 11 November 1994, 1, 28.

20. Sowell, *Race and Culture,* 30; Joel Kotkin, *Tribes* (New York: Random House, 1992), 5.

21. Vine Deloria, Jr., *We Talk, You Listen* (New York: Macmillan Company, 1970), 74.

22. Michael Quintanilla, "Divided We Stand," *Los Angeles Times,* 28 April 1995, E1, E10; Lena Williams, "After the Train Killings, A Rise of Black Anxiety," *New York Times,* 13 December 1993, B6.

23. *Armed & Dangerous: Militias Take Aim At The Federal Government* (New York: Anti-Defamation League, 1994), 1–3; Christopher John Farley, "Patriot Games," *Time* (19 December 1994): 48–49.

24. Jean Caldwell, "Black Williams Student Admits to Racist Notes," *Boston Globe,* 10 February 1993, 25 and 11 February 1993, 34; Lawrence Rubin, "When the Nazis Come to Town: Action and Reaction in the Jewish Community," *Journal of Jewish Communal Service* (Winter 1979–80): 149–56; *Time,* 10 October 1988, 49.

25. Charles M. Sennott, "Case Confirms Some Fears of Racism in S.C. Town," *Boston Globe,* 6 November 1994, 22; Don Terry, "False Accusation in South Carolina Hurts Blacks," *New York Times,* 6 November 1994, 32; Lynda Richardson, "Ex-Farrakhan Aide Speaks at N.Y.U.," *New York Times,* 9 November 1994, A25.

26. Frank C. Nelson, "Norwegian-American Attitudes Toward Assimilation During Four Periods of Their History in America, 1825–1930," *Journal of Ethnic Studies* 9 (Spring 1981): 59; Alan M. Kraut, *Silent Travelers: Germs, Genes, and the "Immigrant Menace"* (New York: Basic Books, 1994), 40.

27. Morris N. Eagle, "Jewish Life in the United States: Perspectives from Psychology," in *Jewish Life in the United States,* ed. Joseph B. Gittler (New York: New York University Press, 1981), 109; William H. Grier and Price M. Cobbs, *Black Rage* (New York: Bantam Books, 1969), 173.

28. "An Open Letter to the President of the United States," *New York Times,* 20 January 1995, A29; *Washington Post,* 24 May 1984, B1; *The Pilot,* 12 April 1985, 16 and 12 November 1993, 11; *Heterodoxy* (January 1995), 3; *Hate Groups in America* (New York: Anti-Defamation League of B'nai B'rith, 1982), 51.

29. Erik H. Erikson, *Identity, Youth and Crisis* (New York: W. W. Norton &

Company, 1968), 59; Irving M. Levine and Judith Herman, "Group Conflict, Group Interest, and Group Identity: Some Jewish Reflections on 'New Pluralism,' " in *Pieces of a Dream,* ed. Michael Wenk, S. M. Tomasi, and Geno Baroni (New York: Center for Migration Studies, 1972), 184–85; *Boston Globe,* 13 March 1994, 71; Richard Weizel, "Of Dancing, Drums and Crafts," *Boston Sunday Globe,* 15 January 1995, A36; Lance D. McCoy, "Native American Cultural Perspectives," *Journal of Intergroup Relations* (Summer 1995): 27.

30.  Charles M. Sullivan et al., eds., *Five Ethnic Groups in Boston: Blacks, Irish, Italians, Greeks and Puerto Ricans* (Boston: Action for Boston Community Development and United Community Services, 1972), 41–44; Rudolph O. De La Garza, "Mexican Americans in the United States: The Evolution of a Relationship," in *Case Studies on Human Rights and Fundamental Freedoms,* Vol. 5, ed. Willem A. Veenhoven (The Hague: Foundation for the Study of Plural Societies, 1976), 274; Neil C. Sandberg, *Ethnic Identity and Assimilation: The Polish Community* (New York: Praeger Publishers, 1974), 64; *Boston Globe,* 4 May 1986, 88; Judith Weinstein Klein, *Jewish Identity and Self-Esteem* (New York: Institute for American Pluralism, 1989), 9.

31.  Lawrence Auster, *The Path to National Suicide* (Monterey, Va.: American Immigration Control Foundation, 1990), 46; Dotson Rader, " 'We Can't Just Sit Back and Hope,' " *Parade Magazine,* 27 March 1994, 4–7.

32.  *New York Times,* 29 June 1993, A12.

33.  Charles Kamasaki and Raul Yzaguirre, "Black-Hispanic Tensions: One Perspective," *Journal of Intergroup Relations* (Winter 1994–1995): 23; Lena Williams, "Blacks Reject Gay Rights Fight as Equal to Theirs," *New York Times,* 28 June 1993, A1; Alice Dembner, "Northeastern Takes Steps to Hire More Gays," *Boston Globe,* 28 June 1994, 20.

34.  William Kai-Shen Wang, "Should Minorities Receive Special Treatment?— A Chinese American View," *Christian Science Monitor,* 26 January 1978, 31; Dante Ramos, "Losers," *The New Republic,* 17 October 1994, 25.

35.  Adam Pertman, "In Calif., Immigrant Proposal Hits Nerve," *Boston Globe,* 23 October 1994, 1; Shelby Steele, "How to Grow Extremists," *New York Times,* 13 March 1994, E17.

36.  Roy Simon Bryce-Laporte, "New York City and the New Caribbean Immigration: A Contextual Statement," *International Migration Review* 13 (Summer 1979): 229.

# 9

# Group Responses to Prejudice and Discrimination

If I am not for myself, who will be for me? And if I am only for myself, what am I? And if not now, when?

—Hillel,
*Sayings of the Fathers*

Personally experiencing discrimination, learning that family and friends were likewise discriminated against, and seeing or hearing that bigotry still exists not only makes group members feel vulnerable, but also affects their sense of justice, relations with other groups, and beliefs about what America is or should be. In this chapter, the focus will be on the many and varied ways groups react to bigotry.

In the present, as in the past, much depends on the size of the group and the size of its attackers; the intensity and persistence of the attacks on it; the group's historical experiences in dealing with enemies; its communal unity and political power; the conditions that prompted members to leave their ancestral home; and the character of the people, economy, laws, and government officials around them. Obviously, the interplay of so many factors makes for generalizations and disputes rather than certainties and agreements about how groups respond—or responded—to bigotry.

To make matters still more complex, a few other qualifications—or, better said, cautions—are in order. First, the nature of bigotry is rife with contradictions and irrationalities, wherein a particular group's members may be praised, damned, or praised and damned, by the same or different members of other groups. Second, not all groups or all members of a group, nor all generations of a group, react in the same way to prejudice and discrimination. Third, the smaller and less organized the group, and the more different it is racially, religiously, and/or ethnically from the dominant society, the greater is its vulnerability to attack and the greater is the attackers' immunity to retaliation. On the other hand, the more a group isolates itself socially and geographically, does not compete economically with other groups, understands and speaks English, and possesses work and family values similar to those of the larger society, the more likely it is tolerated, though not necessarily accepted socially as friends or neighbors.[1]

Lastly, persistent or periodic bigotry does not necessarily prevent the growth and proliferation of particular religious beliefs, groups, and institutions. Nor does it necessarily prevent a significant number of achievers among some groups, such as Armenians, Chinese, Cubans, Greeks, Huguenots, Japanese, Jews, Koreans, Quakers, Mormons, and West Indians. This is equally true of some of today's immigrants, and especially their children, who achieve a higher socioeconomic status than they had, or was available to them, back home, or than their group American-born counterparts have, or that members of some other American-born groups have. For example, a study in 1980 of male immigrants, aged 25 to 64, from ninety-two countries found that those from forty-one countries, mostly European, had greater earnings than American-born Anglo and Asian men, that most of the men born in Latin America had earnings as high as, or higher than, American-born Cubans, Mexicans, and Puerto Ricans, and that wide differences existed within continental groups: European Swiss and British earned more than Greeks and Portuguese; Asian Iranians and Indians earned more than Vietnamese and Laotians; and Latin American Argentinians and Venezuelans earned more than Bolivians and Salvadorans.[2]

Emotionally, too, reactions to bigotry vary, ranging from surprise and resentment to fear and paranoia. For example, a 1985–86 poll of victims of ethnoviolence showed that 80 percent felt "very much" angry at those responsible for attacking them; 69 percent felt "very much" sad about it; 49 percent felt powerless to do anything about it; 47 percent feared that they or their families would be physically hurt; 36 percent feared that they or their families would be killed, and 27 percent expressed suspicion of other people.[3]

Generally, minority responses to bigotry can be categorized as: fatalistic submission, pragmatic accommodation, prudent avoidance, militant defense, retaliatory aggression, geographic resettlement, or defiant determination to prove that members of the group are not what they are accused of being, or that they are as good as—if not better than—their attackers. For example, Hawaiians generally greeted and tolerated European and American intruders. Under American military occupation resulting from the Spanish American War of 1898, Puerto Ricans were usually friendly and accommodating, while Filipinos moved from the latter feelings to those of resentment and rebelliousness. The widely dispersed Eskimos in Greenland, Alaska, Canada, and Soviet Siberia were submissive and over-whelmed by encroaching outsiders and, more recently, by oil and natural gas developers. Like many immigrant parents, early twentieth-century Punjabis in California urged their children to have as little contact as pos-sible with non-Punjabis, to ignore bigoted remarks, to avoid fights, and to do well in school. In contrast, contemporary Asian Indian Americans are urged to "aggressively pursue a policy of social intercourse with other eth-nic groups to educate them about our background and culture."[4]

Depending on the tribe, geographic area, and time period, Native Americans varied in their reactions to foreigners from abroad or from the East Coast. Some Native Americans were immediately helpful to the new-comers, some suspicious and withdrawn, and some resentful and aggres-sive. As noted earlier, some tribes allied themselves with the settlers to fight other tribes or European powers. All belatedly learned that the only way they could have stopped the white man's encroachment, or at least greatly delayed it, was through united tribal opposition. In sharp contrast were many Hutterites and Garveyites, who immigrated respectively to Canada and Africa to escape religious discrimination and racism. Though often armed, Mormons fled from gentile detractors and attackers in New York, Ohio, Missouri, and Illinois (where a mob killed their founder Jo-seph Smith and his brother) and finally settled in the Great Salt Lake Val-ley. Chinese on the West Coast were relatively submissive, but if social and economic conditions became unbearable, wrote Betty Lee Sung, an expert on Chinese Americans, they often moved eastward, and, "If the white man begrudged him a job, he opened a laundry or restaurant or grocery and became his own employer." To avoid being stigmatized, a few minority members passed into the general society, such as white immigrant off-spring who changed their names, religion, and facial features; light-skinned Afro-Americans who hid their roots; and black Caribbean immi-grants who suppressed their ethnicity in public. "I used to be scared to tell people that I was Haitian," said one schoolgirl. "Like when I was in eighth grade there were lots of Haitians in the English as a secondary language (ESL) classes, and people used to beat them up. They used to pick on them. I said to myself I am going to quiet down, say I am American."[5]

To victims and victimizers alike, numbers, resources, and cohesiveness are crucial to successful defense or attack. For example, when Catholics were a tiny minority among Protestants, they were consciously accommo-dating. Before emigrating from seventeenth-century England, Cecil Calvert counseled Catholic immigrants not to offend majority Protestants, but to practice their faith "as privately as may be" and remain "silent upon all occasions of discourse concerning matters of Religion." As Catholics grew in number, however, so did their militancy and organization. Established in

1827, the Catholic Tract Society not only defended the faith, but criticized Protestantism. In some cities, Catholics formed semimilitary units to defend themselves against mob attacks, as in Philadelphia and New York City, where Bishop Hughes devised a plan for filling each church with 1,000 to 3,000 men who would take "as many lives as they could in defence of their property," and, if necessary, give up "their own lives for the same cause." By the late nineteenth century, Catholics gained political power in many large cities where they had become a majority or plurality. Only after the presidential election of John F. Kennedy did many Catholics stop feeling like a "beleaguered community."[6]

Other minority groups, too, formed organizations and developed programs to defend themselves from physical or verbal attack, as well as, of course, to strengthen their group cohesiveness and demonstrate their patriotism:

—The German Turnverein Society, brought from Germany in 1824, originally focussed on gymnastics and politics, and by 1856 had groups in twenty-eight states. Because of nativist attacks in the 1850s, particularly in Hoboken, New Jersey, and Louisville, Kentucky, the society encouraged the formation of paramilitary companies. During World War I, many German, Norwegian, and Danish Lutheran groups cooperated in combatting anti-German and anti-Lutheran prejudice. After the war, amid intense xenophobia, the Steuben Society of America was founded to counter negative images of Germany as a nation of Huns and of German Americans as a people of divided allegiance.[7]

—A few years after arriving in the latter nineteenth century, Japanese immigrants formed the Japanese Association. While most of its activities were social and benevolent, when nativists on the West Coast attacked them, they adopted self-protective measures, such as contacting the police or the Japanese consul for assistance. The second generation created the Japanese American Citizens League, which combined both protective and acculturationalist functions.[8]

—The American Jewish Committee came into being in 1906 to "prevent the infraction of the civil and religious rights of Jews in any part of the world" and "to secure for Jews equality of economic, social, and educational opportunity." Seven years later, the Anti-Defamation League of B'nai B'rith was created to combat anti-Semitism as well as to "secure justice and fair treatment for all citizens alike."

—Between 1909 and 1911, the first national black defense and improvement societies were established: the National Association for the Advancement of Colored People and the National League on Urban Conditions. With the civil rights movement of the 1960s, new and more militant organizations came into being, led mainly or entirely by a younger generation of Afro-Americans: the Congress of Racial Equality (CORE), the Southern Christian Leadership Conference (SCLC), and the Student Non-Violent Coordinating Committee (SNCC).

—Mexican Americans formed mutual aid and protective societies, such as the Alianza Hispano Americana in 1894, the Orden Hijos de America (the Order of the Sons of America) in 1921, and the League of the United Latin American Citizens in 1929, with one of its prime goals being the end of bigotry against Mexican Americans. In 1995, the Mexican American Opportunities Foundation, in California, established a "Hall of Fame," which highlights the lives of outstanding Mexican Americans and thereby countering the negative images of Mexican American gangs, knifings, and illegal border crossings.[9]

—Largely in response to the post–World War I revival of the Ku Klux Klan in the South and rampant antiforeign feelings, a group of Greek Americans in Atlanta, Georgia, formed the American Hellenic Educational Progressive Association (AHEPA) in 1922. While committed to acculturation and the use of English in their official meetings, they vigorously defended their Greek heritage and language.[10]

Similar organizing continues to take place among smaller, more recent immigrant groups. For example, in Cincinnati, where residents of Appalachian descent are second in size to African Americans, a human rights ordinance was passed in 1993 banning discrimination against them, and a political action committee, AppalPAC, was created to support sympathetic candidates. Earlier, in 1985, the Gay & Lesbian Alliance Against Defamation (GLAAD) was organized to oppose media and public prejudice against members. A National Association for the Advancement of Fat Acceptance also came into being, advocating legislation banning height or weight discrimination, which, as of 1995, only Michigan had passed. Ethnically, the American-Arab Anti-Discrimination Committee was formed in 1980 to combat media stereotyping and employment, educational, and political discrimination. Five years later, the Colombian-American Society was created in Miami to assist kinsmen to adapt to American life and to counter jokes and suspicions about all Colombians being criminal drug dealers. For too long, said a society official, "We are getting the bad news and we never took the time to get the good news."[11]

When a group cannot adequately protect itself, or when a local or the federal government offers economic and political protections or benefits to a broadly defined group (such as Hispanics, Asians, or women), it may join with other similarly situated groups in an ad hoc or long-term coalition. What it cannot obtain alone, particularly if it is small, becomes achievable through a confederation of groups, which, if it is to be successful, requires those joining to put aside any significant cultural, linguistic, religious, racial, ethnic, and/or socioeconomic differences they may have.

Some minority groups are fortunate in having their former governments speak in their defense. Throughout the late nineteenth and early twentieth centuries, China, Japan, Italy, and Mexico protested the industrial abuse of workers and nativist attacks on their nationals and, at times, succeeded in forcing federal investigations, formal apologies, or indemnifications for families of the injured. Recently, when California passed a proposition cutting social and educational services to illegal immigrants, El Salvador's president urged expatriates living in America not to react violently and the Mexican government issued a statement criticizing "all open and undercover forms of discrimination and any xenophobic practices," though it was at the same time being criticized by Mexican and Guatemalan human rights advocates for mistreating and expelling Central American illegal immigrants.[12] Totally without foreign governmental support were blacks and early twentieth-century minorities who either had no homeland governments or ones that cared about them, as in the case of Jews, Armenians, and Poles.

Of course, not all groups experiencing discrimination form self-defense structures, either because they are new to the country or too few in number, lack financial resources, have no significant political leaders, are unaccustomed to voluntary group advocacy, or simply believe that nothing can be done to change their situation. Instead, they become the beneficiaries of reforms brought about by more established or militant groups.

Dramatic changes in the situations of minorities began during and after World War II, when large numbers of Americans started abandoning the prejudices of their parents and grandparents as a result of military service, travel abroad, patriotism, religious or political idealism, and compliance with the antidiscrimination laws, or any combination thereof. Ethnic, religious, and racial bigotry were increasingly seen as irrational, unfair, and immoral—and that one's own well-being was best assured when that of other groups was also assured. Moreover, as never before, African Americans challenged institutional and governmental bigotry through mass public appeals, court cases, marches and demonstrations, sit-ins and boycotts, and political action groups and coalitions, all of which influenced other groups to do the same. As Bayard Rustin, in 1965, described the impact of black civil rights activists:

Clearly, it was the sit-in movement of young Southern Negroes which, as it galvanized white students, banished the ugliest features of McCarthyism from the American campus and resurrected political debate. It was not until Negroes assaulted *de facto* school segregation in the urban centers that the issue of quality education for all children stirred into motion. Finally, it seems reasonably clear that the civil rights movement, direct and through the resurgence of social conscience it kindled, did more to initiate the war on poverty than any other single force.[13]

In spite of the physical, socioeconomic, and psychic pains of bigotry, there are always some victimized groups or members who believe that suffering is God-ordained, spiritually uplifting, character strengthening, or essential for survival. Colonial Quakers claimed that, "Persecution endowed them with courage and an ever-deepening faith in the truth of their doctrine." Prosperity and security are believed detrimental to the Hutterite determination to live and work together, thereby confirming to them the old saying, "Good times have never yet made good Christians." Amish do not believe in anger or vengeance, said Arthur Kraybill, author of *The Amish Struggle with Modernity*, but rather have "a deep sense of comfort, assurance that things are in God's hands and in the long run everything will come out OK." To early Mormons, "the blood of the martyrs became the seed of the church" and strengthened their group identity and unity.[14]

From a more practical perspective, one successful businessman claimed that the steadfastness of kindred Albanian immigrants was due to the successive waves of Bulgars, Serbs, Turks, Italians, Greeks, and Nazi Germans who had invaded and oppressed their homeland, so that when "we came here and people pushed, we stood our ground." Jewish commentators often note that anti-Semitism, or the danger of it, increases Jewish identity and communal solidarity. "It's very easy to be Jewish when everybody is anti-Semitic: you're constantly reminded that you're a Jew; it's not even your choice," said Nathan Perlmutter, the late head of the Anti-Defamation League of B'nai B'rith. "But it's a very difficult achievement in an open, secure society. The more we succeed, the more endangered that part of our personality becomes." In his study of Asians in America, Brett Melendy wrote that fear and hatred of the Japanese appeared to be the only unifying force among various Korean groups. Lebanese-American Joseph Jacobs, a highly successful engineering corporation head, remembers being called a "camel jockey" while growing up in Brooklyn, and credits discrimination with giving him an "additional incentive to *accomplish* something and get the respect of your peers."[15]

In the process of group self-defense, each minority group member has to decide not only if, how, and to what extent to respond to bigotry, but also how he or she wants to be defined. "You are compelled to see yourself as different, as a member of a minority group," wrote Magorah Maruyama, a third-generation Japanese-American writer. Facing the truth can be a painful experience. . . . I have finally faced this reality. I am yellow—I cannot change what I am. I can say honestly now that I am proud of being Japanese." Mas'ood Cajee, a 21-year-old Muslim-American student activist, places a lot of responsibility on Muslims themselves for the negative stereotypes about them in the 1990s. "More members of our faith have to reach out and communicate with the non-Muslim world, and communicate what our religion is about . . . not only in America but across the world."[16]

Victims of prejudice and discrimination rarely forget those who cause them pain. A common experience is that of Derald Wing Sue, a California psychologist and teacher who cannot forget when, as a third-grader, he spoke to his brother in Chinese and the teacher told him, " 'You have to speak English if you want to succeed.' I was humiliated. I told my mother I never wanted to speak Chinese again. I felt ashamed of my cultural heritage." Such is equally true of countless other minority group members who speak with an accent. In fact, some neurobiologists found that, emotionally, memories of pain can become permanently imbedded in the brain, subject to suppression but not elimination.[17]

Thus, many victims will distrust and sometimes hold guilty the entire group to which their victimizers belong, or, at the other extreme, wish they had been born a member of the dominant group. Such people usually refuse to acknowledge that prejudice against their group has declined, which it has for all pre–World War II minority groups, or that prejudice in general is lower today than it was a few decades ago, which is true for all groups. These victims refuse to see that they are sometimes treated less harshly than members of other groups, or that members of other groups often want to help them or to support their candidates.

Usually, the persistence and frequency of such beliefs is correlated to the duration and intensity of the group's historic victimization. For example, in a 1981 study of American anti-Semitism, 76 percent of the Jews polled believed that a majority of non-Jews thought they had "too much power in the business world," though in fact only 32 percent actually thought so; 55 percent of the Jews believed that non-Jews saw them as "trying to push in where they are not wanted," but only 16 percent of the non-Jews really expressed such a belief; and, lastly, most Jews believed that non-Jews saw them as unacceptable presidential candidates or marriage partners, though a clear majority of non-Jews actually said the contrary.[18]

W. E. B. Du Bois acknowledged that blacks gradually adopted "the reciprocal habit of hating white skins, of being suspicious of every white action, and particularly of talking and acting as though even those white people who are not prejudiced, or who earnestly desire not to be, belonged to the unfortunate majority." If blacks failed to fulfill white expectations of being unprejudiced, he wrote, the fault was that of whites. "Lay it to the last lynching, or to the last time he was insulted in the theater, or to the last time he went hungry because all available hotels and restaurants were closed against him."[19]

Ironically, the enactment of tougher antidiscrimination laws and affirmative action programs led not only to less bigotry against minorities, but also to more accusations of it, including some questionable ones:

—An African-American father in Nebraska sued the publisher of a CD-ROM encyclopedia for $40 million because of the emotional distress he and his three sons suffered from discovering the word "nigger" was included about six times—such as in reference to a story by Joseph Conrad, a book by Dick Gregory, and an incident in the life of Martin Luther King, Jr. He also claimed damages under the state laws dealing with deceptive trade practices and libel.[20]

—A Polish-American former police chief charged that he had been paid less than the town's Irish superintendent of highways and sewers because a town official had told him that he could not "expect a Polack Chief to be equal with an Irish Street Superintendent." An investigation found the comparison had been made in jest and was unrelated to the chief's desire for higher salary.[21]

—Some Asian-American actors charged discrimination because some major roles of Asians in the Broadway plays *Good Woman of Szechwan* in 1973 and *Miss Saigon* in 1990 were given to Caucasians.[22]

—In explaining increased producer complaints over station programming decisions, a PBS official said that they were simply crying "racism or censorship" to "gain publicity for programs that otherwise wouldn't attract notice."[23]

—A 1995 U.S. Labor Department report found that a "high percentage" of reverse discrimination claims made by whites resulted from "a disappointed applicant failing to examine his or her own qualifications, and erroneously assuming that when a woman or minority got the job, it was because of race or sex, not qualifications."[24]

—A scholar in Asian–Indian American immigration studies claimed that while the 1965 Immigration Act ended invidious national origins quotas, in practical application it still discriminated against "persons from India" because India's quota is "only 20,000 out of 390,000 (5.1 percent of the total) whereas the population of India constitutes 15.3 percent of the world's population."[25]

Because of the range and diversity of minority feelings, fears, and forebodings about being victimized, there are frequent disagreements between a group's leaders and members at large. For example, a 1985 poll comparing the views of blacks in general with those of the leaders of the NAACP, National Urban League, Southern Christian Leadership Conference, Operation PUSH, National Conference of Black Mayors, and the Congressional Black Caucus showed that while 77 percent of the latter believed minorities should receive preferential treatment to make up for past discrimination, an equal percentage of blacks generally believed otherwise; busing to integrate black and white children in the public schools was favored by 68 percent of the leaders, but opposed by 53 percent of the black public; and while 61 percent of the leaders felt that African Americans were making less progress, 66 percent of blacks in general believed more progress was being made.[26]

Some black leaders and organizations have also been accused of sexism and of being more interested in dwelling on social pathology than in recognizing minority success. In 1994, a number of black women criticized the NAACP, Southern Christian Leadership Conference, National Urban League, National Rainbow Coalition, Nation of Islam, and National Baptist Convention for excluding or having relatively few women in executive positions. By presenting "minority problems" as solvable by financial expenditures, wrote Thomas Sowell, minority group leaders distort and reduce the complexities of history, economics, and cultural dynamics "to a simplistic play in which the choice is to blame either 'society' or to 'blame the victim.' "[27]

Similar intragroup differences exist in other groups. Richard Estrada, a contemporary syndicated columnist, claimed that Hispanic leaders in America do not really speak for the larger Hispanic community, but more often represent themselves, their fellow Hispanics of similar socioeconomic background, and the values of non-Hispanic foundations that contribute funds to them, especially on issues like the limiting of immigration, the requiring of a national ID card, abortion, and bilingual education. The leaders of organizations like La Raza, the Mexican American Legal Defense and Educational Fund, and the Puerto Rican Legal Defense Fund, wrote Estrada, frequently "overlook the adverse impact of the policies they promote upon low-wage, low-skill Hispanics, as well as many tax-paying Hispanics in the middle class."[28]

Rose Hum Lee, in her study of Chinese in America published in 1960, accused Chinese association leaders of being "a dividing rather than a constructive force," whose power depended on group separation, and who feared losing their leadership positions to American-born "better-informed Chinese." Fordham University historian John P. McCarthy chastized Irish-American political and organizational leaders for championing homeland causes in order to obtain local Irish-American votes, as well as for being unrealistically nationalistic about Ireland, which is "more concerned with economic development, fiscal stability, European integration, community reconciliation, and the various strains imposed on individual and familial harmony" than irredentist issues. Rabbi Meir Kahane, founder of the Jewish Defense League, claimed that American Jewry "suffers from a massive lack of greatness, from a deplorable and tragic absence of talented leaders." However, to Rabbi Daniel Lapin, founder of the politically conservative group Toward Tradition, American Jews are "disportionately committed to militant liberalism," which they use as "a replacement for their Judaism."[29]

Before Ukrainia became an independent nation, Myron B. Kuropas, a columnist for the American *The Ukrainian Weekly*, criticized his group's leaders for not protesting alleged anti-Ukrainian statements and actions by President Ford in 1976 and Vice President Bush in 1988: "Why can't our leaders understand that when it comes to attacks from outsiders, we need to remember we're family. We can fight all we want among ourselves, but when a family member is maligned from the outside, we need to stand as one." Magnus J. Krynski, chairman of the Department of Slavic Languages at Duke University, charged Polish-American congressmen in 1984 with being alienated from their ethnic heritage and constitutents because they failed to protest "the massive violations of human rights in Poland under martial law" and were "divorced from the problems of repression in Poland and seem unaware of the role the Soviet Union plays in these repressions." Facing a declining membership and financial problems, Denny Yasuhara, elected president of the Japanese American Citizens League in 1994, denied that the organization was unresponsive to younger people. "Today we don't have an issue that cuts across the generations. . . . I've tried to recruit younger members and every other question is 'What's in it for me?' " he said. In the gay world, one conservative criticized the power of gay political leftists, because when they are "confronted with a bothersome truth, they react with threats, intimidation, and terror. Despite their attempts to cloak themselves in the mantle of human-rights advocacy and an opposition to hate, I have observed how vicious and unprincipled they can be toward those who break ranks with them."[30]

In summary, all American minority groups experience some form and degree of bigotry and respond in varying ways—from fatalististic submission to aggressive opposition. The more intense and pervasive the victimization, the longer it is remembered, forming a historical, if not instinctive, reservoir of suspicion, bitterness, and/or hostility toward the victimizers and toward those in society who allow or validate the oppression.

Disagreements among group members and between them and their organizational leaders on how to deal with bigotry and other societal problems is common. The success of a group in combating bigotry depends in large measure on its size, its unity of purpose, its level of political activity, and its ability to attract the support of members of other groups.

How the dynamics of group life thus far discussed impact on American democracy will now be examined.

## NOTES

1. S. M. Silverman, "Victim and Victimizer," *The American Zionist* (December 1971): 29–32.

2. Dudley L. Poston, Jr., "Patterns of Economic Attainment of Foreign-Born Male Workers in the United States," *International Migration Review* (Fall 1994): 489–96.

3. Paul H. Ephross et al., *The Ethnoviolence Project: Pilot Study* (Baltimore: National Institute Against Prejudice and Violence, 1986), 8.

4. Alejandro Portes and Min Zhou, "Should Immigrants Assimilate?" *Public Interest* (Summer 1994): 29; G. S. Sandhu, "Indian-Americans Are Industrious, Resourceful and Prudent," *India Worldwide, North American Edition* (January 1995): 20.

5. Kenneth H. Winn, *Exiles in a Land of Liberty* (Chapel Hill: University of North Carolina Press, 1989), 63–84; B. L. Sung, *The Story of the Chinese in America* (New York: Collier Books, 1967), 240; Mary C. Waters, "Ethnic and Racial Identities of Second-Generation Black Immigrants in New York City," *International Migration Review* (Winter 1994): 812.

6. John Cogley, *Catholic America* (New York: Dial Press, 1973), 10; Ray Allen

Billington, *The Protestant Crusade* (Chicago: Quadrangle Paperbacks, 1964), 47; Edward Wakin, *Enter the Irish-American* (New York: Thomas Y. Crowell, 1976), 83; Christopher J. Kauffman, *Faith and Fraternalism: The History of the Knights of Columbus, 1882–1982* (New York: Harper & Row, 1982), 154; Andrew M. Greeley, *The American Catholic* (New York: Basic Books, 1977), 73.

7. Richard Hofstadter and Michael Wallace, *American Violence* (New York: Vintage Books, 1971), 309; Clifford E. Nelson, *The Lutherans in North America* (Philadelphia: Fortress Press, 1980), 399; Sander A. Diamond, *The Nazi Movement in the United States, 1924–1941* (Ithaca: Cornell University Press, 1974), 57–58.

8. Roger Daniels and Harry H. L. Kitano, *American Racism: Exploration of the Nature of Prejudice* (Englewood Cliffs, N.J.: Prentice-Hall, 1970), 81–84.

9. Marilyn Martinez, "Mexican American Hall of Fame Honors Unsung Cultural Heroes," *Los Angeles Times,* 12 May 1995, B1.

10. Andrew T. Kopan, "Greek Survival in Chicago: The Role of Ethnic Education, 1890–1980," in *Ethnic Chicago,* ed. Peter d'A. Jones and Melvin G. Holli (Grand Rapids, Mich.: William B. Eerdmans, 1981), 117.

11. Judy Pasternak, "Bias Blights Life Outside Appalachia," *Los Angeles Times,* 29 March 1994, A1; Gavin Daly, "Bill Would Ban Weight Bias," *Boston Globe,* 21 March 1996, 71; *New York Times,* 17 August 1985, 24.

12. "Mexico Hits California's 'Xenophobic' Proposition," *Boston Globe,* 10 November 1994, 20; Rosalind Muhammad, "Proposition 187," *The Final Call,* 30 November 1994, 7; Leon Lazaroff, "Mexico Takes Flack Over Its Version of Proposition 187," *Christian Science Monitor,* 20 December 1994, 1, 7.

13. Bayard Rustin, "From Protest to Politics: The Future of the Civil Rights Movement," in *Problems & Prospects of the Negro Movement,* ed. Raymond J. Murphy and Howard Elinson (Belmont, Calif.: Wadsworth Publishing Co., 1968), 414.

14. V. F. Calverton, *The Awakening of America* (New York: John Day Company, 1939), 173; David Flint, *The Hutterites* (Toronto: Oxford University Press, 1975), 69; Val Dan MacMurray and Perry H. Cunningham, "Mormons and Gentiles: A Study in Conflict and Persistence," in *Ethnic Conflicts and Power: A Cross-National Perspective,* ed. Donald E. Gelfand and Russell D. Lee (New York: John Wiley & Sons, 1973), 212; Mary Pemberton, "Amish Show No Anger after Slaying," *Boston Globe,* 13 February 1995, 3; Lewis Coser, *The Functions of Social Conflict* (New York: Free Press of Glencoe, 1956), 110.

15. Tim Golden, "Changes in Albania Rekindle Pride in Immigrants," *New York Times,* 18 March 1991, B4; Edwin Black, "Remembering Nathan Perlmutter," *Greater Phoenix Jewish News,* 5 August 1987, 9, 16; Yen Le Espiritu, *Asian American Panethnicity* (Philadelphia: Temple University Press, 1992), 26; Casey Kasem, "I Want My Son to Be Proud," *Parade Magazine,* 16 January 1994, 5.

16. Maxine Seller, *Immigrant Women* (Philadelphia: Temple University Press, 1981), 321; Charles M. Sennott, "After Bombings, America Faces Up to Prejudice," *Boston Globe,* 21 June 1995, 18; Bob Herbert, "Who Will Help the Black Man?" *New York Times Magazine,* 4 December 1994, 75.

17. "Meet Derald Wing Sue," *NEA Today* (April 1993): 9; Sandra Blakeslee, "Tracing the Brain's Pathways for Linking Emotion and Reason," *New York Times,* 6 December 1994, C1.

18. *Anti-Semitism in the United States,* Vol. 1, The Summary Report (Prepared for The American Jewish Committee, July 1981, by Yankelovich, Skelly and White, Inc.), 28

19. Meyer Weinberg, ed., *W. E. B. Du Bois, A Reader* (New York: Harper & Row, Publishers, 1970), 327.

20. *New York Times,* 9 March 1995, A18.

21. *John F. Skroski v. Town of Deerfield,* The Commonwealth of Massachusetts, Docket No: 79-SEM-0025, October 1, 1980.

22. *New York Times,* Letters to Editor, 28 September 1990, A26; *National Review,* 3 September 1990, 15.

23. Frederic M. Biddle, "Hunter-Gault Criticizes PBS for Lack of Diversity," *Boston Globe,* 12 August 1994, 64.

24. *New York Times,* 31 March 1995, A23.

25. *Journal of American Ethnic History* (Spring 1985): 128.

26. *Washington Post,* 19 September 1985, 1.

27. Steven A. Holmes, "In Fighting Racism, Is Sexism Ignored?" *New York Times,* 11 September 1994, E3; Thomas Sowell, "Ethnicity in a Changing America," *Daedalus* (Winter 1978): 233.

28. Richard Estrada, "Whom Do Hispanic Leaders Speak For?" *Boston Globe,* 24 July 1995, 4.

29. Louis L. Gerson, *The Hyphenate in Recent American Politics and Diplomacy* (Lawrence: University of Kansas Press, 1964), 236; John A. Murphy, "Ireland and Irish America: Strained Relations?" *Boston Irish News,* March 1985, 3; John P. McCarthy, "The Irish Government and Irish America," *Boston Irish News,* April 1983, 1; Rabbi Meir Kahane, *Time to Go Home* (Los Angeles: Nash Publishing, 1972), 280; *Forward,* 30 September 1994, 1–2.

30. *The Ukrainian Weekly,* 16 October 1988, 7; Magnus J. Krynski, "What's Wrong with the Voting Record of Polish-Americans in the 98th Congress," *Perspectives* (January–February 1985): 389; Jane Meredith Adams, "Japanese American Civil Rights Group in Turmoil," *Boston Globe,* 30 April 1995, 2; "The Conscience of a Gay Conservative," *Heterodoxy* (May/June 1994): 1.

# 10

# The Future of Group Life: Survival or Erosion?

And if a house be divided against itself, that house cannot stand.
—Saint Mark 3:24–25.

And now we come to the most difficult part of the book—a discussion of the future of group life in America and how American democracy is changing. Until now I have tried to identify the major factors and processes at work in the formation of group identity—an ever-expanding and diversifying population; the changing ways individuals, groups, and the government identify themselves and their goals; the proliferation, simultaneity and succession of group victims and the differential group patterns of responses to discrimination; and the individual, group, and national benefits and disadvantages of group identity. I also tried to show that each individual and group confronted problems of how to relate to people different from themselves and to the larger society, as well as how to perpetuate their own traditional values, behaviors, and language. By citing examples from many groups, I hoped to show both the uniqueness and yet the commonality of problems that each group faces.

From America's very beginnings as a nation, the goal of reformers, progressives, liberals, and social justice activists, both religious and lay, was generally to maximize individual freedoms and equal rights for all citizens, to prevent or stop the government from interfering with an individual's or a group's beliefs and practices (unless they violated the law), to eliminate interpersonal and intergroup racial, religious, ethnic, and sexual bigotry, and, above all, to maintain a unity of states and citizens. A variety of factors have facilitated such efforts through the years: an expansion of social, political, and economic opportunities outside one's own group; a multiplicity of groups and living styles; a dominance of the English language; a sharp rise in college graduates, especially after the institution of the World War II GI Bill of Rights; an increased need for highly skilled and educated workers and professionals; a relativizing of cultures and values; an availability of inexpensive domestic and overseas transportation; a repudiation of bigotry by mainstream media; a growing ecumenism among Christian leaders and between them and Jewish, Greek Orthodox, Mormon, and Muslim leaders; and a continuing enactment and public acceptance of legislation outlawing racial, religious, ethnic, gender, sex, and age discrimination, as well as discrimination toward the disabled.

The principles and practices of equal protection of the law, of equal opportunities for the bounties of society, and, most recently, of inclusion of minority group members in all aspects of American life, steadily replaced those of invidious restriction and exclusion. While only a few decades ago, discrimination against minorities in employment, housing, education, public accommodations, the executive offices of industry, and high society was common, today it is much less so. The 1990s are a far cry from the early 1960s when sociologist E. Digby Baltzell decried "the White-Anglo-Saxon-Protestant establishment's unwillingness, or inability, to share and improve its upper-class traditions by continuously absorbing talented and distinguished members of minority groups into its privileged ranks."[1]

And, indeed, no longer do white, Anglo-Saxon male Protestants overwhelmingly dominate the executive suites of corporate America, lead philanthropic foundations, or, for that matter, the major arenas of political, social, and educational life. A study of religious presence among America's social, political and economic elites from 1930 to 1992 shows that the percentage of Episcopalian, Presbyterian, and United Church of Christ members relative to their percentage in the total American population dropped from 53 in the early 1930s to 35 in 1992, with Catholics and particularly Jews gaining more access to those elite groups than ever before. Other studies show that by the 1980s, Catholics outnumbered Episcopalians as chief executive officers of major corporations, and that in 1987 over half of the twenty-five highest paid executives identified by *Business Week* magazine were "non-WASPs," with Italian-American Lee Iacocca leading the list and Cuban-American Roberto C. Goizueta ending it.[2]

The increasing presence in recent years of women and minority executives in major foundations is epitomized by Afro-Americans Franklin Thomas as operating head of the Ford Foundation and Clifton Wharton as board chairman of the Rockefeller Foundation; Jewish American Helene Kaplan as chairperson of the Carnegie Corporation's board; and

Puerto Rican Sara Melendez, president of Independent Sector, the nation's largest philanthropic coalition. The number of female college presidents more than tripled in the past few decades, going from 148 in 1975 to 453 in 1995, including Judith Rodin, the first woman head of an Ivy League college, the University of Pennsylvania. "It's exciting," she said, "to be putting the mater back in alma mater." In addition, Ruth Simmons was appointed president of Smith College in late 1994, the first black woman to head an Ivy League college.[3]

At the same time, record numbers of minorities were elected or appointed to national and local government offices. Some thirty years after the Irish Catholic John F. Kennedy was elected to the U.S. presidency, the Greek Orthodox Michael Dukakis ran for the same office, proudly proclaiming himself a son of poor immigrants who couldn't speak English when they arrived in America. His loss of the election, moreover, was not due to any nativist attacks on his roots or on the Jewish heritage of his wife.

In the once exclusive halls of the State Department, a Pole, Edmund Muskie, and then a Jew, Henry Kissinger, became the secretary of state. Anton Scalia became the first Italian-American Supreme Court justice, and the Mexican-American Lauro Cavozos became secretary of education. Similarly unprecedented was the appointment of the African-American Thurgood Marshall as a Supreme Court justice and General Colin L. Powell as chairman of the Joint Chiefs of Staff, who in turn was succeeded by the foreign-born General John Shalikashvili, of Polish and Russian parents. After the 1992 national elections, the number of Hispanics in the House of Representatives rose from 10 to 17, blacks from 25 to 38 (which included 9 black women, aside from the first black woman senator, Carol Moseley-Braun), women from 28 to 47 (in addition to two Jewish women senators, Dianne Feinstein and Barbara Boxer), the first Puerto Rican woman, Nydia Velazquez, and the first Korean, Jay Kim. Even the number of elected, self-acknowledged gay public officials increased from 63 to 140 after the 1992 elections.[4]

What is unique in many of the elections of minorities is that while candidates were frequently helped with votes or funds from their group members, they still needed the support of nongroup members to win. A candidate's position on economic and social issues, such as jobs, street crime, quality education, and taxes, often proved more important to voters than his or her religious, racial, ethnic, or sexual group identity. For example, in recent years, Afro-Americans by themselves could not have elected Douglas L. Wilder as governor of Virginia, Alan Wheat as a congressman from Missouri, Gary Franks as a congressman from Connecticut, J. C. Watts as a congressman from Oklahoma, or as mayors, Norman Rice of Seattle, Wellington Webb of Denver, Emanuel Cleaver of Kansas City, Dwight Tillery of Cincinnati, John Daniels of New Haven, Chester Jenkins of Durham, N.C., Sharon Sayles Belton of Minneapolis, or John Jenkins and William Burney, respectively, of Lewiston and Augusta (Maine), whose black populations are less than one-half of 1 percent. In fact, from 1967 to 1993, African Americans won mayoral elections in seventy cities with populations of 50,000 or more, though blacks constituted less than a majority of the electorate in most of them and less than one-third of the electorate in thirty of them.[5]

Italians could not, by themselves, have elected Mario Cuomo as governor of New York or Thomas M. Menino as mayor of Boston; nor Jews, Madeline Kunin as governor of Vermont or Bernie Sanders as its congressman; nor Armenians, George Deukmejian as governor of California; nor Swedes, Kay Orr as governor of Nebraska; nor Lebanese, James Abourezk and Spencer Abraham as senators respectively from South Dakota and Michigan; nor Filipinos, Ben Cayetano as governor of Hawaii; nor Asians, Sheng H. Chang as councilman in Arcadia, California, the city's first Asian American and minority member.

Trite but true, today's minorities have positions or opportunities that their parents and certainly their grandparents never had. When a 1993 *New York Times/CBS News* poll asked blacks and whites if there had been "significant progress toward Martin Luther King's dream of equality," 62 percent of blacks and 64 percent of whites believed there had been. A *Los Angeles Times* poll the following year probing black and white assessments of race relations in the workplace found that 83 percent of the respondents felt that relations were good to excellent, including 52 percent of the blacks surveyed. In addition, as never before, society, schools, and even families stress the need for greater intergroup respect. For example, a 1993 Phi Delta Kappa/Gallup poll found that 96 percent of parents believed their children should be taught to respect those of different racial and ethnic backgrounds, 87 percent to respect people with different religions, and 50 percent to respect those of different sexual orientations.[6]

As has also been seen, upon arriving, most immigrants begin a process of acculturation that accelerates with each successive generation, whose members usually complete more education than their forebears, abandon traditional trades and jobs, and leave parental homes, farms, and neighborhoods for better economic or living conditions in another neighborhood, city, or state. Also, unlike prior generations, twentieth-century immigrants and their offspring interacted with a greater variety of people in the workplace and in the armed forces, particularly during World War II, the Korean War, the Vietnam War, and the Gulf War. Fast meals and fast-food stores rather than homecooking and extended family meals have become the norm. Plastic surgery, hair dyes, and cosmetics are used to alter physiognomies and complexions. Full religiosity and ethnicity are reserved for funerals, weddings, holy days and celebrations, though American influences are evident in the music played, foods served, clothes worn, and

languages spoken. The rate of interfaith and interethnic dating and marriages continues to rise. Among racial minorities similar developments are
taking place, though to a lesser extent. Under such conditions, it is not
surprising that individual or group isolation has become more difficult,
though not yet impossible, for Chassidim, Amish, Black Muslims, Mormons, and the many small cultist and millennialist communities that periodically come into being.

Today, those wishing to perpetuate group identity as their ancestors
lived it, or as they inherited it, or as they would want to bequest it to the
next generation, confront a series of interrelated problems, which though
not entirely new, are more difficult to solve simply because parents and
religion do not have the influence and control they once had: how to create foreign language fluency and pride in past history in the younger generations; how to prevent the steady loss of members because of assimilation
and intermarriage; how to stop the late marriages and decline in the birthrates of married children; how to create a family, group, and societal environment responsive to the here-and-now emotional, intellectual, and social
needs of the young; how to maintain local and national social, religious,
and cultural organizations; and how to respond to prejudice and discrimination, which though much less severe than in prior generations, still exists—these are all difficult questions without easy answers in today's
world.

Compounding the problems of group survival are the increasing number
of Americans born of mixed marriages, who are either ignorant, indifferent, or unwilling to identify with any one branch in their family tree. For
example, when Alyson Todd, a student, attended a mandatory intercultural awareness workshop at Wellesley College in 1989 and was asked to
bring an item expressing her cultural identity, she was baffled:

Like many Americans, my heritage is a mix of many different nationalities, including Irish, English, Dutch, German, French and a dash of Italian. I did not really
have any possessions which expressed the essence of any of those cultures. . . .
So I decided that I am an American, and that I would bring to the workshop
something that expressed American culture: the American dollar bill.[7]

Of course, the above situation is not unique. Census and survey data
for 1980 and 1990 reveal sizable numbers of whites who did not affirm
any specific European ancestry, or who simply identified themselves as
Americans. In the 1990 census, just under 10 percent (almost 24 million)
did not report any ancestry; 5 percent (some 13 million) simply reported
"American" or "United States"; and 30 percent reported having more
than one ancestry (almost 74 million).[8]

In contrast, but concomitant with the above pattern of acculturation
and assimilation, is a rising desire and effort by some minority group

members to retain and reaffirm group identity. Name-changing to eliminate any non–Anglo-Saxon connotations, whether motivated by self-
hatred, social acceptance, or professional advancement, has all but ended,
as epitomized by entertainment superstars like Sylvester Stallone, Arnold
Schwarzenegger, and Barbra Streisand. Some blacks assume a Muslim or
African name, as when Cassius Clay renamed himself Muhammad Ali; the
writer Le Roi Jones, Amiri Baraka; and academic Arthur Smith, Molefi
Kete Asante. In schools and colleges across the country, minority students
increasingly want to learn more about their history and language, and as
a result, minority courses, departments, caucuses, clubs, faculty members,
and scholarships have multiplied. For example, in 1991, at the University
of California Los Angeles, there were more than sixty-five Asian-Pacific
student organizations, in comparison to less than ten twenty years earlier.[9]

Of no less impact are the calls of some minority intellectuals and leaders
for the restructuring of American society along group lines. To them the
problems of group identity, well-being, and racism are interlinked, with
economic progress coming too slowly, bigotry too entrenched, and exclusions from positions of authority too frequent. Change for the better, they
say, can only come about through the restructuring of society, the institutionalization of group interests, and the equalizing of economic rewards.
As society is presently constituted, "Black people will never gain full
equality in this country," said law professor Derick Bell, but only "short-
lived victories that slide into irrelevance as racial patterns adapt in ways
that maintain white dominance."[10]

Implicit in such arguments is a belief that racial, gender, and cultural
group differences are fixed characteristics, as well as a pessimism about
the ability of members of some groups to achieve in the same way that
members of other groups do. Blindfolded justice, it is argued, must be
replaced by group-conscious compassion and remedial preferences. Terms
like individual opportunities, achievement, merit, and competition are dismissed as ways by which majorities exclude and subjugate minorities. It is
also argued that continuity rather than disappearance of groups is needed,
and the government's responsibility is to include and empower groups in
all aspects of society. Failure to do so is interpreted as perpetuating socioeconomic and political inequity, injustice, racism, and sexism.

For example, Harold Cruse, in *The Crisis of the Negro Intellectual,* argued for amending the Constitution "to reflect the social reality of
America as a nation of nations, or a nation of ethnic groups." Similarly,
Vine Deloria, Jr., in *We Talk, You Listen,* wants groups to become the
basic elements of American society. "To continue merely on the basis of
an abstract individual contracting with other individuals would be to court
disaster." Law professor Lani Guinier proposed a number of ways to further racial justice: an electoral system based on "proportionate interest
representation," a "minority veto for legislation of vital importance to mi-

nority interests," and instituting "cumulative voting and legislative super-majority requirements." Charles Lawrence, another law professor, called for "liberating action" or "freedom now," in which "the only remedy for racial subordination" is through "the systemic disestablishment of those structures, institutions and ideologies" that produced it. Some white and black intellectuals have repudiated what they term "Eurocentric" values of the commonality of people, the universality of ideals, and the objectivity of observation and interpretation. For Black Studies professor Molefi Kete Asante, African values should be central to "any analysis that involves African culture and behavior." Likewise, with some feminists, the consideration of gender is central to understanding their values, thinking, and position in society.[11]

And so, as minority members and groups philosophically, legally, politically, or vicerally demand more recognition and power, government increasingly complies, legitimating groups as basic units of society. While being a member of a minority group before the 1960s' civil rights movement—particularly a racial one—was a sure invitation to discrimination, today it can be a passport for preferential treatment, wherein the concepts of fairness, justice, and democracy are redefined to favor group affiliation over individual qualifications. To prove discrimination, it is no longer necessary to point to an individual's present or past exclusion, but to a group's absence or underrepresentation in a given arena of life. Thus, in seeking city, state or federal business contracts, a person's race, ethnicity, or sex can be a positive factor, particularly when few or no members of the group do business with the contracting agency.

To insure the hiring and promoting of minorities and women, some large private and public employers change or suspend their usual standards, tests, or scoring of tests, either because the tests are deemed culturally biased, or they do not reveal the talents of job applicants, or they do not result in a given number of qualified applicants. Other employers simply restrict job openings to women or minority applicants, as when the Detroit Symphony Orchestra abandoned its blind audition hiring policy in order to hire an Afro-American musician or when the Minnesota State Arts Board limited a new grant program to "artists or individuals of color."[12]

City, county, state, and federal electoral districts have been redrawn or created to insure minority representation, particularly for blacks and Hispanics. Some experts claim such actions contributed to the Democratic Party's loss, in 1994, of a majority in the House of Representatives by drawing off regular white Democratic votes from white districts and removing black Democratic votes from marginally Republican districts. While the Supreme Court in 1995, by a 5 to 4 decision, declared a Georgia congressional district unconstitutional because its boundaries were "predominantly motivated" by race, the Court approved without comment a

California plan to create or strengthen a dozen black- and Hispanic-major-ity districts.[13]

Of course, there is much debate over whether such developments are good or bad—and for whom. How government should relate to individu-als, groups, bigotry, and societal problems generally involves at least three basic questions: First is whether or not American democracy should change from its historic emphasis on guaranteeing individual rights *regard-less* of one's race, religion, ethnicity, or sex to guaranteeing individual rights *because* of one's race, religion, ethnicity, or sex. Up to 1965, civil rights reformers generally sought the former—equal protection of the law and equal opportunity for all citizens in employment, housing, education, voting, and public accommodations, with legally imposed segregation for none, particularly in schools, where the Supreme Court in 1954 declared separate facilities "inherently unequal" and therefore unconstitutional. The phrase "affirmative action" was first used to redress unfair labor prac-tices as defined in the Wagner Act of 1935 and then in a 1961 executive order by President Kennedy ordering federal contractors to "ensure that applicants are employed, and that employees are treated during employ-ment, without regard to their race, creed, color, or national origin." In those years an individual's merit was still considered the determining fac-tor in hiring and promotion.[14]

Such thinking was reaffirmed in the 1964 Civil Rights Act, which stipu-lated that all people are to be treated "without regard to their race, color, religion, sex, or national origin." In securing its passage, Senator Hubert Humphrey emphatically assured legislators that the act did not compel any employer "to hire on the basis of percentage or quota related to color, race, religion, or national origin" and that if anyone could find such word-ing in the act he would "start eating the pages one after another."[15] And indeed, Title VII of the act specifically bars requiring any employer to "grant preferential treatment to any individual or to any group because of race, color, religion, sex, or national origin of such individual or group on account of an imbalance."

Nevertheless, changes in interpretation and implementation of the law began taking place. Believing that laws banning discrimination were not sufficient to undo centuries of oppression, President Johnson in 1965 de-clared that the government must not only seek "equality as a right and a theory, but equality as a fact and equality as a result." Similarly, though not endorsing quotas, the Supreme Court and some federal agencies began validating race-conscious programs to remedy past discrimination or racial imbalances. Chief Justice Warren Burger claimed in the 1971 *Griggs v. Duke Power* case that the 1964 Civil Rights Act proscribed "not only overt discrimination but also practices that are fair in form, but discrimi-natory in operation." Justice Harry Blackmun went further in the 1978 *Bakke* decision. "In order to get beyond racism, we must first take account of race. There is no other way. And in order to treat some persons equally, we must treat them differently." Within a decade at most, Blackmun stated that American society "must and will reach a stage of maturity where acting along this line is no longer necessary." [16]

Such a development, of course, has not yet occurred. Instead, the government and the courts have adopted or permitted preferential group classifications and programs, in some cases even where no past or present history of group discrimination existed. Included were immigrants from such far-off countries as Pakistan, Bangladesh, Sri Lanka, Bhutan, the Maldive Islands, and Nepal, though they were few in number, had no personal or group history of being discriminated against in America, and, in some instances, notably among Asian Indians, earned more than white Americans.[17]

In mid-1995, the Supreme Court, by a 5 to 4 vote, in *Adarand Constructors v. Pena,* did express serious doubts about federal programs classifying people by race, even for benign purposes, but instead of banning them outright, as two justices recommended, the majority ordered that they be subject to strict judicial scrutiny to " 'smoke out' illegitimate uses of race" and insure "the personal right to equal protection of the laws has not been infringed." In a dissenting opinion, Justice John Paul Stevens defended "remedial race-based preferences" as a way of eradicating racial subordination and fostering equality in society.[18]

While experts immediately disagreed on whether the decision signaled the beginning of the end of affirmative action, a month later President Clinton strongly defended affirmative action as morally and politically good for the country, but acknowledged that it needed some corrections and that it should not be carried on forever. Affirmative action, he said, "does not mean, and I don't favor, the unjustified preference of the unqualified over the qualified of any race or gender. It doesn't mean, and I don't favor, numerical quotas. It doesn't mean, and I don't favor, rejection or selection of any employee or student solely on the basis of race or gender without regard to merit." [19]

Clearly, as indicated by both the *Adarand* decision and the president's policy speech, some kinds of affirmative action programs would no longer be adopted, while others would be ended or changed. However, just as clearly, the president said, "The job of ending discrimination in this country is not over," and a majority of justices affirmed the government's responsibility to respond to the "unhappy persistence of both the practice and the lingering effects of racial discrimination against minority groups in this country." [20] Unresolved were the inherent tensions within and between both sets of views—insuring individual rights and opportunities while ending past and present discrimination against specific groups.

The second basic question is whether or not government should do for groups what they cannot or will not do for themselves. Until recent decades, except for American Indians, with whom formal treaties were made, and regularly broken, and for blacks, who were provided with special educational and economic programs during the Reconstruction period, the U.S. government refrained from direct involvement in the maintenance of minority group life, though some nineteenth-century European groups requested help in immigrating and settling here and some twentieth-century religious groups sought financial aid to maintain their schools. The general attitude of the government was that groups wishing to immigrate here, to live within their own communities, and/or to educate their children in their own ways, were free to do so, as long as it was at their own expense and did not violate the law.

In more recent decades, however, the calls and demands for governmental assistance have increased, based on a number of new moral and political rationales: If the government had no hesitancy in oppressing some people because of their group affiliation, why shouldn't the government redress wrongs committed on the same basis? Also, it is argued that the government has a responsibility to eliminate all gross group socioeconomic disparities, which it institutionalized or allowed others to do so along racial, ethnic, or sexual group lines. Moreover, if the government really believes in diversity and multiculturalism, then it has an obligation to make these concepts everyday realities.

How government relates to individuals and groups—and vice versa—are not new problems, nor as we shall see, unique to America. The framers of the Constitution and the Bill of Rights emphasized the separation of governmental powers; freedom of religion, speech, and petition; due process; and equal protection of the law. Though immigrants were expected to discard ancestral prejudices and loyalties, the framers never enacted laws defining America as a land of one faith, one race, one language, or one God. Rather, they wanted no religious tests for government officials, and no requirement that office-seekers be born in America, except for those seeking the presidency.

While none of the Founding Fathers foresaw the evolution of today's enormous multicultural population, they knew the dangers of a divided people and of a government that bestowed privileges on some groups, whether royal, religious, or political. George Washington visualized an America that "gives to bigotry no sanction, to persecution no assistance," and that "requires only that they who live under its protection should demean themselves as good citizens." And by "good citizens," he meant people with a "pacific and friendly disposition" that induces them "to forget their local prejudices and policies, to make those natural concessions which are requisite to the general prosperity, and in some instances, to sacrifice their individual advantages to the interests of the Community." With equal simplicity and sagacity, John Quincy Adams, three decades later, wrote that America "is a land, not of *privileges,* but of *equal rights*

. . . *privileges* granted to one denomination of people, can very seldom be discriminated from erosions of the rights of others." [21]

Such early views, plus the guarantees of the Bill of Rights, form the basis of the American ideal, though often not of its reality. It is the contradiction between the ideal and the reality that leads to the third and most difficult question: What kind of governmental system best insures the greatest freedoms for individuals and groups, as well as the greatest possibilities of undoing wrongs among and between them, with the least injury to any person or group and to the nation's unity?

The very phrasing of this question will be repudiated by some people as being overly utilitarian or for ignoring or denying the centrality of institutionalized racism and socioeconomic inequities. And to some extent, at least semantically, they are correct, but not if one agrees that maintaining a healthy, democratic society is and should remain central to solving human rights injustices and social problems among all citizens, not just those of a select or privileged few groups. There is no evidence that governments based on racial, ethnic, religious, or sexual preferences, or on proportional representation, provide more personal and group freedom and self-respect, socioeconomic equality, surcease of bigotry, domestic well-being, national security, intergroup cooperation, and democratic solutions to societal problems than governments based on individual rights and liberties, equal opportunities for all, and blind justice.

In theory, governments based on proportional representation may appear fairer and more attractive, because they seem to—and sometimes do—offer some immediate redress and representation to minorities, but in reality they also can and do generate, multiply, and perpetuate intergroup tensions and conflicts, which delay or derail needed reforms, undermine the progress that has been or could be made, and endanger the future well-being of all citizens and society itself.

There are other and more immediate dangers as well, which neither the Founding Fathers nor the later civil rights reformers anticipated. By providing benefits to some groups on a preferential basis, a disrespect, if not contempt, for the recipients, the providers, and the law is created or reinforced. Bitter questions are asked. Why should all members of a group be eligible for benefits, while no members of other groups are eligible? Why must there be lower standards for some groups and higher ones for others—for the same job, promotion, or entrance to college? Is there, as various racists and sexists have long claimed, something biologically, intellectually, and/or socially amiss with blacks, Hispanics, Indians, and women? Or is there, as some militant group-rights advocates claim, something biologically, intellectually and/or socially superior in such groups?

If it is believed that all people are equal, or equally endowed, or equally entitled to certain inalienable rights, opportunities, and guarantees, why do some of those same believers insist on differential treatment in obtaining them, whether it be through quotas, goals, and timetables, set asides, or exemption from standard procedures? Is it not hypocritical for an individual or group to deplore being denied equal treatment and then defend the denial of such consideration to others or to denounce the misbehavior of others and defend the very same behavior by members of one's own group?

Who can respect the beneficiaries of favoritism, except for gaining something not fairly earned or that has been denied others? And how can such recipients respect themselves, except for the same reasons? And what is one to say about laws and legislators who validate such behavior? Much like that of majoritarian patronage and nepotism, a process of minority bestowal is seen to be at work, wherein positions are believed given those of the correct racial, ethnic, or sexual makeup—and denied those of the wrong racial, ethnic, or sexual makeup.

In cities across the country, local minority group leaders, like their white Anglo-Saxon Protestant and European ethnic counterparts, seek power by bloc voting, gerrymandering, the control of community development funds, and through the distribution of patronage jobs. At times, some programs are implemented in violation of the law. In New York City, for example, dozens of leaders of supposed coalitions of blacks, Hispanics, and women were indicted in 1993 for extorting money and no-show jobs for themselves and friends from construction builders, who were promised enough minority workers to meet federal contract requirements. A few years later, two members of the Mafia were indicted for fraudulently obtaining city and state minority contracts by establishing three front companies, which they actually owned but said belonged to a black, a woman, and a Hispanic, respectively.[22]

In other communities, minority and women contractors established paper offices, padded payrolls with female family members, or sold their company name to non–minority-owned companies so that the latter could obtain government contracts. One Native American leader obtained millions of dollars worth of government-owned construction and farming equipment free in the name of helping unemployed tribal members, and then sold it at a great profit elsewhere through a company he and two non–Native Americans had formed.[23]

When such programs are criticized for inefficiency, unfairness, or corruption, some minority leaders accuse the critics of being racist for seeing only wrongs that minorities commit or, worse yet, for wanting to undo the progress that has been made; or they will acknowledge that some wrongs do occur, but that they are few in number; or they will agree with the criticism, but note that it was not Afro-Americans, Hispanics, Native Americans, Asians, or women who throughout American history practiced political wrongdoing and instituted laws and legislation to limit, restrict, segregate, or exclude minorities.

A second danger to society resides in what has been termed "dumbing down," that is, the lowering of standards of performance and the ending of distinctions between high and low achievers in the belief that: minority performance, role models, and self-esteem will be improved; minority individuals and groups will no longer be viewed as genetically or culturally intelligent or unintelligent because of school performance; students will be encouraged to take courses beyond their immediate interest; work and school settings will more accurately reflect societal diversity; racism and bigotry will be diminished; problem-solving ability will be improved; and a more democratic society will result. The impetus for such changes comes from a variety of sources: minorities who want group representation in areas in which they are not present or have long been excluded from, and who believe existing tests and standards are structurally biased against them; educators who believe much greater attention should be given to underachievers or potential achievers; laws and legislation that penalize employers and businesses for employing a disproportionately low number of minorities; and politicians, social policy analysts, and community leaders who seek a classless, statusless, or more egalitarian society.

To achieve those goals in the workplace and schools, a variety of techniques are employed, such as inflating or eliminating school grades, admitting or hiring lower qualified or underqualified people, excluding or restricting higher or highly qualified people, passing all students, adding numerical handicaps to test scores, using different performance measurements for different groups, recruiting on the basis of group affiliation, padding salaries and perquisites of minority professionals, eliminating competency tests and evaluations that result in disparate group results, awarding group-based scholarships and contracts, ending separate classes or tracks for talented students, and projecting group numerical goals and timetables for minorities.

At many educational institutions, admission standards have been lowered, coursework has been eased, graduation requirements have been reduced, classroom distinctions in achievement have been eliminated, failing grades and dropped courses have not been entered in student records, and deceptive statistics on student achievement have been publicized. One researcher, in 1994, noted that 75 percent of colleges offered remedial reading, writing, and math courses and 23 percent gave credit for such courses toward graduation.[24]

In its desire for African-American and Mexican-American students, the University of Texas Law School admitted a given number of these students even though they had substantially lower academic scores than applicants of other groups. Likewise, African-American and Hispanic students with lesser scores than whites and Asians were admitted to a California medical school. "Medical school is not a reward for high test scores and grades," said an attorney for the school. "Medical schools have to decide who is going to fulfill the most pressing needs of society, and that doesn't correlate extremely well with test results and grades." At Harvard University, by the early 1990s, the grade C all but disappeared and the incidence of A grades went from 22 percent in 1966–67 to 43 percent in 1992. At Princeton University, the incidence of A grades rose from 16.9 percent in 1965 to 41.2 percent in 1994, while C grades dropped from 40 to 12 percent. Before F grades were reinstituted at Stanford University in 1995, Cs had declined from 16 percent in 1968–69 to 6 percent in 1986–87, while in the same period As went from 29 percent to 35 percent. Students at Brown University can take any course on a pass or fail basis—and if they fail, not have it or the course noted on their records.[25]

A similar devaluation is taking place in elementary and secondary schools, especially in high-poverty areas. For example, in one federal study, more than two-thirds of all eighth graders got As and Bs in English and math classes, though when such youngsters took tests also given to students from affluent schools, they scored only as high as the C and D students from the latter schools. Elsewhere, a philosophy of outcome based education (OBE) is gaining popularity, wherein the emphasis is on the teaching of values, feelings, attitudes, and beliefs rather than on facts and knowledge, and wherein no students fail. Any procedure differentiating students by individual merit is rejected. As one OBE educator put it, "Everyone trying out for the football team should make it; every girl or boy that wants to be a cheerleader should make it; everyone who comes to the program for the gifted and talented should make it."[26]

A growing number of junior colleges and four-year colleges engage in "dumbing down" as a way of solving financial and enrollment problems. "In their panic to keep numbers up, some of the four-year schools, both public and private, have been accepting every warm body that applies," said David Bartley, president of a Massachusetts two-year college. Wanting to appear attractive to parents and prospective students, some colleges deliberately send publishers of educational guidebooks inflated statistics on their students' SAT scores and graduation rates, wherein the scores of low-achievers and foreign students are simply excluded from the averages presented. Not immune to such practices are some Ivy League college departments and professors, who seek to attract or maintain enrollments by "competitive standard-cutting." As a Yale professor said, "If you want students to come to your classes, you have to inflate grades so that they are not afraid of not getting an A."[27]

At the same time, among some minority students, a culture of peer group pressure to not achieve is spreading. Studying, speaking standard English, being on time, using the library, and getting an A are belittled and therefore to be avoided. As columnist Rachel Jones recalled, "As a child I heard the same chant over and over: 'Why are you trying to act like a white person?' I was threatened and harassed because I liked to read, for using correct English and for striving to articulate my words as my older brothers and sisters had taught me." A similar pattern was found among Mexican Americans in a small California community, where students who studied were ridiculed as "schoolboys" and "schoolgirls" or "wannabes." The "in" behavior among some minority students is to cut classes, sit in the back of the class and not participate, not carry books to school or take difficult classes, and do the least needed to get by.[28]

The proverbial "best and brightest" are no longer sought, nurtured, or produced—to the extent they were in past decades. A number of federal studies in 1992–93 found that 25 percent of four-year college graduates had not studied history, 30 percent had not studied math, almost 40 percent had not studied literature, and more than 50 percent had not studied a foreign language. Another federal study of talented U.S. schoolchildren, including the poor and minorities, found many were bored and unchallenged in classrooms, did poorly on international assessments of achievement, underperformed on domestic tests, and were offered less difficult courses, books, and homework assignments than their counterparts in other countries. In a third study, many schools did not require daily homework in all subjects, more than 90 percent of 17 year olds were unable to do rigorous academic work in basic subjects, and only 2 percent of eleventh graders met national goals in writing skills.[29]

Historically, "dumbing down" is not new. Throughout much of American history those of the "right" religion, ethnicity, socioeconomic class, family, political connections, or athletic prowess—chiefly white, Anglo-Saxon Protestants—benefited from mediocre standards and performances, as epitomized by the almost proverbial satisfaction in earning a "Gentleman C" grade. At many turn-of-the-century Ivy League colleges, anti-Catholicism, anti-Semitism, racism, social snobbery, and anti-intellectualism were common—and athletic prowess was highly prized. "Scholarship has apparently declined throughout the country; certainly at Yale," lamented a 1903 faculty committee report. "In fact, in late years the scholar has become almost taboo." Only lower-class students from the public schools and those of southern, central, or eastern European and Asian origins were expected to study hard, for which they were ridiculed.[30]

By the 1940s, dramatic changes in attitudes toward those engaged in sports took place. College athletic stars were now often caricatured as dumb Irishmen, Poles, or Swedes, who, for example, when asked how much 2 plus 2 equalled, answered 5, to which the coach approvingly said, "Close enough." These were also years when many white female college students deliberately underachieved, particularly in mathematics, lest they be considered intellectual and therefore sexually cold.

Professional sports organizations were likewise bigoted toward minorities. In the 1880s, African Americans began being barred from major and minor league baseball, and after 1911, from being jockeys at major races.

Though able to compete in boxing, they were barred from seeking the world heavyweight title until 1908, when Jack Johnson won it in a fight held in Australia. Jews were believed lacking in the cultural resources needed to excel in some sports. Though skillful boxers and ring strategists, noted a popular sports writer in 1935, Jews "did not have the background to stand out in a sport which is so essentially a team game as baseball."[31]

A third danger results from the growing debate over what rules, regulations, and laws should exist to combat negative group descriptions, invidious stereotyping, verbal abuse, insulting gestures and symbols, and physical attacks motivated by racial, religious, ethnic, sexual, national origin, age, or physical hatred of others. The line between actual and imagined, acceptable and unacceptable, and legal and illegal, invidious speech, gestures, and behaviors is becoming a major source of intergroup controversy and an impediment to free speech. Some examples:

—One New York law firm instituted a personnel code penalizing employees who suggest that minority colleagues are somehow less qualified and were hired only because of "affirmative action."[32]

—The speech code of the University of Massachusetts at Amherst bans harassment based on "race, color, national or ethnic origin, gender, sexual orientation, age, religion, marital status, veteran status, disability, citizenship, culture, HIV status, language, parental status, political affiliation or belief, and pregnancy status." At the University of Connecticut, "inappropriately directed laughter" and "conspicuous exclusion" of another student from conversation is forbidden.[33]

—In Seattle, Washington, a compulsory employee tolerance training program urged that words like "gals," "ladies," "yuppies," and "geriatrics" not be used.[34]

—The *Los Angeles Times* style manual no longer allows use of "invalid" and "New World," because they are offensive respectively to the handicapped and pre-Columbian cultures.[35]

—The U.S. Marine Corps ordered personnel not to make "statements or gestures or engage in any action that could be interpreted as racial, gender or ethnic prejudice or bias."[36]

—Changes in the sign language of the deaf were made to avoid certain stereotypes, such as twisting one's little finger next to the eye for "Japanese," swishing one's wrist for "homosexual," and flattening the nose for "Negro."[37]

Such well-intentioned proscriptions and prescriptions are bitterly resented when ambiguously worded, selectively applied, or zealously enforced. Many people complain of having been unfairly accused of bigotry because of comments they made or allowed others to make, which are said to slight, demean, insult, caricature, or criticize a group or hurt the feelings of some group members. "Open discussion of many major public questions has for some time now been taboo," wrote Nobelist and author Saul

Bellow. "We can't open our mouths without being denounced as racists, misogynists, supremacists, imperialists or fascists. As for the media, they stand ready to trash anyone so designated."[38]

In fact, some programs designed to improve intergroup relations resulted in the opposite. In 1993, the U.S. Department of Transportation suspended an 11-year-old diversity awareness training program after receiving complaints of male participants being groped, women sobbing, and blacks and whites being urged to insult each other. In another program, employees resented being asked whether as children they had been sexually abused, when they first had sex, and whether they had undergone an unwanted pregnancy or an abortion. The National Association of Scholars criticized some efforts to combat sexual harassment, such as compulsory sensitivity training programs that are "an assault on individual dignity and freedom" and in which being white, male, or heterosexual frequently constitutes "a presumption of guilt." Some college professors avoid controversial topics and request students to write reports that are then read to the class anonymously. "What really bothers me," said one law professor, "is that the views that students hold privately differ from what they express publicly."[39]

In some communities, differences over hurt feelings have led to bitter intergroup friction or violence. In mid-1993, some Japanese Americans in Rhode Island objected to celebrating V-J Day (Victory over Japan Day), saying the name should be changed because it encourages racist insults and attacks. In the same year, after a 13-year-old Jewish student in New Hampshire protested that her public school had Merry Christmas signs and that carols like "Jingle Bells" and "Silent Night" were sung, making her feel uncomfortable, she was "threatened, jostled and ostracized" by other students, who felt their values had been insulted. In San Jose, California, when a memorial for the Japanese Americans interned during World War II was dedicated in 1994, some German Americans and Italian Americans complained that their fellow ethnics had also been mistreated and should be officially remembered. "Unlike blacks and other racial minorities, poor and mostly rural whites have few defenders," wrote poet Lloyd Van Brunt, saying they are, like Polish Americans, "the one group everybody feels free to belittle, knowing that no politically correct boundaries will be violated." Evangelical Christians can be called "born-again bigots" and nonfeminist women can be called "bimbos" or "Barbie dolls," wrote theologian Richard John Neuhaus, because it has become respectable to label some people bigots, such as those "who think homosexuals should not have special legal entitlements as a minority group, parents who do not want their eight-year-olds instructed in the use of condoms, those who insist that abortion is very bad for unborn children and their mothers. . . ."[40]

At times, some real or imagined violators of speech codes target members of their own groups, as in the case of some black rap music stars, whose recordings so denigrate black women and sensationalize violence that the National Political Congress of Black Women pressured music stores in 1994 to no longer stock them. Nevertheless, such recordings and speech have been defended as: mere expressions of profound cultural feelings and frustrations, examples of multiculturalism and free speech, reflections of social reality, and, above all, not articulated to incite violence. As rapper Snoop Doggy Dogg told an interviewer, "When I was nine years old, one of my homeboys got shot in some gang violence. And wasn't no rap music being played then. So you tell me the music we make now made him die? If they're saying that, well, country music makes white motherf____ go kill horses and tie horses and do all that crazy-ass s__ they be doing at rodeos."[41]

Still, it is all too clear that until recent decades group slurs, stereotypes, put-downs, and even physical attacks on minorities were tolerated, validated, and perpetuated by various levels of government and society. Minorities learn early in life that words, like sticks and stones, do hurt, and that name-calling can reflect an underlying societal hostility that precedes or accompanies physical aggression against them. In protesting a radio talkmaster's comments, in 1994, the Reverend Jesse Jackson, said: "It may be free speech, but it's foul speech. It's divisive speech. It's provocative speech, and in many ways it's violent speech."[42]

However the problems of speech are viewed, it is clear that the time is gone when a student, scholar, or political leader can freely discuss minority group life or be admired for affirming Voltaire's statement, "I disapprove of what you say, but I will defend to the death your right to say it." And if one does speak up in a class or forum, and some people don't like what he or she says, the speaker is subject to being accused, condemned, or even sued for everything from insensitivity to bias.

In the process of favoring all individuals of some groups resides a fourth danger to society—the debasement of individual achievements in all groups—particularly in the arts, business, education, and government. Instead of encouraging credible norms and role models, those of dubious distinction are often created and pointed questions raised. Why should one study, save, sacrifice, or stand in line, if another person can move ahead by doing less, little, or nothing, other than "working or beating the system," or, at best, barely meeting a minimum requirement? Instead of rewarding people for outstanding or greater effort, they can be ignored, bypassed, punished, or deemed expendable, though regrettably so. As a result, lack of personal effort, product, and consistency of evaluation encourages cynicism, conflict, and corruption.

In recent years, an increasing number of minorities and local community groups and leaders, especially black academics and intellectuals, have emphasized the need for greater self-help group efforts, while questioning the value of affirmative action programs and the tendency to blame a group's plight on racism. Some examples:

—Shelby Steele, a professor of English, faulted the lowering of standards to increase black representation because it "puts blacks at war with an expanded realm of debilitating doubt, so that the doubt itself becomes an unrecognized preoccupation that undermines their ability to perform, especially in integrated situations." Furthermore, it "nurtures a victim-focused identity in blacks and sends us the message that there is more power in our past suffering than in our present achievements." [43]

—Economist Glenn Loury noted that distributing opportunities on the basis of color "may have the unintended effect of dulling the incentive to acquire skills for those whom the policy is intended to benefit. . . . The point is that the incentive to acquire a skill can be lowered by either reducing the likelihood that a skilled worker will succeed or increasing the likelihood that an unskilled worker will succeed." [44]

—Walter E. Williams, another economist, stressed the need for more black self-help, claiming that most of the problems college blacks face do not stem from official campus discrimination, but from poor academic preparation. By continually "focusing on affirmative-action programs at the college level, while ignoring the massive educational fraud taking place at the primary and secondary schools blacks attend, means that campus problems will exist in perpetuity." And such may well occur among college faculties, where in 1991 only 2 percent of the professors (excluding those at traditional black colleges) were black, at a time when less than 1,000 blacks received a Ph.D. degree, in comparison to almost 22,000 for whites. [45]

—William Raspberry, a syndicated columnist, charged that African Americans "expend precious resources, time, energy, imagination and political capital searching, always successfully, for evidence of racism, while our problems grow worse. . . . It is clear that recently arrived Asian Americans spend none of their time proving that white people don't love them. The differences between us and them is in our operating myths. Our myth is that racism accounts for our shortcomings. Theirs is that their own efforts can make the difference, no matter what white people think." [46]

Decrying or outlawing negative perceptions or statements of minority inability to achieve or compete will not change them or their underlying causes. Nor will compelling people to confess to racism for having such thoughts, blaming all minority group problems on majority society, or hiring people simply because of their group being. Observable achievements are the best antidotes to imagined or actual failures. As law professor Stephen Carter, a self-described "affirmative action baby," wrote, black achievers should commit themselves "to battle for excellence, to show ourselves able to meet any standard, to pass any test that looms before us, in short, to form ourselves into a vanguard of black professionals who are simply too good to ignore." [47]

And, indeed, such achievement among all minorities has been increasing in a number of areas on both a relative and absolute basis. In the case of American blacks, the number of professionals in law, medicine, and engineering has risen dramatically, and in some fields blacks earn as much as or more than whites, and their percentage within a given job area sometimes exceeds their percentage of the general population, such as bank tellers, cashiers, social welfare workers, telephone operators, and bus drivers. While black earnings for the most part do not equal those of whites, the gap is narrowing. The earning ratios of full-time black workers to white workers went from 61 percent in 1955 to 73 percent in 1990, and for black women from 61 percent to 90 percent. [48]

In other areas, changes for the better have also taken place. In 1970, there were 11 blacks in Congress and 168 in state legislatures, but in 1993, there were 39 and 406 respectively; from 1 black in the president's cabinet in 1968 (Robert Weaver), there were 4 (Mike Espy, Hazel O'Leary, Ron Brown, and Jesse Brown) in 1993; blacks completing high school went from 33.7 percent in 1970 to 66.7 percent in 1990; those attending college skyrocketed from 522,000 in 1970 to 1,187,000 in 1990; the number of black military officers went from 6,351 in 1965 to 20,861 in 1991; the number of black business managers and administrators went from 243,000 in 1972 to 858,000 in 1991; and while in 1973, the leading 100 black businesses had total annual revenues of $473 million, in 1993 the total was $9 billion. [49]

Such improvements do not mean that all or most blacks have made it or will make it, that they are generally as well off as whites, that there isn't a growing proportion of poor blacks, or that many other minorities don't face severe socioeconomic problems, but rather to stress that progress can and is being made. To be sure, affirmative action programs provide income, jobs, psychological security, and visibility to many minority members who otherwise would not have obtained them, just as patronage, nepotism, or payola do and did for many other people. However, as a number of critics of affirmative action have pointed out, overall black, as well as Asian-American and Mexican-American, progress began before affirmative action programs were fully implemented in the early 1970s, and is more related to the growth of the economy generally, the increasing enforcement of antidiscrimination legislation, and the rising skill and educational levels of minority workers in particular. The importance of education is underscored in a 1992 census study, which found the median income of full-time, year-round black workers 25 years old and over with a bachelor's degree or more to be 66 percent higher than that of comparable blacks with only a high school diploma. [50] Unfortunately, in most cases, affirmative action programs do not reach the poor, uneducated, and non-English-speaking.

There is much controversy over how to best maintain progress and insure its continuity among succeeding generations. Group rights, preferences, and quotas are effective, but only for a particular group or for those socioeconomically better off within the group. Largely excluded are the needs or reactions of other groups and the unifying ideals of the country as a whole. No advocates of affirmative action for racial, ethnic, or sexual groups have explained how and when preferential group measures, even those originally proposed as temporary, would be capped or deactivated (other than through a court decision, which they usually oppose, or through expressing a hope that they would end, without specifying when).

Should members of a group not be admitted to colleges, hired for jobs, or nominated for elected offices—or should they be dismissed from such—for exceeding a numerical group allotment? So far no activists have called for such reductions for members of their own group or have themselves volunteered to give up their positions to an underrepresented group member—whether in the overrepresentation of blacks in social welfare positions and sports, Jews and Asians in academia and the medical professions, or women as librarians and teachers, gays in design and fashion professions, or Cambodians and Asian Indians in the donut and motel businesses, respectively, in California.[51]

And how are people of mixed racial, ethnic, or sexual makeup to be identified? Shall legal distinctions be reinstituted between those of "pure" and "mixed" blood, as well as the generational gradations among the latter, as the Spanish and Germans once did? In order to attract underproportionalized people or avoid attracting overproportionalized ones, will the old European *numerus clausus* laws restricting admissions by group in universities be reintroduced—or signs and ads saying, no Irish, Jews, blacks, Chinese, Japanese, women, and so forth, need apply?

Nor have the above advocates explained how their programs can be implemented without violating the actual or desired equal rights of people from more than 200 ancestral groups, as well as greater numbers and combinations of racial, religious, ethnic, sexual, and linguistic groups. True, not all groups, nor all members of a single group, are or were equally disadvantaged or discriminated against, but relativity of suffering doesn't soothe or prevent a victim's anguished feelings, scarred memories, and fervent hopes for equal or preferential redress.

On a community level, intergroup jealousies and tensions over government policies grow between old and new immigrants, between immigrants and native-born Americans, and between immigrant groups. Some examples follow.

In Miami, Haitians resented the government's benign treatment of Cu-

ban refugees while their countrymen were stopped from entering or im-
prisoned and returned home. In Philadelphia, Polish-American groups discovered that because of governmental regulations they, unlike Asian or
Hispanic groups, did not qualify for funds to help fellow refugees from
Poland. In Brooklyn, many longtime Italian-American residents resented
new Jewish-Russian immigrants, whom they accused of being pushy, not
understanding American culture, and too readily going on welfare. In
Massachusetts, Hispanic leaders demanded more representation in state
government, complaining "that all minority programs are currently designed and staffed as if the minority population were almost exclusively
African-American." Blacks and Mexicans in Houston differed over who
gets what and first from government. "There's not much sympathy for
immigrants," said one Afro-American woman, who runs a food program
for the homeless, because "there is only so much food and you have to
decide if it should go to blacks or Mexicans." In Garden City, Kansas,
longtime Mexican migrant workers resented a federally funded resettlement program giving more access to new Vietnamese immigrants than to
them. The ease with which some new Chinese immigrants in California
got welfare infuriated other longtime Chinese residents. "I worked here
. . . and paid taxes for 30 years," said one, "yet they come in without
having worked a day, and get a welfare check twice as large as my Social
Security check." In Detroit, a plan to establish Arabic-English classes in
some elementary public schools further exasperated interethnic tensions,
with one parent protesting: "These are American schools. We never taught
Polish kids in Polish or Italian kids in Italian, and that was to their benefit." [52]

Resentments and recriminations between minority ethnic, racial, and
gender groups have also increasingly affected political decisions and parties. A 1985 Democratic party survey found that a significant number of
white men had voted for Republican candidates in two prior presidential
elections because "women get advantages, the Hispanics get advantages,
Orientals get advantages. Everybody but the white male race gets advantages now." An "angry white male" syndrome was largely credited in the
1994 congressional elections for the Republican candidates attracting 60
percent of the white male vote as they won majority control of the U.S.
House and Senate. The following year, resentment over affirmative action
was further reflected in a *Newsweek* telephone poll, in which 75 percent of
the respondents opposed qualified blacks receiving preference over equally
qualified whites in gaining college admissions or jobs. [53]

As yet no modern or developing country (at least one that is democratic)
can serve as a model for America, particularly after the dissolution of the
Soviet Union, the fragmentation of Yugoslavia, the political repression in
China, the continuing exodus of Cubans to Florida, and the hundreds of
thousands of people who leave or want to leave once-praised egalitarian

societies. On the other hand, if it is believed that America should lead the way, the recommended solutions are often confusing, contradictory, divisive, and unconvincing, wherein a variety of logical, judicial, political, and mathematical claims are projected based on a group's: race, ethnicity, religion, sex, or sexual orientation; history of victimization; proportion of city, state, or national population (whichever is higher); socioeconomic standing; and, most recently, a social policy of diversity premised on compassion rather than merit.

The rhetoric and reasoning behind each group's claims are often similar, as if all groups or all members of each group suffer or had suffered equally, which is, in reality, not true. And therein lies another constellation of questions and problems:

—On what moral, philosophic, or legal principles should competing or conflicting group claims be resolved? And what should the criteria and process be for preventing fraudulent individual claims for group-specific benefits? Shall group or government boards be created to certify purity of group background? How should those of mixed marriages or births be evaluated? Will a threshold lineage percentage be established for inclusion or exclusion, and will it be 100, 75, 50, 25, or less?

—To bring about electoral proportional representation why shouldn't the concept of "one man, one vote" be replaced or added to by "one group, one vote," or by giving some groups or individuals a number of additional votes to insure their victory? If proportional representation in employment is given some minority groups why not to all such groups—or to a group plurality or majority?

—Why not redraw all city, state, and federal voting boundaries to insure the elections of various minority candidates (as happened with blacks and Hispanics in some states and with whites for a long time through gerrymandering)—and, more effective yet, why not have separate elections for different groups and reinstitute restrictive housing covenants and clauses to insure minority representation or control?

—In addition to making the District of Columbia a separate state, why not divide California, Texas, and Florida and thereby insure still greater black, Hispanic, and Asian federal representation and funds and do the same for some large U.S. cities, which already have a "little" Korea, China, Italy, Saigon, Russia?

—Should the concept and practice of "segregation" or "separate but equal" group facilities be reestablished in order to foster group identity, role models, or a better learning atmosphere? Or, perhaps, America, like the Turkish empire of yore, should allow autonomous communities, wherein each religious or cultural group rules itself.

—Since many Supreme Court cases have been decided by 5 to 4 decisions, perhaps the number of justices should be increased to a few hundred to reflect the full diversity of America's racial, ethnic, religious, and sexual makeup. In fact, why should any racial, ethnic, religious, sexual, or special interest group not be represented on the Supreme Court and on every level of government?

—To inspire the bringing about of diversity and inclusiveness, why not change our national ideal of "united states" to "united groups"?

The possibilities and probabilities of all such changes occurring are slight, though some are already in the making. However, if actualized, the odds of their causing more injustices, severe civic unrest, and national fragmentation are high, at least if world history is any guide.

What is presently happening abroad between various ethnic, racial, and religious groups in the same country or in adjoining ones over minority rights, self-determination, immigration, and old and new feuds should serve as a warning to America. In countries like India, Nigeria, Australia, Guyana, Malaysia, Sri Lanka, Pakistan, and Indonesia, Thomas Sowell found that affirmative action and preferential programs originally designed to be temporary were expanded and became permanent; were often disproportionately helpful to group members who were better off financially; frequently led to people fraudulently claiming membership in a designated preferred group; and, lastly, evoked a range of negative reactions by non-beneficiaries—from political backlash to civil war.[54]

In Western Europe, into which some 15 million immigrants entered between 1980–1992, incidents of xenophobia, racism, anti-Semitism, attacks on foreigners, and right-wing nationalist parties have been increasing, and, as a United Nations report on human rights noted, pseudoscientific beliefs about biological inequality are giving way to seemingly benign beliefs about "insurmountable differences between cultures," which "justify the need to keep human communities separate." At the same time, calls for autonomy, separatism, and secessionism resurface in countries where they had either been long suppressed by the government or where they had been relatively dormant for many decades. "Canada copes with Quebec's secessionism," wrote scholar Patrick Glynn, "the United Kingdom with Scottish separatists, Italy with increasing tensions between its north and its south. In Germany, as well as in France and Britain, ethnically motivated violence has become a major factor in politics, and rebellious youths are inflamed by a puzzling new ideology of ethnic hatred." In eastern and central Europe, independence movements have been more successful. In 1992, the United States recognized twelve new independent republics in the former Soviet Union, three independent states in the former Yugoslavia, and, in the following year, two independent states within the former Czechoslovakia.[55]

Similarly, in many African and Asian countries, racial, religious, ethnic, and cultural tensions and conflicts multiply over group rights and boundaries between various tribes, nationality groups, whites and blacks, Arabs and black Africans, Hindus and Muslims, Muslims and Christians, Chinese and Tibetans, and Hindus and Buddhists, to cite a few broad categories. The reciprocal slaughter of Hutus and Tutsis in Rwanda, as well as of Serbs, Croats, and Bosnians in the former Yugoslavia, are stark reminders of the dangers of group passions. "The defining mode of conflict in the era ahead is ethnic conflict," said Sen. Patrick Moynihan, in 1993. "Get ready for 50 new countries in the world in the next 50 years. Most of them will be born in bloodshed." By 1990, more than half the world's 30 million refugees were "fleeing from civil wars and repression which were the result of communally-based conflicts." Three years later, the number of refugees had risen to 44 million people, with the largest numbers in Asia (7.2 million), Africa (5.4 million), and Europe (3.6 million). Equally ominous are the deaths from small wars in the fifty years since World War II, which exceed those of the war itself.[56]

Whereas self-determination was once sought largely in the name of national self-fulfillment, it is also increasingly being sought to repress, segregate, or get rid of minorities within a country, without interference by other countries and the United Nations in particular. In the process, some foreign governments—like some American minority groups—are redefining racism and human rights, which they do not want measured by any universal standards, but rather by their own national ones. At the very least, they don't want the world's more industrialized countries, especially America, to link issues of free trade with those of human rights, child labor, or environmental protection. We "reject the unilateral application of any political, economic, social and environmental linkage regarding market access in international trade relations," declared a group of Latin American foreign ministers meeting with their European counterparts in Brazil, in 1994.[57]

A year earlier, at a United Nations conference on human rights in Vienna, Indonesia's foreign minister acknowledged that while human rights are "vital and important," so are "efforts at accelerated national development," which must, in his opinion, take priority. China's foreign minister denied the right of other countries to interfere in his country's affairs, arguing that individual rights should never prevail over those of the state and society. Cuba's foreign minister accused America of trying to impose its human rights concepts on developing countries, while cruelly maintaining an economic boycott of his country. And Singapore's foreign minister warned, "Too much stress on individual rights over the rights of the community will retard progress." Though U.S. Secretary of State Warren Christopher declared, "We cannot let cultural relativism become the last refuge of repression," he defended the renewal of China's most-favored-nation trading status in mid-1994, while acknowledging that China had not made the "overall, significant progress" in human rights required for such a continuation.[58]

At the Fourth World Conference on Women, held in China in 1995, First Lady Hillary Rodham Clinton stressed the connection between women's right and human rights. "It is a violation of human rights when babies are denied food, or drowned, or suffocated, or their spines broken, simply because they are born girls . . . when women and girls are sold into slavery or prostitution for human greed . . . when women are doused with gasoline, set on fire and burned to death because their marriage dowries are deemed too small . . . when thousands of women are raped in their own communities and when thousands of women are subjected to rape as a tactic or prize of war." [59]

The attempts of some countries to deny any violations of human rights within their boundaries, to reject the existence of universal standards of human rights, to relativize or rationalize all forms of behavior, to blame the West or Satan for all domestic problems, and to place national rights above individual ones are disturbingly similar to what some minority leaders and intellectuals are seeking in America: placing the well-being of the group above that of the individual and of the nation as a whole, denying the need for general standards of behavior and achievement, justifying certain values and behaviors that violate those of society in general, establishing proportional representation on all levels of society, and blaming all individual or group misbehavior on society at large and on racism, bigotry, and sexism in particular.

Ironically, such developments in the United States and abroad are often defended in the name of compassion, peace, progress, democracy, or group tradition, though only a few decades ago they were denounced as discriminatory, racist, imperialist, uncivilized, or, of course, undemocratic. And yet, when looking at American or world history, some truths emerge that transcend the geographic situation, group, or country—whether the latter be developed or Third World. If one believes in reason, science, justice, compassion, and the sanctity of human life, then that person cannot support a group or society that allows slavery, cannibalism, human sacrifice, blood feuds, torture, mutilation, self-immolation, female infanticide, clitoridectomies, suttee, wife beating, forced prostitution, child labor and marriages, arbitrary arrest, secret imprisonment, starvation, deprivation of health and medical care, "ethnic cleansing," collective punishment for the sins of the few in the present or past, or mistreating people on the basis of their race, religion, ethnicity, or sex.

In terms of religion, at least if one believes in Judeo-Christian traditions, certain commandments, proscriptions, and laws are not only spiritually uplifting, but civically necessary as well. Six of the Judaic Ten Commandments deal with interpersonal relations, wherein people are enjoined to honor their parents, not commit murder, not engage in adultery, not steal, not bear false witness, and not covet a neighbor's wife or possessions (Deut. 5:6–18). On a more theological, but no less pragmatic, note, the Second Vatican Council stressed the existence of evil acts per se, which are independent of their circumstances:

Whatever is hostile to life itself, such as any kind of homicide, genocide, abortion, euthanasia and voluntary suicide; whatever violates the integrity of the human person, such as mutilation, physical and mental torture and attempts to coerce the spirit; whatever is offensive to human dignity, such as subhuman living conditions, arbitrary imprisonment, deportation, slavery, prostitution and trafficking in women and children; degrading conditions of work which treat labourers as mere instruments of profit, and not as free responsible persons.[60]

Whether the above are imposed by a majority or minority group led by an indigenous or foreign governor, commissar, general, religious leader, king, or president, both the imposers and that which they impose are—or should be—abhorrent to the enlightened mind. Unfortunately, there are individuals, groups, and countries that defend or rationalize many of the above actions and accuse those opposing them of being racists, cultural triumphalists, or simple bigots. For example, when the *New York Times* columnist A. M. Rosenthal condemned female circumcision and supported a congressional bill that would prohibit the practice in America, Maynard H. Merwine, a history instructor at a Pennsylvania community college, disagreed, claiming that "from the African viewpoint the practice can serve as an affirmation of the value of woman in traditional society" and that any congressional action to change "a tradition central to many Africans and Arabs is the height of ethnocentrism."[61]

In the name of cultural relativity, diversity, or religious freedom, other behaviors considered illegal or inhumane in America, but not within a particular group or in a group's ancestral homeland, have been defended or rationalized, such as assisting a Buddhist in Connecticut to set himself on fire, a South American woman in Georgia stroking the genitals of her male child to help him fall asleep, a Chinese husband in New York City killing his wife because of infidelity, an Asian Indian husband in New York beating his wife because her parents back in India had failed to deliver a dowry, Hmong males in Wisconsin 16 years and older impregnating very young Hmong girls, some being sixth graders, and an Indian tribal court in Oregon ordering the whipping of a young female member because of her socializing with gangs, failing in school, drinking, and running away from home.[62]

Just as ignorance of the law should be no excuse for violations of it, so the existence of some moral and behavioral codes in other parts of the world should be no rationale for their practice in America or continuance abroad. For example, the slave trade, human sacrifice, and headhunting in Africa, the Pacific islands, and Central America were rightfully outlawed by European occupiers, much to the unhappiness of their practitioners. Though voodoo gives comfort and strength to its believers, particularly Haitians, in no way should it be considered a substitute for regular medical attention, the use of the courts to obtain justice, or for running a democratic government. Similarly with hoodoo, a variation of voodoo and Catholic beliefs practiced in rural Louisiana, where two sisters in 1994 gouged out the eyes of their third sister in order to dispossess her of a demon. Not only did the blinded sister defend the action, but when a jury found her sisters guilty, their lawyers claimed that the jury, eleven of whom were white, did not understand the nature of supernatural forces and Louisiana's black culture. Nor should ancient Gypsy practices of exorcising curses, enhancing sexual potency or attractiveness, or foreseeing the future be considered as anything other than entertainment at best, though in a recent case of alleged fraud by four Romani women in San Diego such actions were defended on the basis of First Amendment rights and the need to respect cultural diversity.[63]

Acknowledging cultural differences should not mean tolerance or approval of whatever an individual, group, or nation does or wishes to do, unless we are to regret having outlawed the above-noted practices, plus such "crowd-pleasers" as public whippings, the quartering of bodies, auto de fe's, the cutting off of fingers, tongues, ears, or testicles, and being thrown to the lions. Simply put, all cultural beliefs and practices are not equal, nor equally good for their adherents or other people, at least if one believes in protecting human life and working for a society that is free of disease, bloodshed, and tyranny. Intelligence is preferable to ignorance, and ability is preferable to incompetence, though there are nice, loving, and law-abiding people who are ignorant and incompetent, as well as cruel, hateful and law-violating people who are intelligent and competent. It is also true that intelligence and ability by themselves do not guarantee civilized or civil behavior, but ignorance and incompetence surely decrease the possibilities of such.

It is the Matthew Arnold "best" of thoughts, ideas, and knowledge that society should applaud and adopt, without regard to the color, religion, ethnicity, or sex of their propounders. Science is and should be more preferable than astrology and numerology, no matter how personally consoling the latter. Licensed doctors and prescription drugs are and should be more valued than shamans and faith healing, no matter the few cures the latter have achieved. Democracy is and should be more respected than fascism, nazism, or communism, no matter how well the latter ideologies made trains run on time, provided full employment, or equalized incomes. And chewing gum, collecting baseball cards, and going to the movies are and should be more desirable than eating people, sacrificing them to Gods, or shrinking and collecting their severed heads, though doing so nourished and abetted communal pride and organization.

Last, for Americans to cite differences between their country and others is not chauvinisitic nationalism, but admirable government in which a core body of beliefs and values is maintained that transcends the public's mood of the moment or its racial, ethnic, religious, or sexual components, particularly when it is to America that so many people from other countries have fled, are fleeing, and want to flee. America is not heaven on earth, but it is far more humane than the tribes, city-states, kingdoms, nations, and empires of the past and present. If, or until, the First or Second Coming takes place, only by the rule of equal laws and unitary moral standards consistently defined and applied can a pluralistic democracy like America endure—or a world of peaceful nations come about. The alternatives are rule by self-interest, multiple-standard morality, armed might, and the separation, segregation, or secession of groups.

In its 200-plus years of existence, America has undergone only one major and violent internal threat to its united existence—the Civil War, which was approved of and overwhelmingly fought by whites differing over the right of individuals to own slaves and the right of states to withdraw from a union they had voluntarily entered. Though xenophobia and paranoia have periodically swept the country (usually born of wars abroad, fear of domestic revolution and revolutionaries, or economic recessions or depressions), they were short-lived, resulting in isolated cases of bloodshed.

Happily, Americans never nurtured the kinds of enduring intergroup feuds and hatreds that Europeans, Africans, and Asians did and still do. That is why most Americans with different ancestral roots, and particularly their children, live more in peace with each other than do their counterparts in their homelands. That is also why relatively few Americans leave America or renounce their citizenship, even when they start a new life in another country. American Irishmen and Englishmen, Armenians and Turks, Frenchmen and Germans, Russians and Poles, Chinese and Japanese, Muslims and Christians, Israelis and Arabs, Hindus and Sikhs, Vietnamese and Cambodians, or Africans from different tribes do not and have not fought each other here as they do or have done back home. It is no wonder that a 1994 *Reader's Digest* poll asking whether people believed, as prior generations did, that America was "the very best place in the world to live," 80 percent agreed, with relatively little difference between races or educational levels—82 percent of whites and 74 percent of blacks, as well as 84 percent of college graduates, 81 percent of high school graduates, and 74 percent of non–high school graduates.[64]

For all the gun ownership, violence, and bigotry which are found in America, Americans remain a basically friendly people, whether in helping others or allowing them to immigrate. When any natural catastrophe occurs abroad, American voluntary and governmental aid is there first and with the most, as epitomized by the recent massive food and medical aid to Somalia, where the United States had no pressing national military or economic interest.

Also, though 61 percent of Americans in a 1993 *New York Times CBS News* poll opposed increasing the level of immigration and though California voters in particular, by a ratio of 3 to 2, supported a proposition ending social and educational services to illegal immigrants, Americans generally opposed immigration not out of xenophobia but rather a concern over the economy, job cutbacks, and, in some states, skyrocketing costs of aid to illegal immigrants. In spite of this concern, almost 50 percent of Americans polled said that "today's immigrants work harder than people born here," and 67 percent said they would welcome some new immigrants into their neighborhoods. "You want to give them a fair shake," said one respondent. A 1994 study reaffirmed the openness of the American public. In response to the question of what values Americans want the public schools to teach their children, 95 percent favored "respect for others regardless of their racial or ethnic background," 81 percent favored not bringing guest speakers into schools who argue that "the Holocaust never happened," 80 percent favored teaching that "girls can succeed at anything boys can," and 61 percent favored teaching "respect for people who are homosexual." The following year, a national survey by *USA Weekend Magazine* of nearly a quarter of a million sixth to twelfth graders indicated that 72 percent had a close friend of another race and 71 percent would date a person of another race.[65]

Perhaps, as a nation, the United States is still too young, too energetic, too naive, too rich, and too geographically distant from other countries to really feel threatened by them, to suspect all who are different, or to maintain hatred for any significant time period against those with whom we disagreed or warred with in the past.

The dominant characteristics of American government have been ever-expanding civil rights, civil liberties, due process, free elections, social reform, national unity, and intergroup cooperation, with ever *decreasing* forms and degrees of bigotry in laws, legislation, social policies, religious teaching and preaching, and individual behaviors. Political parties, assorted demagogues, voluntary organizations, and legislation based on fear and hate failed to have any lasting impact—such as the Alien and Sedition Acts, the Know-Nothing Party, the Ku Klux Klan, loyalty oaths, and dozens of extreme right- and left-wing groups and leaders. With relatively few exceptions, the rights of dissent and protest have been continually strengthened, as long as individual life or national survival were not clearly threatened. Tongue piercing, whipping, branding, imprisonment, banishment, or hanging for alleged or actual religious blasphemy or heresy long ago became historical footnotes. Social reform—moderate rather than radical—continues to be favored by the overwhelming majority of Americans.

It is of course also true that all too often justice was delayed, denied, or abused, particularly for blacks, Indians, and Asians, and that racism, anti-Semitism, anti-Catholicism, anti-Asianism, sexism, poverty, and political corruption still exist, but the more salient truth is that such injustices and others are generally fewer, less severe, and more open to correction than ever before in America than in any other country. That pattern of meliorism is endangered today by (1) the steady replacement of individual rights with group rights; (2) the increasing polarization of relations between minority groups; (3) the continuing abandonment of broad coalitional politics and reform; (4) the adoption of social policies predicated on unchangeable group identities and differential group standards of behavior and achievement; and (5) the granting of opportunities, preferences, and benefits—or the denying of them—on the basis of a group's race, religion, ethnicity, or sex.

"Instead of a nation composed of individuals making their own unhampered choices," wrote historian Arthur M. Schlesinger, Jr., "America increasingly sees itself as composed of groups more or less ineradicable in their ethnic character," wherein the proverbial *unum* is belittled and the *pluribus* glorified. Likewise, Daniel J. Boorstin, former Librarian of Congress, said that too much emphasis has been placed on groups seeking power and on the diversity of our peoples, with too little emphasis on "what has built our country . . . the willingness of people to build together." [66]

By themselves, groups and new immigrants pose no danger, though in each century some Americans want to reduce or stop the immigration of non–English-speaking Protestant Anglo-Saxons, fearing that their sheer number and diversity would overwhelm and destroy American democracy. Early on, Alexander Hamilton warned that in "the compositon of society, the harmony of the ingredients is all important, and whatever tends to discordant mixture must have an injurious tendency." Before becoming president, Thomas Jefferson feared that an unrestricted number of immigrants would infuse our legislation with a foreign spirit, "warp and bias its directions, and render it a heterogeneous, incoherent, distracted mass." John Quincy Adams had no illusions about those who immigrated here— "none come from affection or regard to land to which they are total strangers. . . . We know that they come with views, not to our benefit but to their own—not to promote our welfare, but to better their own condition." [67]

Of course, history has proven such fears wrong. The multiplicity of groups, individuals, and beliefs did not result in a loss of national unity. Rather, by accepting the primacy of national well-being, one nation indivisible, or *e pluribus unum,* people and groups enriched American culture, and by their work, conformity with the law, and voluntary organizations helped society and government become more responsive to the needs of all of its citizens, while preventing any one group from dominating all others. Many of the Founding Fathers recognized the value of diversity in spite of its inherent dangers. To James Madison, "Security for civil rights must be the same as that for religious rights; it consists in the one case in a multiplicity of interests and the other in a multiplicity of sects." American statesman Edmund Randolph believed that a multiplicity of sects would prevent "the establishment of any one sect, in prejudice to the rest." And Patrick Henry insisted that "no particular sect or society ought to be favored or established, by law, in preference to others." Though writing of England at the time, Voltaire also recognized the value of diversity as an antidote to tyranny. "If there were one religion in England, its despotism would be terrible; if there were only two, they would destroy each other; but there are thirty, and therefore they live in peace and happiness." [68]

American democracy was defended in foreign wars by a multiplicity of foreign- and native-born citizens and their offspring, whose loyalty to America transcended that to their ancestral homeland. If not intellectually, then behaviorally, they believed that as Americans they possessed, or should possess, the hallowed rights of life, liberty, and the pursuit of happiness. They readily supported freedom of speech, assembly, and petition; insisted upon due process of law; yearned for equality of opportunity, treatment, and protection; wanted reform and representation through ballots rather than bullets; rejected a philosophy of one people, one land, one language, and one God; opposed discrimination because of race, religion, ethnicity, or sex; and generally sought to accommodate, acculturate, or assimilate with other Americans. Very few individuals or minority groups ever sought separation, secession, or flight from America. When sharp differences and conflicts erupted between or among individuals and groups, or with the government, it was generally expected that they would be resolved on the basis of fairness, compromise, majority rule, and coalitional group efforts, *regardless of* or *in spite of* the disputants' racial, religious, or ethnic affiliations.

Until recent decades, social critics, minority leaders, and politicians usually agreed on the value of such principles and procedures. They were leery of government responding to special interest groups, becoming identified with any particular religious, racial, or ethnic groups, or favoring or empowering only one or a few groups. Historically, they knew that to do so could provoke enormous controversy, violence, and bloodshed between and among individuals, groups, and countries. As a result, the U.S. government guarantees the wall of separation between church and state, the proscribing of religious tests for public office, the separation of governmental powers, and no requirement of American birth as a requisite for elected office, except for the presidency.

That informed caution and the societal progress it facilitated are now being forgotten—or rejected—as government wittingly and unwittingly strengthens the existence of old and the creation of new racial, ethnic, religious, and sexual groups and tensions by providing some of them with benefits and rights on an absolute or preferential basis, thereby doing what it avoided and legislated against doing in the past—the invidious treatment of people based on their group affiliation. If continued, these practices can only lead to a nation divided into competing and resentful groups, with more privileges and favoritism for some groups and less liberty and justice for all citizens.

## NOTES

1. E. Digby Baltzell, *The Protestant Establishment* (New York: Random House, 1964), x.

2. James D. Davidson, Ralph E. Pyle, and David V. Reyes, "Persistence and Change in the Protestant Establishment, 1930–1992," paper delivered at the annual meeting of the Association for Sociology of Religion, August 1994, 21; Robert C. Christopher, *Crashing the Gates* (New York: Simon and Schuster, 1989), 16–20, 99, 120–121.

3. Kathleen Teltsch, "Philanthropic Coalition Names a New President," *New York Times,* 20 May 1994, B3; *Boston Globe,* 4 October 1995, 6; Alice Dembner, "In Academia, Women Taking Hold at the Top," *Boston Globe,* 31 July 1994, 1.

4. Brian McGrory, "Gays See Growing Backlash," *Boston Globe,* 28 November 1993, 20.

5. Abigail Thernstrom, "Redistricting, in Black and White," *New York Times,* 7 December 1994, A23.

6. *New York Times,* 4 April 1993, 16; John Balzar, "Majority Support Steps to Diversity in the Workplace, *Times* Poll Finds," *Los Angeles Times,* 28 November 1994, A13; *Teaching Tolerance,* semi-annual publication, (Fall 1994): 6.

7. Alyson Todd, "Growing Up Absurd at Wellesley," *Heterodoxy* (March 1993): 1.

8. Stanley Lieberson and Mary C. Waters, *From Many Strands: Ethnic and Radical Groups in Contemporary America* (New York: Russell Sage Foundation, 1988), 265; *Detailed Ancestry Groups for States,* 1990 CP-2-1-2 (Washington, D.C.: U.S. Department of Commerce, 1992), 111-1-3.

9. Haruna Bab and Richard Chung, "How Many Asian Pacific Groups Exist at UCLA?" *Crosscurrents, Newsmagazine of the UCLA Asian American Studies Center* (Summer 1991): 1.

10. James Traub, "For Whom Bell Tolls," *The New Republic* (1 March 1993): 17.

11. Harold Cruse, *The Crisis of the Negro Intellectual* (New York: William Morrow and Co., 1967), 394; Vine Deloria, Jr., *We Talk, You Listen* (New York: Macmillan, 1970), 152; David Twersky, "Radical Prof May Become Reno Deputy," *Forward,* 23 April 1993, 5; Lani Guinier, "What I Would Have Said," *Boston Globe,* 17 June 1993, 23; Charles R. Lawrence, "Beyond Redress: Reclaiming the Meaning of Affirmative Action," *Amerasia Journal* 19, no. 1 (1993): 4; Steven Yates, "Multiculturalism and Epistemology," *Network News & Views* (August 1993): 10–11.

12. Philip Perlmutter, *Divided We Fall: A History of Ethnic, Religious, and Racial Prejudice in America* (Ames: Iowa State University Press, 1992), 323; "Reductio Ad Absurdum," *Heterodoxy,* January 1994, 3.

13. Steven A. Holmes, "Did Racial Redistricting Undermine Democrats?" *New York Times,* 13 November 1994, 32; Linda Greenhouse, "Justices in 5-4 Vote,

Reject Districts Drawn with Race the 'Predomiant Factor,' " *New York Times,* 30 June 1995, A1, A22; Steven A. Holmes, "Voting Rights Experts Say Challenges to Political Maps Could Cause Turmoil," *New York Times,* 30 June 1995, A23.

14. Hugh Davis Graham, "The Origins of Affirmative Action: Civil Rights and the Regulatory State," *Annals of the American Academy of Political and Social Science* (September 1992): 54.

15. Paul Craig Roberts and Lawrence M. Stratton, Jr., "Color Code," *National Review,* 20 March 1995, 38.

16. Graham, "The Origins of Affirmative Action: Civil Rights and the Regulatory State," 56; Roberts and Stratton, Jr., "Color Code," 46; *New York Times,* 29 June 1978, A21.

17. Thomas Sowell, *Preferential Policies* (New York: William Morrow and Company, 1990), 122.

18. Linda Greenhouse, "By 5-4, Justices Cast Doubts on U.S. Programs That Give Preferences Based on Race" and idem, "Excerpts from the Decision on Justifying Affirmative Action Programs," *New York Times,* 13 June 1995, A1, D24–25.

19. "Excerpts from Clinton Talk on Affirmative Action," *New York Times,* 20 July 1995, B10.

20. Todd S. Purdum, "President Shows Fervent Support for Goals of Affirmative Action," *New York Times,* 20 July 1995, A1; Tamar Lewis, "5-4 Decision Buoys Some; For Others It's a Setback," *New York Times,* 13 June 1995, D25.

21. Bertram W. Korn, "Jews and the American Revolution," *Jewish Digest* (July 1975): 10; Merle Curti, *The Roots of American Loyalty* (New York: Atheneum, 1968), 24; Moses Rischin, *Immigration and the American Tradition* (Indianapolis: Bobbs-Merrill Company, 1976), 46.

22. Richard D. Lyons, "Extortion Scheme in Minority Hiring Is Charged by U.S.," *New York Times,* 30 June 1993, A1, B3.

23. Selwyn Rabb, "12 Charged in Minority Businesses Scheme," *New York Times,* 19 May 1995, B2; Alan Levin and Jack Meyers, "Contractors Scoff at Lax Enforcement," and Jack Meyers, "Biz Program Fraud Goes Far and Wide," *Boston Herald,* 11 August 1993, 1, 7; *New York Times,* 9 October 1994, 25.

24. *Academic Questions* (Summer 1995): 13.

25. Richard Bernstein, "Racial Discrimination Or Righting Past Wrongs?" *New York Times,* 13 July 1994, B8; idem, "Moves Under Way in California to Overturn Higher Education's Affirmative Action Policy," *New York Times,* 25 January 1995, B7; Craig Lambert, "Desperately Seeking Summa," *Harvard Magazine* (May–June 1993): 36–40; Davidson Goldin, "In a Change of Policy, and Heart, Colleges Join Fight Against Inflated Grades," *New York Times,* 4 July 1995, 8; David Margolick, "Stanford Brings Back the F and Toughens Rules on Course Selection," *New York Times,* 4 June 1994, 7.

26. Albert Shanker, "All 'A's' Are Not Equal," *New York Times,* 11 September 1994, E7; Charles J. Sykes, "Dumbing Down Our Kids," *Network News & Views* (February 1994): 12.

27. Alice Dembner, "Educators Agree: Standards Dropping at State's Public Colleges," *Boston Globe,* 19 November 1993, 1; Robert M. Costrell, "Letter to Editor," *Boston Globe,* 28 November 1993, A6; Steve Stecklow, "Colleges Inflate SATs and Graduation Rates in Popular Guidebooks," *Wall Street Journal,* 5 April

1995, A1; Christopher Shea, "Grade Inflation's Consequences," *Network News & Views* (February 1994): 93.

28. Jared Taylor, *Paved with Good Intentions* (New York: Carroll & Graf Publishers, 1993), 294; Rachel L. Jones, "Striving for Success Doesn't Make Us 'White,' " *Boston Globe,* 6 September 1994, 11; Alejandro Portes and Min Zhou, "Should Immigrants Assimilate?" *Public Interest* (Summer 1994): 27.

29. Alice Dembner, "Study of College Puts Emphasis on Core Values," *Boston Globe,* 6 December 1993, 3; Lynda Richardson, "Public Schools Are Failing Brightest Students, a Federal Study Says," *New York Times,* 5 November 1993, A23; Taylor, *Paved with Good Intentions,* 152–53; Catherine S. Manegold, "U.S. Students Are Found Gaining Only in Science," *New York Times,* 18 August 1994, A14.

30. Dan A. Oren, *Joining the Club: A History of Jews and Yale* (New Haven: Yale University Press, 1985), 20.

31. Frederic Cople Jaher, "White America Views Jack Johnson, Joe Louis, and Muhammed Ali," in *Sport in America,* ed. Donald Spivey (Westport, Conn.: Greenwood Press, 1985), 148; William M. Simons, "The Athlete as Jewish Standard Bearer: Media Images of Hank Greenberg," *Journal of Social Studies* (Spring 1982): 96.

32. Heather MacDonald, "The Diversity Industry," *The New Republic,* 5 July 1993, 25.

33. Taylor, *Paved with Good Intentions,* 48.

34. Timothy Egan, "Teaching Tolerance in Workplaces: A Seattle Program Illustrates Limits," *New York Times,* 8 October 1993, A18.

35. Steven Pinker, "The Game of the Name," *New York Times,* 5 April 1994, A21.

36. Eric Schmitt, "Japanese-American Proves Marine Bias," *New York Times,* 2 January 1994, 10.

37. Jennifer Senior, "Language of the Deaf Evolves to Reflect New Sensibilities," *New York Times,* 3 January 1993, A1.

38. Saul Bellow, "Papuans and Zulus," *New York Times,* 10 March 1994, 16.

39. "U.S. Offered Unusual Class on 'Diversity,' " *New York Times,* 2 April 1995, 34; Kara Swisher, "Diversity Training: Learning from Past Mistakes," *Washington Post National Weekly Edition,* 13–19 February 1995, 20; *The New Republic,* 14 March 1994, 9; Arlynn Leiber Presser, "The Politically Correct Law School," *Network News & Views* (October 1991): 96.

40. Carolyn Thompson, "R. I. Japanese See Racism in 'Victory Day,' " *Boston Globe,* 8 August 1993, 34, 24 December 1993, 13, and 7 March 1994, 7; John Leo, "The Gay Tide of Catholic-Bashing," *The Pilot,* 17 May 1991, 15; Jacuelyene E. Adams, "If Liberals Are So Troubled by Words," Letters to the Editor, *Boston Globe,* 12 July 1995, 8; Lloyd Van Brunt, "Whites Without Money," *New York Times Magazine,* 27 March 1994, 38.

41. "Hip to Hate," Anti-Defamation League special report, June 1992; John Leo, "City Rage and Revival," *U.S. News & World Report,* 1 November 1993, 21; *Boston Globe,* 6 January 1994, 3; Christopher Farley, "The Dogg is Unleashed," *Time,* 13 December 1993, 78.

42. James Barron, "State Agency Suspends Ads on Talk Show," *New York Times,* 26 October 1994, B1.

43. Shelby Steele, "A Negative Vote on Affirmative Action," *The New York Times Magazine,* 13 May 1990, 49.

44. Glenn C. Loury, "Incentive Effects of Affirmative Action," *Annals of the American Academy of Political and Social Science* (September 1992): 20–21.

45. Walter E. Williams, "Race, Scholarship, and Affirmative Action," *National Review* (5 May 1989): 36; Peter Applebome, "Duke Learns of Pitfalls in Promise of Hiring More Black Professors," *New York Times,* 19 September 1993, 34.

46. Taylor, *Paved with Good Intentions,* 120–21.

47. Steven L. Carter, *Reflections of an Affirmative Action Baby* (New York: Basic Books, 1991), 60.

48. Dave M. O'Neill and June O'Neill, "Affirmative Action in the Labor Market," *Annals of the American Academy of Political and Social Science* (September 1992): 88, 98–99; Sam Roberts, "The Greening of America's Black Middle Class," *New York Times,* 18 June 1995, 1E, 4E.

49. *Boston Globe,* 4 April 1993, 72 and 24 September 1993, 14; Editor's Comment, "The State of Race Relations: Perception vs. Reality," *Lincoln Review* (Winter-Spring 1993): 7, 8; Calvin Sims, "Black Enterprises Grow and Get Noticed," *New York Times,* 11 July 1993, 20E.

50. O'Neill and O'Neill, "Affirmative Action in the Labor Market," 88–89; William L. Taylor and Susan M. Liss, "Affirmative Action in the 1990s: Staying the Course," *Annals of the American Academy of Political and Social Science* (September 1992): 32–33; Sowell, *Preferential Policies,* 141; Claudette E. Bennett, *The Black Population in the United States: March 1992* (Washington, D.C.: U.S. Department of Commerce, 1993), 1–2.

51. Sam Roberts, "Women's Work: What's New, What Isn't," *New York Times,* 27 April 1995, B6; "Modest Proposals for Pulling Down the Overrepresented," *The American Enterprise* (May/June 1995): 9.

52. Robert Bach, *Changing Relations: Newcomers and Established Residents in U.S. Communities* (New York: Ford Foundation, 1993), 42, 44, 65; Yen Le Espiritu, *Asian American Panethnicity* (Philadelphia: Temple University Press, 1992), 97; Efrain Hernandez, Jr., "Report on State's Hispanics Seeks Services, Business Aid," *Boston Globe,* 20 September 1993, 6; Garry Pierre-Pierre, "A Slow Boil in the Melting Pot," *New York Times,* 8 August 1993, 39; Norman Matloff, "Easy Money, Lost Traditions," *National Review,* 21 February 1994, 47; Ron Russell, "Will Arabic-English Classes Make Grade?" *Network News & Views* (July 1995): 86.

53. Lawrence J. Block and David B. Rivkin, Jr., "Auxiliary Precaution," *Policy Review* (Winter 1990): 66; *Newsweek,* 3 April 1995, 25.

54. Thomas Sowell, " 'Affirmative Action': A Worldwide Disaster," *Commentary* (December 1989): 21–41.

55. H. D. S. Greenway, "Racism That Wears a Multicultural Cloak," *Boston Globe,* 10 June 1993, 19; Patrick Glynn, "The Age of Balkanization," *Commentary* (July 1993): 21; John Darnton, "Western Europe Is Ending Its Welcome to Immigrants," *New York Times,* 10 August 1993, A8.

56. David Binder with Barbara Crossette, "As Ethnic Wars Multiply," *New York Times,* 7 February 1993, 1, 14; Rita Jalali and Seymour Martin Lipset, "Racial and Ethnic Conflicts: A Global Perspective," *Political Science Quarterly* 7, no. 4 (1992):587; Paul Lewis, "Stoked by Ethnic Conflict, Refugee Numbers Swell,"

*New York Times,* 10 November 1993, A6; William J. Olson, "Preface: Small Wars Considered," *Annals of the American Academy of Political and Social Science* (September 1995): 8.

57. *Boston Globe,* 24 April 1994, 4.

58. Christopher Reardon, "Talk of 'Universality' Dominates UN Rights Conference," *Christian Science Monitor,* 18 June 1993, 7; *New York Times,* 17 June 1993, A15 and 21 June 1993, E5; *Boston Globe,* 19 June 1993, 2; Ellen Goodman, "The Darker Image of Multiculturalism," *Boston Globe,* 17 June 1993, 23; *Los Angeles Times,* 28 May 1994, A15.

59. Patrick E. Tyler, "Hillary Clinton, in China, Details Abuse of Women," *New York Times,* 6 September 1995, A1.

60. Pope John Paul II, "Encyclical Letter, Veritatis Splendor" (Vatican City: Libreria Editrice Vaticana, 1993), 123.

61. Maynard H. Merwine, "To the Editor," *New York Times,* 24 November 1993, A24.

62. Ricard Lacayo, "The 'Cultural' Defense," *Time, Special Issue* (Fall 1993): 61; Constance L. Hays, "Enduring Violence in a New Home, *New York Times,* 6 December 1993, B3; Roy Beck, "The Ordeal of Immigration in Wausau," *The Atlantic Monthly* (April 1994): 89; *New York Times,* 30 October 1994, 38.

63. *New York Times,* 25 September 1994, 23; Tony Perry, "Gypsy Clan Facing Test as Psychics," *Los Angeles Times,* 27 February 1995, A3, A18.

64. Robert J. Samuelson, "America the Caricature," *The Washington Post National Weekly Edition,* 10–16 July 1995, 5.

65. Seth Mydans, "Poll Finds Tide of Immigration Brings Hostility," *New York Times,* 27 June 1993, 1; Daniel B. Wood, "Immigration Issue Fueled by Highest Rate in Years," *Christian Science Monitor,* 27 July 1993, 2; News Release, The Public Agenda Foundation, 5 October 1994, 2; William Raspberry, "What Teens Think about Race," *Boston Globe,* 22 August 1995, 15.

66. Arthur M. Schlesinger, Jr., *The Disuniting of America* (New York: W. W. Norton, 1992), 16–17; Ted Szulc, "The Great Danger We Face," *Parade Magazine,* 25 July 1993, 4.

67. Frances Kellor, *Immigration and the Future* (New York: George H. Doran Co., 1920), 246; Curti, *The Roots of American Loyalty,* 69; Rischin, *Immigration and the American Tradition,* 48.

68. Leo Pfeffer, *The Liberties of an American* (Boston: The Beacon Press, 1956), 34, 84; Thomas J. Curry, *The First Freedoms* (New York: Oxford University Press, 1986), 197.

# Bibliographical Essay

There is an old Hasidic story of a Jewish congregant who repeatedly tells his rabbi that he loves him, only for the rabbi to say he doesn't believe it. The more the congregant affirms his love, the more the rabbi refuses to believe it. "But why don't you believe me?" asks the bewildered congregant. "Because," says the rabbi, "in all your professed love for me, you never once asked what pains me."

Simply put, to have credibility with other people or groups, it is not enough to avow affection or admiration. One must also know and understand what pains them.

Even then, one can learn much about a group, but understand little of its everyday problems, as with people who recite statistics or historical facts about groups in general, but know little about their daily living problems and struggles. A person can know much about a group's everyday problems, but not about its religion, beliefs, customs, or past history.

Ideally one should know and understand a group in terms, concepts, and emotions acceptable to most of the people in the group. There are many ways of learning to understand a group, such as reading newspapers, books, periodicals, and articles about the group; seeing movies and television programs dealing with other groups; attending a group's meetings, celebrations, and conferences; living or working among or near members of a group; having minorities as professional and social friends; visiting their homes or neighborhoods and, if possible, their ancestral homelands; and always being attentive to how they react to bigotry.

The following periodicals and books will hopefully serve as a basis for understanding: minority group life in America; the historical tenacity and variety of bigotry and racism; the multifaceted nature of majority-minority relations; and the changing nature and problems of American democracy.

Because of the complexity of the problems involved and the growing vastness of material available, I have selected materials that should be interesting, readily accessible, and largely general in scope, hopeful they will inspire newcomers to the world of minority group relations to read and probe deeper. More specialized works are cited in the footnotes to this book and in the works noted below.

## PERIODICALS AND REFERENCE SOURCES

Books and articles on minority groups range from the popular to the scholarly, from the contemporary to the historical, and from the relatively objective to the clearly filiopietistic. It is important for the serious reader to gain a familiarity with them all.

One of the most convenient ways of learning about a group is to read its weekly press. Every group has some weekly newspaper and/or monthly publication, which tells of what is occurring in its community or homeland. Usually the larger the group, the more periodicals it has, which are obtainable through subscriptions, at large newsstands in major cities, or in stores in a group's neighborhood. A full listing of ethnic, racial, religious, and gender periodicals by state is found in the *International Year Book of Editor and Publisher* and in the annual *Gale Directory of Publications and Broadcast Media* (which also provides circulation figures). For a more detailed and historical perspective, *The Ethnic Press in the United States,* edited by Sally M. Miller (Greenwood Press, 1987) is excellent, as is *The Religious Press in America* (Holt, Rinehart and Winston, 1963), which focuses on the Protestant, Catholic, and Jewish press.

The differences in group interests and priorities begin to become evident when reading and comparing front-page stories in a half dozen or so weekly newspapers. The *Armenian Weekly* focuses on Armenia and its problems, the *Forward,* a Jewish publication, on Israel, the *Irish Echo* on Northern Ireland, and so forth, in addition to, of course, on how local or national politics impinge upon their respective group interests, such as immigration and holidays. In some communities, a group may have two or more competing weekly newspapers.

Though highly ethnocentric, such publications nevertheless reflect a group's concerns, problems, and achievements as well as revealing who its leaders and high achievers really are. With the huge increase in recent years of immigrants and the growing acceptance of multiculturalism, many urban general newspapers have begun covering minority group life and problems as never before—and hiring minority reporters to report on them. In fact, newspapers like the *New York Times* and the *Washington*

*Post,* as well as weekly national news magazines like *Time* and *Business Week* have become prime sources of information about minorities (as is evident from the footnotes in this book).

For a deeper knowledge of a group, however, scholarly publications and books must be utilized. Here, too, there is an abundance of material and resources, due largely to the explosion of group pride and the establishment of minority courses on high school and college campuses.

Also, most groups have local, regional and/or national historical societies, which focus on their history in America and publish newsletters, periodicals, studies, and/or books. A full listing of such societies can be found in *The Directory of Historical Organizations in the United States and Canada* (American Association for State and Local History Press, 1994).

Academically, the best and most authoritative source on the origins, history, and status of major ethnic groups in America is the *Harvard Encyclopedia of American Ethnic Groups,* edited by Stephan Thernstrom (Harvard University Press, 1980). On the lighter and more entertaining side is *The Ethnic Almanac* by Stephanie Bernardo (Dolphin Books, 1981), which provides information ranging from the trivial to the significant about group history, personalities, and customs. For statistical year-to-year information on group immigration and settlement in America, as well as comparisons to past decades, the *Statistical Yearbook of the Immigration and Naturalization Service* (U.S. Government Printing Office) is a must.

To aid in the location of periodicals and books about specific groups, the *Guide to American Educational Directories* by Barry T. Klein and the *Bibliography of American Ethnology* by Marc Cashma (both published by Todd Publications, 1976) are both very useful. In addition to such group-specific sources, there are a number of scholarly and professional quarterly journals, usually of a interdisciplinary nature. The *Journal of American Ethnic History* focuses on immigration and group history in North America. *Ethnohistory* specializes in past cultures and societies, especially early American aboriginal people. The *Amerasia Journal* deals with scholarship, criticism, and literature of Asia and the Pacific islands. The *International Migration Review* presents a wealth of material on all aspects of immigration and refugee developments and problems. The *Journal of Intergroup Relations* deals with human rights issues in America and abroad as seen by human rights professionals.

## BOOKS

As for popular and scholarly books on minority groups, immigration, and intergroup relations, I have selected those that cover different time periods and some which provide a variety of perspectives.

For pre-Columbian peoples and migrations *America B.C.: Ancient Settlers in America,* by Barry Fell (Quadrangle, 1977) is a good start. As evident by the title, *Coming Over: Migration and Communication between England and New England in the 17th Century* (Cambridge University Press, 1989) by David Cressy focuses on the English colonists. Spanish and Portuguese behaviors and influences are dealt with in the essays in the *History of Latin Civilization,* edited by Lewis Hanke (Little, Brown and Company, 1973). Sixteenth- and seventeenth-century Franco-American Indian contacts, both negative and positive, are concisely explored in *Friend and Foe* by Cornelius J. Jaenen (Columbia University Press, 1976). Patrick Mannings' *Slavery and African Life: Occidental, Oriental, and African Slave Trades* (Cambridge University Press, 1993) supplies fascinating background on how Africans and Europeans cooperated in the economics and politics of the African slave trade. The dismal record of broken written and verbal promises and agreements made with Native Americans by the European invaders and colonists are revealed in *Of Utmost Good Faith,* edited by Vine Deloria, Jr. (Straight Arrow Books, 1971).

For a more general picture of immigration, a number of excellent books are available, such as Philip Taylor's *The Distant Magnet* (Harper Torchbooks, 1971), Maldwyn Allen Jones' *American Immigration* (University of Chicago Press, 1970), Marcus Lee Hansen's *The Atlantic Immigration, 1607–1860* (Harper Torchbooks, 1961), and John Higham's *Strangers in the Land: Patterns of American Nativism 1860–1925* (Atheneum, 1971). *Immigrant Women,* edited by Maxine Schwartz Seller (Temple University Press, 1981), deals with the experiences of European, Asian, Hispanic, and black immigrant women as reflected in their memoires, oral histories, and fiction.

Though as yet not as extensively researched as European immigration, that of Asians—specifically Chinese, Japanese, Filipinos, Koreans, and Asian Indians—is interestingly recounted by Ronald Takaki in *Strangers from a Different Shore* (Penguin Books, 1989). Similarly helpful, though less extensive, is the collection of short essays in *Crossing the Waters: Arabic-Speaking Immigrants to the United States before 1940* (Smithsonian Institution Press, 1987), edited by Eric J. Hooglund. How foreign and domestic policy considerations determined who and how many immigrants could enter America in recent decades is well analyzed in *Calculated Kindness: Refugees and America's Half-Open Door 1945–Present,* by Gil Loescher and John A. Scanlan (Free Press, 1986).

The experiences of various groups and their impact on American life is another area of growing interest, particularly to teachers and historians interested in conveying their contributions to American democracy. Two texts that are valuable for their scope and readability are Peter C. Marzio's *A Nation of Nations* (Harper & Row, 1976) and Robert Kelley's *The Shaping of the American Past to 1877* (Prentice Hall, 1975). More analytical is Kelley's *The Cultural Pattern in American Politics* (Alfred A. Knopf,

1979), which focuses on how various immigrant groups influenced American politics.

What various foreign visitors thought of America and Americans is essential to an understanding not only of why so many millions of people immigrated here, but also why some foreign governments resented or admired the American people and their form of government. A broad variety of opinions and observations is contained in the four-volume set of extracts (Pendulum Press, 1974): *America Perceived: A View from Abroad in the 17th Century* and *America Perceived: A View from Abroad in the 18th Century* by James Axtell; *America Perceived: A View from Abroad in the 19th Century* by William J. Baker; and *America Perceived: A View from Abroad in the 20th Century,* by Orm Overland.

There is also a variety of books dealing with the similarities and differences within and between minority groups, how they organized themselves, related to each other and society, and reacted to bigotry. From a sociological and theoretical perspective, *Assimilation in American Life,* by Milton M. Gordon (Oxford University Press, 1964) provides an invaluable insight into the nature and dynamics of religious, racial, and ethnic group life in America. Though dealing with one group, Simon N. Herman's psychosocial analysis of the dynamics of identity in *Jewish Identity* (Sage, 1977) has much relevance for understanding other groups as well.

Central to the understanding of minority group life is learning how bigotry—racism, anti-Semitism, anti-Catholicism, anti-Asianism, and sexism—affected it. Here, too, there are a large number of general to specific books. *The Nature of Prejudice* by Gordon W. Allport (Doubleday Anchor, 1958) remains the most readable introduction to the subject from a psychological perspective. Also helpful is Erich Fromm's psychoanalytical *The Anatomy of Human Destructiveness* (Holt, Rinehart & Winston, 1973). How language is used and misused to provoke or perpetuate bigotry is described in *The Language of Ethnic Conflict,* by Irving Lewis Allen (Columbia University Press, 1983).

*Sanctions for Evil,* edited by Nevitt Sanford and Craig Comstock (Jossey-Bass, Inc., 1971), contains fascinating essays on the societal destructiveness of racial, ethnic, and political bigotry. Michael Banton, in *Race Relations* (Basic Books, 1967) explores the tenacity and variety of race relations in different countries, at different times. *American Racism* by Roger Daniels and Harry H. L. Kitano (Prentice-Hall, 1970) presents a sociological and historical perspective on the nature of racism as it affected American blacks, Chinese, Japanese, Asians, Pacific Islanders and Mexicans. From a theoretical and politically pragmatic perspective, the dangers and dysfunctions of group identity and its politicization are explored by Harold R. Isaacs in *Idols of the Tribe* (Harper & Row, 1975). By way of contrast, Lewis Coser's *The Functions of Social Conflict* (Collier-Macmillan Limited, 1964), analyzes some of the positive values of conflict for a group and for society.

For a broad historical perspective on the who, what, when, where, and how of intolerance, Gustavus Myers' *History of Bigotry in the United States* (Capricorn, 1960) provides an interesting overview from colonial times to the 1960s. My own *Divided We Fall: A History of Ethnic, Religious and Racial Prejudice in America* (Iowa State University Press, 1992) traces the origins, growth, and similtaneity of victims and victimizers from pre-Columbian years to the present. *The Ethnic Dimension in American History* by James Stuart Olson (St. Martin's Press, 1994) succinctly portrays the variety of problems that many ethnic, racial, and religious groups faced throughout American history. Ruth Miller Elson's *Guardians of Tradition* (University of Nebraska Press, 1964) is valuable for its depiction of how ethnic, racial, and religious stereotypes were nurtured and portrayed in nineteenth-century American schoolbooks. The interactions and tensions for relatively recent ethnic groups caused by American foreign policy (for the period between 1890 and 1956) are perceptively described in Louis L. Gerson's *The Hyphenate in Recent American Politics and Diplomacy* (University of Kansas Press, 1964).

For books dealing specifically with historical intergroup conflict, *Race Relations in British North America, 1607–1783,* edited by Bruce A. Glasrud and Alan M. Smith (Nelson Hall, 1982), has a variety of essays that focus on blacks, Indians and British colonists. Ian K. Steel's *Warpaths: Invasions of North America* (Oxford University Press, 1994) is superb for its analysis of Indian-Indian, Indian-European, and Indian-colonist conflict. Though not as analytical, Stan Hoig's *Tribal Wars of the South Plains* (University of Oklahoma, 1993) is also interesting.

The difficulties of early twentieth-century European immigrants in American cities is captured by John Bodnar in *The Transplanted* (Indiana University Press, 1985). For information on more recent immigrants to American cities and how they helped to renew them, there is Thomas Muller's *Immigrants and the American City* (New York University Press, 1993). The experiences of Irish, Jews, Greeks, Ukrainians, Italians, Germans, and Japanese are succinctly recounted by a variety of scholars in *Ethnic Chicago,* edited by Peter d'A. Jones and Melvin G. Holli (William B. Eerdmans Publishing, 1981). How Irish, Germans, Jews, and Italians confronted, competed, and conflicted with each other from the Great Depression to the start of World War II is explored in *Neighborhoods in Conflict,* by Ronald H. Bayor (Johns Hopkins University Press, 1978). The life and problems of African Americans, Chicanos, and Native Americans is found in *Three Perspectives on Ethnicity in America,* an anthology of writings, edited by Carlos E. Corest, Arlin I. Ginsburg, Alan W. F. Green, and James A. Joseph (G. P. Putnam's Sons, 1976).

For a fascinating insight into the problems and politics of ethnic and panethnic identity among the increasing number of Asian-American groups, especially Chinese, Japanese, Filipino, Korean, and Vietnamese, there is Yen Le Espiritu's *Asian American Panethnicity* (Temple University Press, 1992).

*The Politics of Religious Conflict* by Richard E. Morgan (Pegasus, 1968) and *Religion and Social Conflict* edited by Robert Lee and Martin E. Marty (Oxford University Press, 1964) are valuable introductions to the dynamics and complexities of church-state relations. *The Protestant Establishment* by E. Digby Baltzell (Random House, 1964) traces the decline of those who long dominated and influenced the social, economic, and political life of America, at least until the onset of pluralism.

To varying degrees, all immigrant groups evoked fears of subversion, disloyalty, un-Americanism. The multiplicity of such paranoid and nativist fears—anti-Catholic, anti-Mormon, anti-Mason, anti-Japanese—is reported by a number of writers in *Conspiracy: The Fear of Subversion in American History* (Holt, Rinehart and Winston, 1972), edited by Richard O. Curry and Thomas M. Brown. For an understanding of nativism and its lingering impact on American society, *The Protestant Crusade 1800– 1860* by Ray Allen Billington (Quadrangle Paperbooks, 1964) remains essential. Violence against various ethnic, racial, and political groups is described from a variety of academic perspectives in *Violence in America,* edited by Hugh Davis Graham and Ted Robert Gurr (Signet Books, 1969). Of the many books on anti-Semitism, Leonard Dinnerstein's *Anti-Semitism in America* (New York, 1994) is the most up-to-date.

In dealing with contemporary issues like multiculturalism, affirmative action, and intergroup tensions, which are growing more intense and complex, newspapers and political journals are an excellent source of information, as evidenced in my frequent use of them in writing this book. A good academic introduction to these topics and their complexities and passions can be gained from *The Disuniting of America* (W. W. Norton & Company, 1992), by Arthur M. Schlesinger, Jr., who is highly critical of exaggerated multiculturalism. Historically more informative is Lawrence H. Fuchs's study of race, ethnicity, and American culture, *The American Kaleidoscope* (Wesleyan University Press, 1990). Also, the issue of *The Annals of the American Academy of Political and Social Science* entitled "Affirmative Action Revisited" (September 1992) provides a number of excellent analyses of the historical, legal, political, economic, and educational problems involved in the affirmative action question.

For a broader understanding of American minority group life, a look at what is occurring in other countries is essential, at least if comparisons are to be made. Cynthia H. Enloe's *Ethnic Conflict and Political Development* (Little, Brown and Company, 1973) provides a solid perspective on the tensions in other countries between minority group desires and those of the government, especially those seeking modernization. How race, economics, politics, intelligence, slavery, and history interact are often provocatively explored by Thomas Sowell *in Race and Culture* (Basic Books, 1994). For case studies of how race, religion, and identity affect the success of some groups that moved beyond their homelands (namely, Jews, the British, the Japanese, Asian Indians, and the Chinese) Joel Kotkin's *Tribes* (Random House, 1992) is most informative.

In summary, the works cited above provide a good basis for understanding minority groups and minority group life in America and elsewhere by showing that group diversity is not new, that each group struggles with defining itself and its relationship to the country, that intergroup conflict between and among new and old groups always occurs, that similar and often more severe problems exist in countries other than the United States, and that hopefully some solutions to today's group and intergroup problems can be found by studying the past.

# Index

# About the Author

PHILIP PERLMUTTER is the former executive director of the Jewish Community relations council of Greater Boston and the author of *Divided We Fall: A History of Ethnic, Religious, and Racial Prejudice in America* (1992), the recipient of the outstanding book award by the Gustavus Myers Center for Study of Human Rights.

ISBN 0-275-95533-8

90000>

EAN

9 780275 955335

HARDCOVER BAR CODE